THROUGH THE SEASONS

THROUGH THE SEASONS

CHRISTEN SVEAAS ART FOUNDATION

CONTENT

FOREWORD

The Henie Onstad Kunstsenter was founded on two individuals' passion for art. The private collection that Sonja Henie and Niels Onstad donated to the museum is a testament to their shared interests, travel patterns, personal and professional networks, and of course their tastes. It is only natural then that the Henie Onstad Kunstsenter has a long tradition of presenting private collections. As early as 1971, just three years after the museum opened, a selection of the Norwegian art collector Rolf Stenersen's paintings were on display. Since then, many important well-known collections have filled the museum's exhibition halls, such as Her Majesty Queen Sonja's collection, Pontus Hultén's, Haaken A. Christensen's and Erling Neby's collections, to name just a few.

Prior to the establishment of the museum, Sonja Henie and Niels Onstad's collection toured Europe in a two-year traveling exhibition displayed at 17 leading art institutions. This was an important move, not only to fuel enthusiasm for and engagement with art, but to raise awareness of their collection and build networks and knowledge around it. Opening an art institution bearing their name was a natural extension of this commitment and willingness to share.

Not unlike the Henie Onstad Kunstsenter, the Christen Sveaas Art Foundation is the result of a substantial private donation. Established by Christen Sveaas in October 2019, the Foundation is a significant actor in the arts community in Norway and internationally. In 2020, roughly 800 works from the private collection that Sveaas had built up over nearly 40 years were donated to the Foundation. The collection is one of Norway's largest and is anchored in two core areas: Norwegian modernism and international contemporary art.

The many parallels in their establishment and connections to artists such as Anna-Eva Bergman, Per Inge Bjørlo and Jakob Weidemann, who are also key figures for Henie Onstad, create common ground for the two collections. International names like Catherine Opie and Marina Abramović also resonate with both.

Our presentation of the Christen Sveaas Art Foundation's collection is thus a continuation of Henie Onstad's long tradition of exploring and celebrating the idiosyncratic nature and inner logic of private collection with a fresh eye and in a new context. Utilising the four seasons as a thematic underpinning, this exhibition offers a rich selection of Norwegian and international contemporary art from the Foundation's collection. It has been curated by Lydia Yee, an independent curator and art historian with extensive experience from chief curator positions at Whitechapel Gallery, the Barbican Centre and the Bronx Museum. We thank her for creating a curatorial narrative that presents this collection in exciting and unexpected ways.

And many thanks to the contributors to the accompanying catalogue; William Flatmo for giving an insight to the history of the collection, Lydia Yee for her curatorial view, and MaryAnne Stevens for giving a historical depth to the seasonal painting in Norwegian art, and to designer Anette L'orange for her thorough and vibrant design.

Many thanks to William Flatmo and Anja Grøner Krogstad for their magnanimity and faith in bringing the Foundation's collection to Henie Onstad's visitors. Henie Onstad's own team deserves thanks for indefatigable effort in producing an exhibition of uncompromising quality.

Most of all, we would like to thank Christen Sveaas for his openness and generosity in allowing us the opportunity to explore and gain insight into his collection, and to share that insight with others.

ANNE HILDE NESET
DIRECTOR,
HENIE ONSTAD KUNSTSENTER

WILLIAM FLATMO, DIRECTOR
CHRISTEN SVEAAS ART FOUNDATION

MAN ON A MISSION

The many stories about Christen Sveaas as a young boy growing up in Oslo all involve some form of exchange, whether acquiring Norwegian antique coins from abroad to sell at a profit on the Norwegian market, renting out his comic books to fellow pupils, or how at age 10 he obtained share certificate number one of Kistefos Træsliberi A/S, the Sveaas family's pulp mill and hydroelectric power plant. The art of trade is undeniably linked to the art of collecting, and many collectors 'trade up' as their taste and collections evolve. For Sveaas, distinguishing the interest in trade per se, as he acquired start capital trading an array of commodities on the rise to becoming a successful businessman, and collecting, as a deepened interest in a work of art and its enjoyment, is important in a discussion of the art collection's beginnings. The instinct to trade was always there, inherited from both sides of his family, from his paternal grandfather Consul Anders Sveaas, and his maternal great grandfather Consul Hans Jørginus Hansen. A true collector, I would argue, is unwilling to part with his most cherished possessions. To build up a strong attachment to a work, knowledge about the artist, sensitivity and appreciation of a work's qualities, recognition of its relative merit in comparison to other work in the artist's oeuvre are all requirements. For Sveaas, who did not grow up in a home where art was part of the daily conversation or great masters adorned the walls, passion for art was to be an edifying journey, one in which taste and connoisseurship evolved along the way.

In the late 1980s, Sveaas made his first purchase at an international auction house (three cases of 1945 Taylor Vintage Port from Christie's London) and bought his first Norwegian 18th-century silver tankard via a newspaper notice. The thrill of studying an object, its engravings and provenance—and of winning at auction—stirred something in him. Upon returning from studies in Switzerland and on his way to building his business empire, Sveaas passed through numerous business headquarters and spent a great deal of time in meetings in other people's offices. What struck him was the pictures on their walls, and those of one in particular, lawyer Erik Wahlstrøm, who had a work by Harald Sohlberg (1869–1935). The charming landscape entitled *Sittpå, Maridalen* (1925) is not one of Sohlberg's most important works, but it had an effect on Sveaas, and today he is its proud owner. Christen Sveaas, aged 29 and guided primarily by instinct, was gradually entering the art world. Other early acquisitions included artworks by the late-19th century Norwegian artists Frits Thaulow (1847–1906) and Arne Kavli (1878–1970) as well as lesser-known names, such as Ludvig Ravensberg (1871–1958), Lars Jorde (1865–1939) and Bjarne Eriksen (1882–1970). Common among them are landscapes, interiors and figure studies infused with a certain melancholy. Early sources included Galleri Haaken, established by Haaken A. Christensen in the 1960s, arts and antiques dealer Kaare Berntsen, national and international auction houses, and Galleri K, established by Kristin and Ben Frija. A year after Sveaas acquired his first Sohlberg, Galleri K organised an exhibition of paintings and prints by the artist that Sveaas describes as having had a great impact on him. The exhibition led to a deepened interest in Sohlberg and also marked a change of direction in the collection toward a soulfulness and exploration of the relationship between man and nature.

Among the Oslo galleries Sveaas frequented, Galleri K had the most forward-looking exhibition profile and would come to play an important role in securing contemporary cornerstones for the collection. In 1990, when the collection was still quite modest in size and scope, Sveaas was looking to broaden its range beyond Norwegian artists and sought Ben Frija's advice. The first artist they looked at was the British painter, Howard Hodgkin (1932–2017). By this time, Hodgkin had made his international breakthrough with gallery representations on both sides of the Atlantic, represented the United Kingdom at the Venice Biennale and won the renowned Turner Prize. The first work Sveaas aquired was *On the Riviera* (FIG. 1), a large and vibrant work on board, painted between 1987 and 1988, and typical of Hodgkin's classical period; you can literally dive into colours and emotions that spill out beyond the canvas onto the frame. The

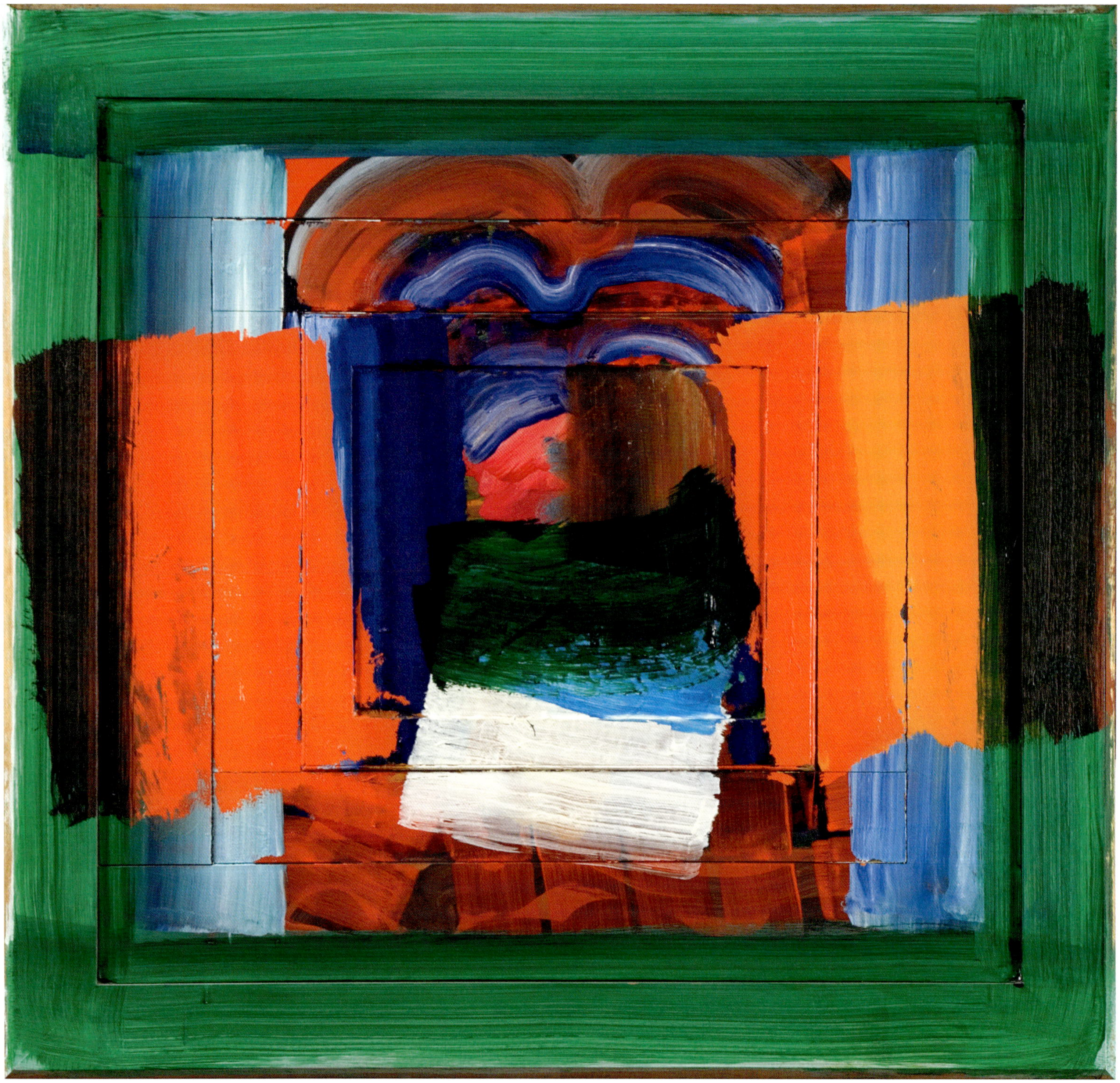

FIG. 1
HOWARD HODGKIN, *ON THE RIVIERA*, 1987–88
OIL ON BOARD, 104.5 X 111.5 CM
PRIVATE COLLECTION; COURTESY OF
CHRISTEN SVEAAS ART FOUNDATION

acquisition demonstrated a willingness and commitment to acquiring important works of art, and in doing so, entering a different league of collecting.

COLLECTING WITH HEART

Christen Sveaas' decision to acquire an artwork is made on instinct, based on a personal reaction upon seeing the work. This passion, at times almost sweeping him off his feet, has resulted in the collection we see today. Sveaas remains true to the idea of being a private collector and, while always remaining open and curious about artists introduced to him by advisors, consistently believes that he must have a personal emotive response to any work that enters the collection.

While Howard Hodgkin's works hold a unique place in the collection, they are also typical of the loyalty and conviction with which Sveaas continues to collect the work of an artist, once they are in the fold. Since 1990, eleven paintings by Hodgkin have been acquired. While this is not a particularly large number by a single artist in the context of Sveaas' collection, it does make it one of the most important collections of Hodgkin's work in the world. To that end, another important work by Hodgkin, *In the Honeymoon Suite* (1983—85), was added in 1994, shortly before being requested for Hodgkin's first major exhibition in the US, at The Metropolitan Museum of Art (The Met) in New York. Hodgkin and Sveaas both attended the private view. It was the only time they met, and in hindsight, Sveaas has said he regrets not getting to know Hodgkin better.

BUILDING RELATIONSHIPS

Just a few weeks prior to the Hodgkin retrospective in 1994, Sveaas had succeeded in acquiring *An Eruption of Vesuvius* (1824) (FIG. 2) by Norway's preeminent painter of romantic landscapes, Johan Christian Dahl (1788—1957). The underbidder was The Met. Through Lord Mark Poltimore, Christie's Director of 19th Century Pictures at the time, contact was established to try to convince the successful buyer to then sell the work to one of the world's most important museums. As someone who has witnessed Sveaas acquiring works of art, I can attest to the way his estimation for a work instantly accrues once acquired. In the case of the Dahl, I whole-heartedly agree! It was a monumental bargain for the masterpiece commissioned by Prince Christian Frederik of Denmark, on whose invitation Dahl visited the bay of Naples before painting the work between 1821 and 1824. The Met's request to sell was met with a firm NO. Sveaas would, however, happily lend the work to the museum. This was the beginning of a lasting friendship with Gary Tinterow, then on the rise to become The Met's Engelhard Chairman of the Department of Nineteenth-Century, Modern, and Contemporary Art. Today, The Met owns three Dahl paintings donated by Christen Sveaas, and its collection of Northern Romantic paintings has grown around these very pictures. Additional donations of works by Peder Balke (1804—1887), Christian Krohg (1852—1925), Frits Thaulow, and Thomas Fearnley (1802—1842) followed over the years.

The stage was thus firmly set not only for acquiring international works of art and bringing them to Norway, but also for Norwegian works of art to take to the international stage. It is remarkable that these two strategies, which have come to define the collection for more than three decades, occurred simultaneously. A third and equally important decision, also made around the same time, in the fall of 1995, was to establish the museum and sculpture park, Kistefos. From tender beginnings in the late 1990s and early 2000s, Kistefos is today considered one of the pre-eminent destinations for international contemporary sculpture in Europe. When the museum organised its first exhibitions in the old industrial buildings erected by Consul Anders Sveaas a century earlier, Dahl was among the first artists shown. When its new exhibition building, The Twist, opened in 2019, it was with works by Hodgkin, celebrating Sveaas' love for painting and coming full circle since acquiring the Dahl and Hodgkin's first works 30 years prior.

ARTISTS FROM SVEAAS' OWN GENERATION

The late 1990s and early 2000s mark a period in which many key works from artists of Sveaas' own generation were collected. Works by Christopher Wool (1955–), Albert Oehlen (1954–), Andreas Gursky (1955–), Thomas Ruff (1958–) and Martin Kippenberger (1953—1997) were all acquired during these years and, perhaps for that reason, are works that Sveaas remains strongly attached to and that continue to excite and move him to this day. Behind each acquisition lies a story, some more unique than others, like in 1996, when Martin Kippenberger was reluctantly convinced to sell one of his most important works just days before going on his honeymoon to Venice. Each encounter with a work of art is also a story of excitement, thrill and emotion, and a desire to own the work, as at Haus der Kunst in Munich in 2007 when standing in front of a unique monumental work by Anish Kapoor (1954—), Sveaas, after some debate, was able to acquire it. Or when offered a monumental work by Louise Bourgeois (1911—2010) in the private viewing room of a Chelsea gallery, simply standing in the presence of such a masterpiece was a challenge. In some cases, the urge alone is enough, like when Sveaas stands in front of Ed Ruscha's (1937–) *OOF* (1962) at The Museum of Modern Art in New York (a work he will never own, although he has acquired others) and reads its title out loud with great empathy. Common to all of these moments is art's ability to stir and excite. It is perhaps in Sveaas' own excitement when looking at great art that his motivation to share this excitement with others arises.

MEN ON A MISSION

I first met Christen Sveaas in the spring of 2010, at my final interview to become director of his art collections. I already knew that he was the owner of a Michelin-starred restaurant in Oslo and that he was a great collector of wine, and while preparing for the interview, I learned that he was also an avid collector of silver, as well as art. From the limited material I found about his art collection came hints of its eclectic nature, spanning from the Norwegian romantic era and German photography from the 1990s, to American post-conceptualism and old master portraits, a combination rarely seen in Norway. At the interview in the densely hung office space, my conservative London attire prompted the first of many jokes and laughs, but his clear-headedness and intensity were what struck me most. Months before officially starting as director, plans for meetings in London and Basel were arranged, and introductions were made to Sveaas' key people. This was clearly a man on a mission who would waste no time in acquiring the next addition to his collection.

Diving into the rich collection, I was amazed at how little was known, even within the world of museums and collectors. Sveaas is a collector with serious ambition who expects to be first in line when the will to acquire asserts itself, but the secrecy of the collection's content and importance was, in my opinion, a hindrance to operating on a top international level. Many works had been acquired anonymously through intermediaries, shielding the name of the collector from those who ought to know it in order to be able to offer him the next important artwork.

In the decades over which the collection has grown, the art world has gone through significant structural changes, moving towards greater transparency. As art has increasingly become an object for speculation, careful vetting of buyers, collector ratings and track records have become part of most contemporary art transactions.

The relationship with The Met was already well established and evolved naturally with Tinterow's successors in Sveaas becoming a founding member of their international council and naming a gallery. The experience from The Met inspired Sveaas to

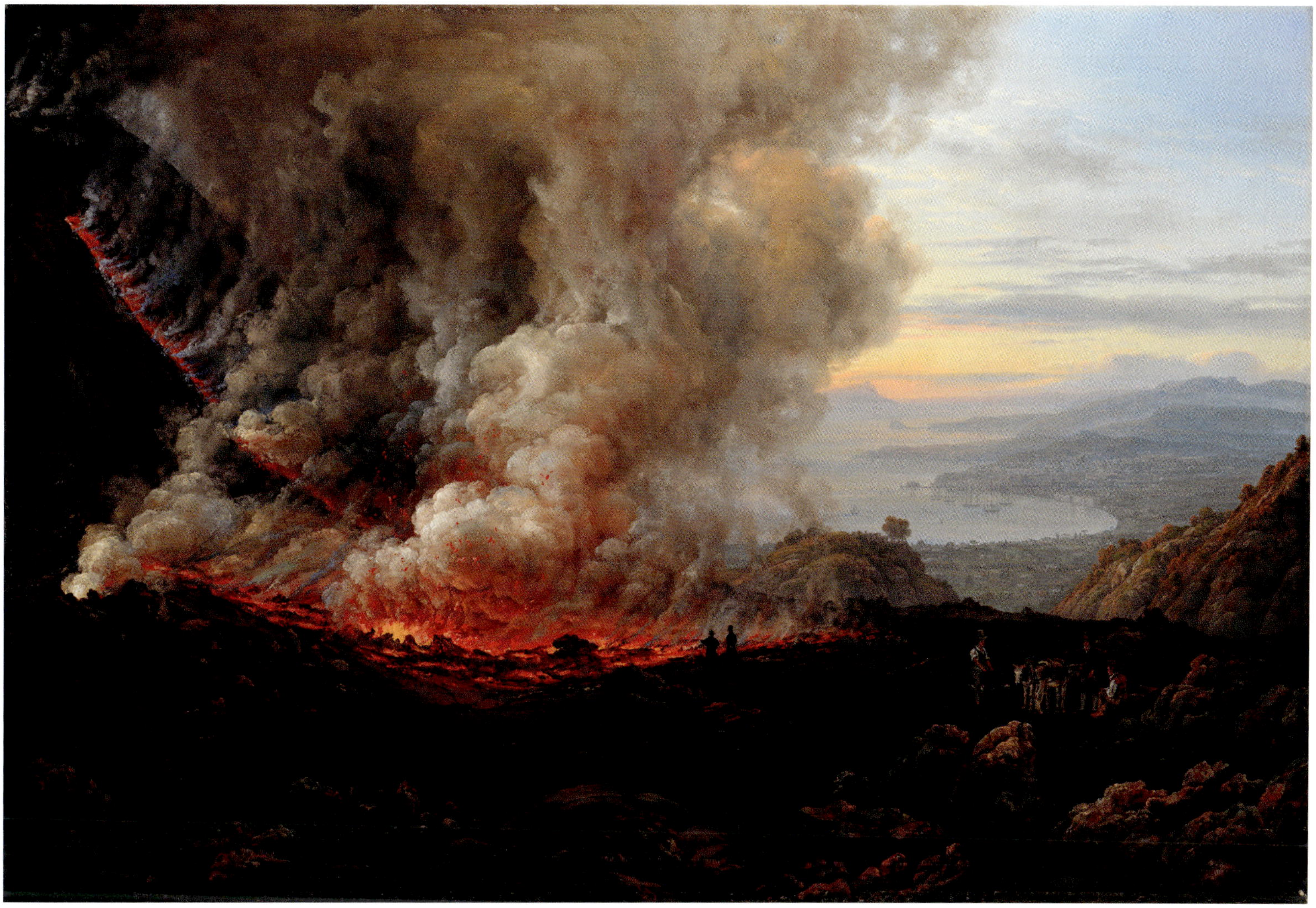

FIG. 2
JOHAN CHRISTIAN DAHL, *AN ERUPTION OF VESUVIUS*, 1824
OIL ON CANVAS, 94 X 139.1 CM
THE METROPOLITAN MUSEUM OF ART
GIFT OF CHRISTEN SVEAAS, IN CELEBRATION OF THE
MUSEUM'S 150TH ANNIVERSARY, 2019

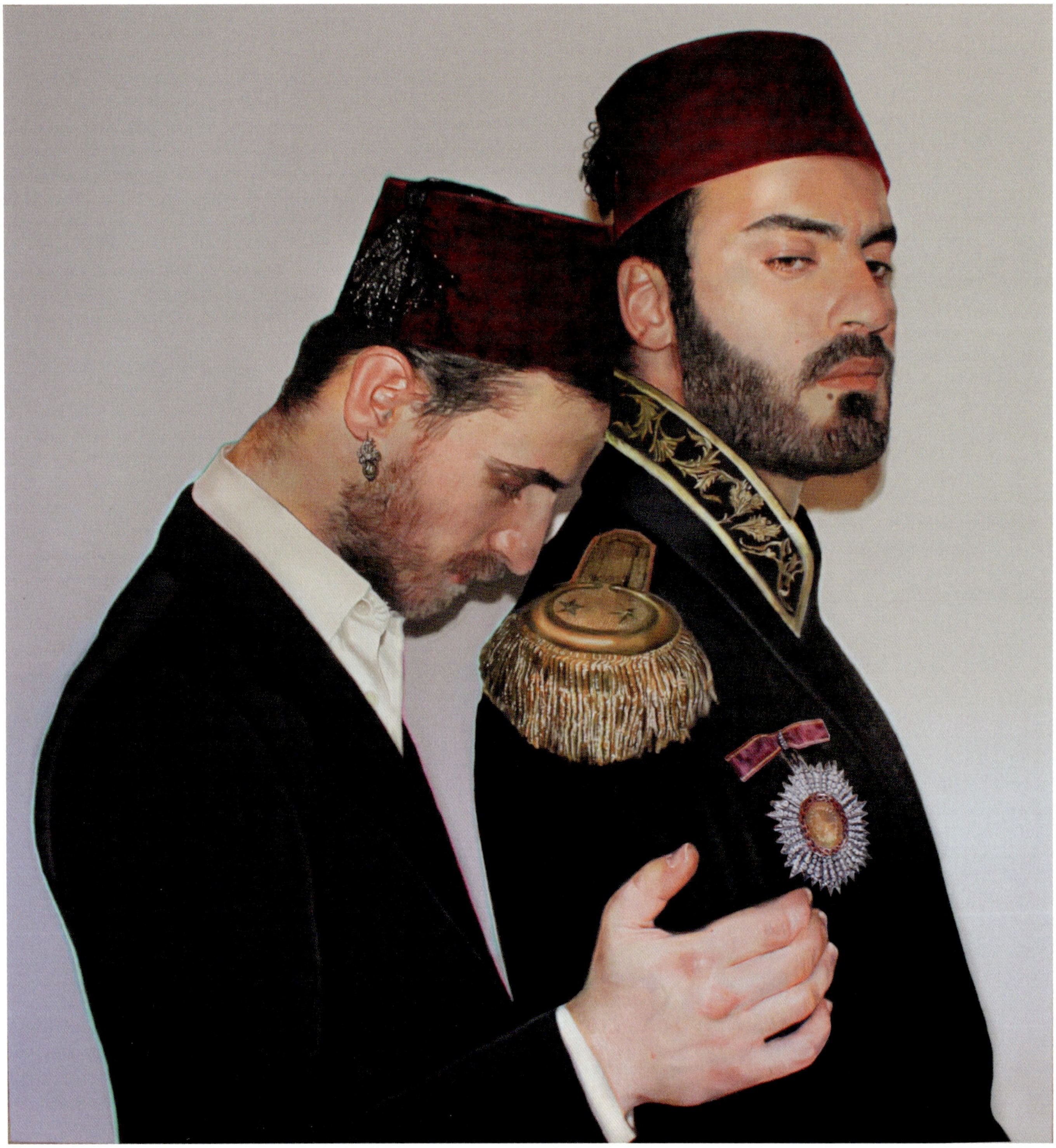

FIG. 3
TANER CEYLAN, *1923 (FROM THE LOST PAINTING SERIES)*, 2010
OIL ON CANVAS. 170 X 180 CM
PRIVATE COLLECTION; COURTESY OF
CHRISTEN SVEAAS ART FOUNDATION

embark on similar initiatives with Kunsthaus Zürich and the Museum of Fine Arts, Houston, both of which now have significant holdings of Norwegian 19th century pictures thanks to Sveaas. Through such institutional bonds, in meeting fellow collectors and museum founders, learning about how different audiences react especially, and seeing how these donations can be transformative, both to curatorial staff and the institutions at large, the vision of creating something with permanence and significance in Norway has surely been fuelled. With every relationship the collection and Kistefos have gained a friend and an ambassador. The network of artists, curators and collectors, and the exchange and support that comes with these relationships, is not only enriching, but essential to the unique journey of forming a collection and insititution.

PLANNING FOR THE FUTURE

2019 saw the opening of The Twist at Kistefos and also marked the beginning of a new chapter for the collection, when Christen Sveaas decided to establish the Christen Sveaas Art Foundation with a donation of 800 works from his private collection. The donation spans 100 years of art, from 1920 to 2020, and includes works by such key artists as Thorvald Hellesen (1888–1937), Anna-Eva Bergman (1909–1987), Jakob Weidemann (1923–2001), Louise Bourgeois, Howard Hodgkin, and Albert Oehlen. In addition to exhibitions marking the donation at Kistefos and KODE Museum in Bergen, works from both collections (the Foundation's and Sveaas' own) were also shown in a series of four exhibitions at the Whitechapel Gallery in London. The decision to establish the foundation firmly cemented the vision of making the collection accessible to a broad Norwegian audience and placed Sveaas among a modest number of Norwegian philanthropists and collectors who contribute to Norway's cultural landscape and legacy while also putting a personal stamp on it.

The shift from private to public has been gradual and has undoubtedly influenced the way the collection has developed in more recent years. With the exception of work by the Norwegian artist Arne Ekeland (1908–1994), the core collection established in the 1990s and early 2000s had few works that could be categorised as political. Rooted in performance, Marina Abramović's (1946–) work from the late 1990s addresses the political unrest in the Balkans during the same period. Similarly, South African Robin Rhode (1976–) comments on a post-apartheid diasporic experience. With these and other additions, the collection today reflects a greater diversity and gender balance, promoting free speech and opposition to discrimination on the basis of race, gender, or sexual orientation. While seeking to better balance the collection has never been an overt objective of acquisition, a certain admiration and respect is acknowledged in acquiring works by artists whose positions necessitated additional struggle. Like that of Taner Ceylan (1967–), for example, a Turkish artist and remarkable practitioner of photorealist painting. One of his works, *1923* (*From the Lost Painting series*) (2010) (FIG. 3), presented at ArtBasel in 2010, depicts two men, one gently resting his forehead on the neck of the other as they say a final farewell. The work tells a different side of the fall of the Ottoman empire and the Turkish revolution. Getting to know the artist, visiting him in Istanbul and learning about his own struggle, living in constant fear of the possible repercussions of simply being himself and in daring to question stories of Turkish history, truth and culture, the significance of the support and promotion becomes that much more important.

Christen Sveaas once said that 'artists dare first'. This statement can be interpreted on many levels: artists are originals and pioneers, they are also highly private and personal in exposing their innermost feelings. This bravery must be rewarded with an openness and humility in experiencing their unique works of art. Perhaps the most defining characteristic of the collection today is in being a meeting place between the artists' output and the collector's curiosity and openness to seeing things from different perspectives.

LYDIA YEE

THROUGH THE SEASONS

Nature has been a recurring subject in art since humans painted animals on the walls of caves with charcoal and iron oxide some 40,000 years ago. From Brueghel's genre scenes of 1565 depicting hunters in winter, the hay harvest and other seasonal activities, to Monet's haystacks or *Meules* (1890–91) painted in different types of weather, light and atmospheric conditions throughout the year, artists have depicted seasonal subjects and the changing rhythms of nature. With the onset of modernism in the late 19th and early 20th century, many artists moved away from naturalistic representation and traditional genres yet continued to bring new interpretations to this timeless motif.

The exhibition *Through the Seasons* and its accompanying catalogue explore modern and contemporary art from the Christen Sveaas Art Foundation through the framework of the seasons. Is it possible to glean both traditional and contemporary seasonal concerns in the eighty selected works (primarily paintings along with a handful of photographs, sculptures and videos) from the collection? I have attempted to arrange the works like an almanac, according to the four seasons. But of course, artworks are open to many interpretations, and my readings of them are subjective and contingent.

Spring

I.
SPRING

'Hark, hark, the lark...' This call to arise from William Shakespeare's play *Cymbeline* is also the title of an abstract, gestural painting by Gillian Ayres from 1984—90 (→ p.23). Associated with both the break of day and the arrival of springtime, the lark is known for its prominent contribution to the dawn chorus, singing while ascending and descending in the sky. In Ayres' painting, yellow-green, pink, violet and blue-green squiggles emerge from a thick impasto of earthen colours—reddish-brown ochres, siennas, and umbers—much like young shoots pushing through the soil towards the light. 'In a mad sort of way,' Ayres affirms, 'I saw nature like paint'. Made from pigments derived from finely ground clay, mineral salts and other geological sediments suspended in oil, paint is indeed like nature, and nature like paint.[1] Juan Uslé's painting *Al Clarear* (2014) (→ p.25) is also abstract, yet its title ('to dawn' or 'to become lighter or clearer' in Spanish) calls forth an image of early morning light, gradually erasing the darkness with pulsating, striated brushstrokes that evoke sky and water.

According to the meteorological calendar, spring starts on the 1st of March, but wintery conditions may persist in northern regions well into March. Early spring is a time of year marked by transition but also variability. Global warming has had an undeniable impact on our understanding of phenological shifts in 'nature's calendar' to the degree that the traditional signals of the start of spring—the flowering of plants, emergence of insects and the appearance of migratory birds—are now occurring several weeks earlier than in previous decades.

1. *Gillian Ayres*, with a foreword by Andrew Marr, texts by Martin Gayford and David Cleaton-Roberts, Art/Books, 2017, p60. https://pifo.cn/press/12/

In the Northern Hemisphere, the vernal equinox occurs around the 20th of March when the sun moves north across the equator, and day and night are equal in length, marking the astronomical start of spring. Meanwhile, the Southern Hemisphere sees the onset of autumn. When atmospheric temperatures begin to rise above zero degrees Celsius, the earth begins to thaw. Resembling the sun, Anish Kapoor's *Untitled* (2011) (→ p.26), a golden concave mirror, turns the world upside down, reminding us of the dualities of day and night, north and south, Eastern and Western. Although spring is not necessarily a wet season in many parts of the world, rain is often associated with spring. The warmer temperatures cause heat to rise from the earth's surface, and the atmosphere becomes unstable, producing rain clouds and precipitation. In an abstract canvas from 2013, Mona Orstad Hansen plays with framing, perhaps a view through a window, and painting so that the 'downpour' that gives the work its title can be read both as a rain shower and the gravitational pull of paint on a vertical surface (→ p.27).

T.S. Eliot's poem *The Waste Land* (1922), written in the ruinous wake of the First World War, opens with the declaration 'April is the cruellest month', a stark refute to Chaucer's restorative image of spring from *The Canterbury Tales*. In his *Study for the Waste Land* (1987—90) (→ p.29), R. B. Kitaj draws on Eliot's imagery—including Tiresias, the blind yet clairvoyant prophet who was transformed into a woman for seven years; the Fisher King in search of the Holy Grail; the tarot card reader Madame Sosostris and Phlebas, the drowned Phoenician sailor who has pearls in his eyes—and collages the fragments together much like Eliot's poem.

Painted at the end of the Second World War when the German occupation in Norway came to an end, *Fugl* (*Bird*, 1945) by the Norwegian late modernist Jakob Weidemann (→ p.30) features a white bird—perhaps a dove, a Biblical symbol of renewal and new beginnings after the deluge—set against a geometric background. Titled *Pica-Pau* (2016), Portuguese for woodpecker, Luiz Zerbini's painting

(→ p.31) features a tree awakening from its winter dormancy and stirring with new green growth. Though the focus is on the tree and with no bird to be seen, the woodpecker's rhythmic tapping to mark territory, create a nesting cavity and attract mates is nonetheless sensed in the wavy, reverberatory patterns surrounding the tree. These marks also resemble the wood grain often imprinted on cast concrete walls in the brutalist architecture of Zerbini's native Brazil.

Traditional symbols of spring—particularly flowers, gardens and maidens—can be found in the works of Norwegian artists in the modern era. These subjects derive in part from Flora, the Roman goddess of spring, flowers and fertility, but depart from allegorical painting based on classical mythology, such as Botticelli's *Primavera* (*Spring*, c. 1480). Paintings by Edvarda Klaudine Lie (→ p.32), Johs. Rian (→ p.33) and Lars Tiller (→ p.35) mix elements of portraiture and still life, featuring girls or young women holding flowers or fruit. These simplified figures presented against flat areas of colour bear the influence of French modernists such as Matisse or Léger. Else Hagen's *Oppstilling* (*Still Life*, 1939) (→ p.36), rendered in a warm and vibrant, springtime colour palette, contrasts with the compositions of her Cubist precursors. Still life, or nature morte ('dead nature' in French), has generally been understood as a reminder of the transience of life rather than a celebration of the abundance of nature. Using loose daubs of colour favoured by French Impressionists and Fauves, Thore Heramb conveys the transient effects of sunlight and budding flora pushing through the warming spring soil in *Hage* (*Garden*, 1953) (→ p.37).

Seasonal renewal and regeneration take another form in the work of Robin Rhode. The greenery in his sculpture *Empties* (*Green*) (2007) (→ p.39) are elongated glass bottles. The reedy green stalks have shot up from a red SAB (South African Breweries) crate like fast-growing giant knotweed.

Dance and springtime have been inextricably linked for centuries through celebrations of pagan and folk fertility rituals in Europe, from the Maypole tradition to the once infamous *Le Sacre du printemps* (*The Rite of Spring*, 1913) by composer Igor Stravinsky and choreographer Vaslav Nijinsky, which was commissioned by Sergei Diaghilev for the Ballet Russes. In *Russisk ballett, Stuttgart* (*Russian Ballet, Stuttgart*, 1925) (→ p.40), Rolf Nesch uses bold colours in an expressionist style to convey a frenetic fight scene from a ballet inspired by Russian folk traditions. Thorvald Hellesen's *Dans* (*Dance*, 1921) (→ p.41) draws from Cubism, Léger's populist figuration and Orphism to depict couples dancing a waltz, the foxtrot or another modern ballroom style. In *Le serpent qui danse* (*The Dancing Snake*, 2020) (→ p.43) by Julie Curtiss, the conflation of a nude female figure and a snake plant conjures a serpent, a symbol of evil as well as sexuality, fertility and rebirth. American dance pioneer Ruth St. Denis created the sensual Cobra dance, and the serpent as a woman appears in Greek, Indian and Japanese mythologies, among others.

The title of Wangari Mathenge's painting, *After Eight (There Is A Moment, Fleeting, When One Returns To Self And Feels, As if For The First Time, Alive)* (2022) (→ p.44—45), and the clock on the chest of drawers in the background make reference to the chocolate after-dinner mint. The scene depicted is ambiguous: Are the woman and man enjoying a moment of post-coital bliss on a warm, late spring evening, or have they withdrawn into their own worlds?

The eve of May Day, also known as Walpurgis Night or Saint John's Eve, is observed on the 30th of April in parts of Northern Europe with bonfires to ward away evil, bringing together pagan celebrations of spring and fertility rites with the veneration of the Christian Saint Walpurga. In the dreamlike forest of *Walpurgis* (2016) (→ p.47), the German painter Daniel Schwarz uses a scumbling technique to insinuate a fairy, a fox and other creatures to the landscape. May Day is both a celebration of spring and a commemoration of the labour movement. Andreas Gursky's *Mayday IV* (2000) (→ p.48—49), a five-metre-wide chromogenic colour print, is a vast aerial panorama of revellers at a German rave, capturing a mass anti-establishment celebration of May Day with astonishing precision.

GILLIAN AYRES
HARK HARK THE LARK
1984–90

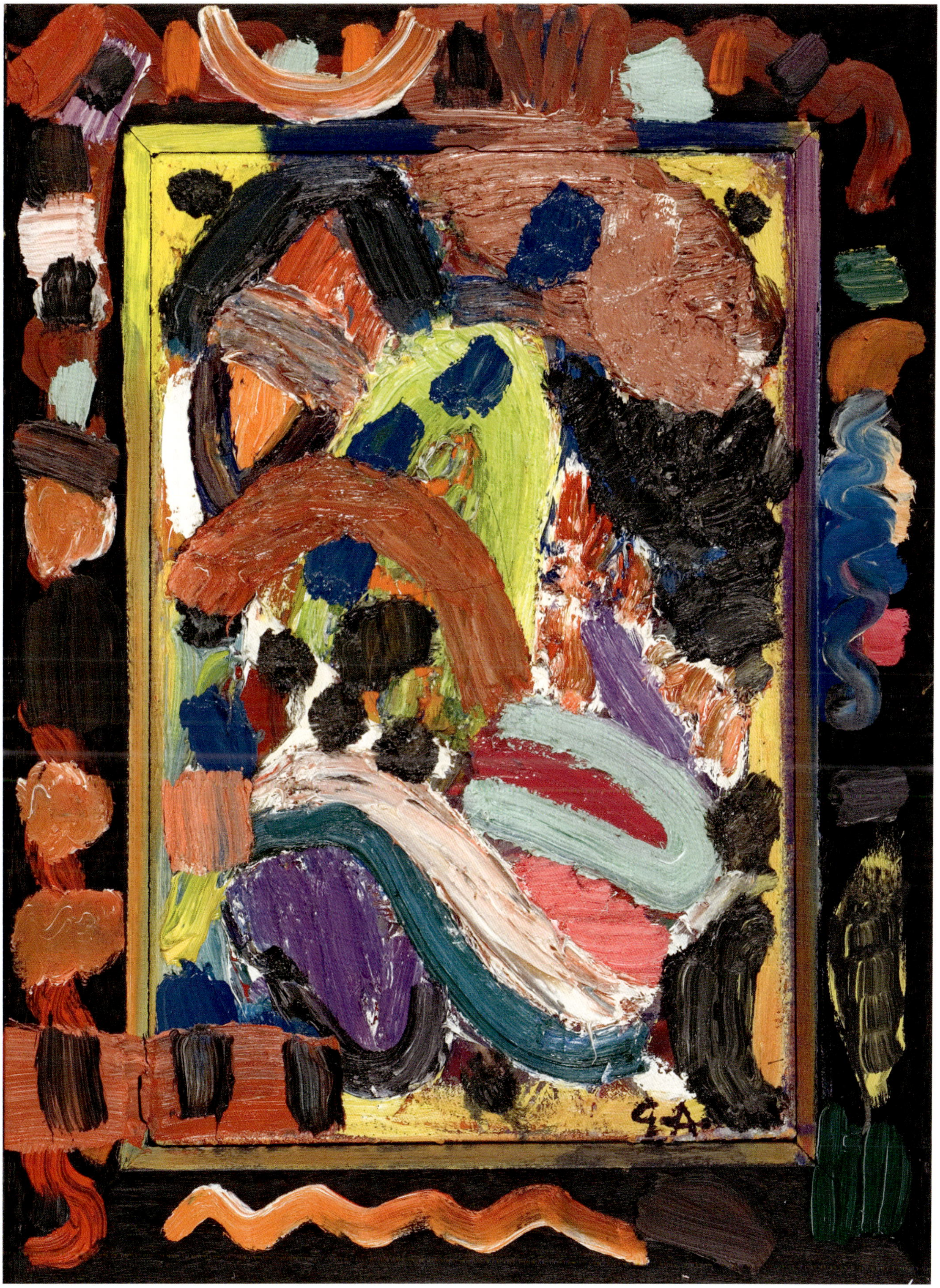
G.A.

JUAN USLÉ
AL CLAREAR, 2014

P.26
ANISH KAPOOR
UNTITLED, 2011

P.27
MONA ORSTAD HANSEN
DOWNPOUR, 2013

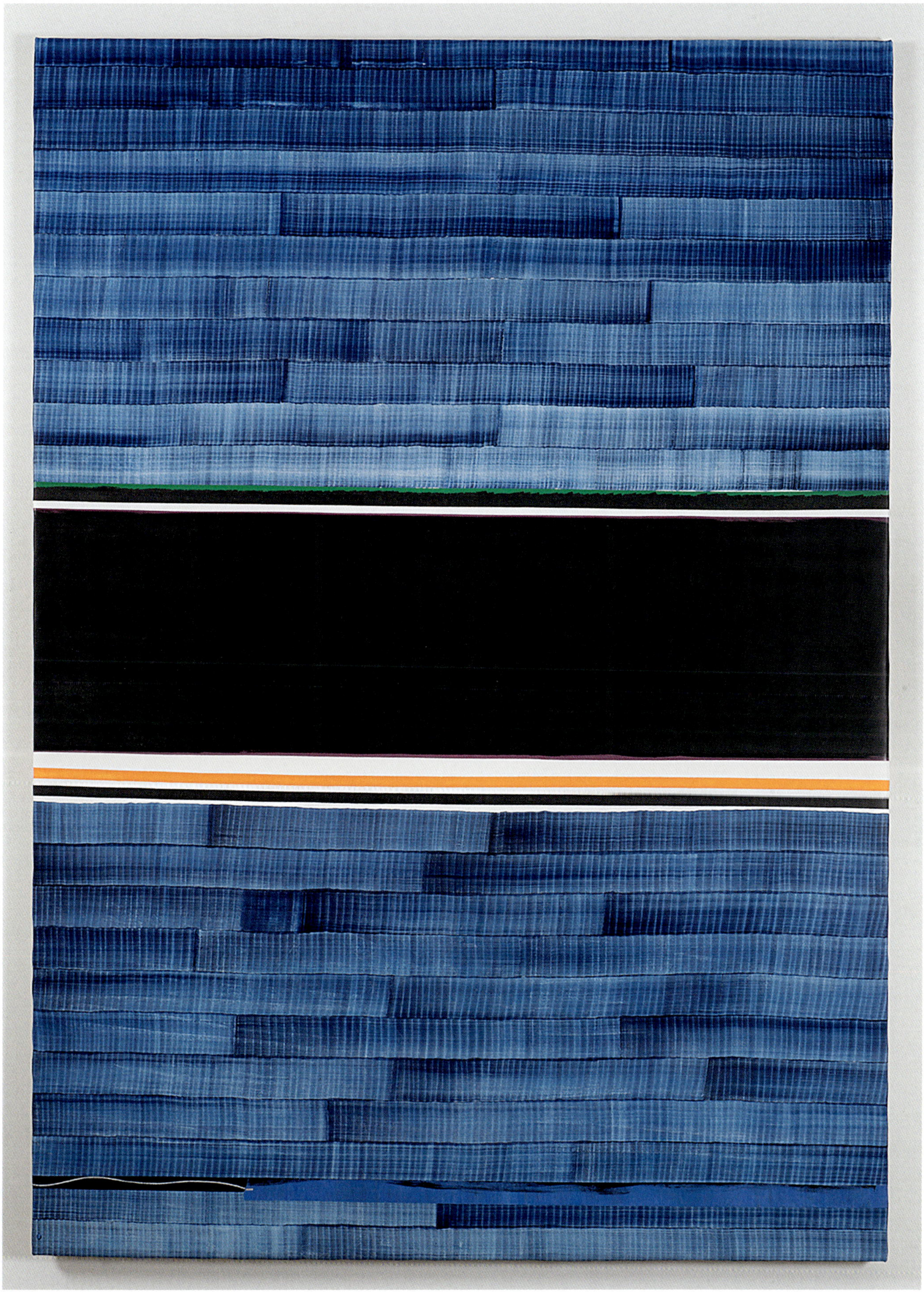

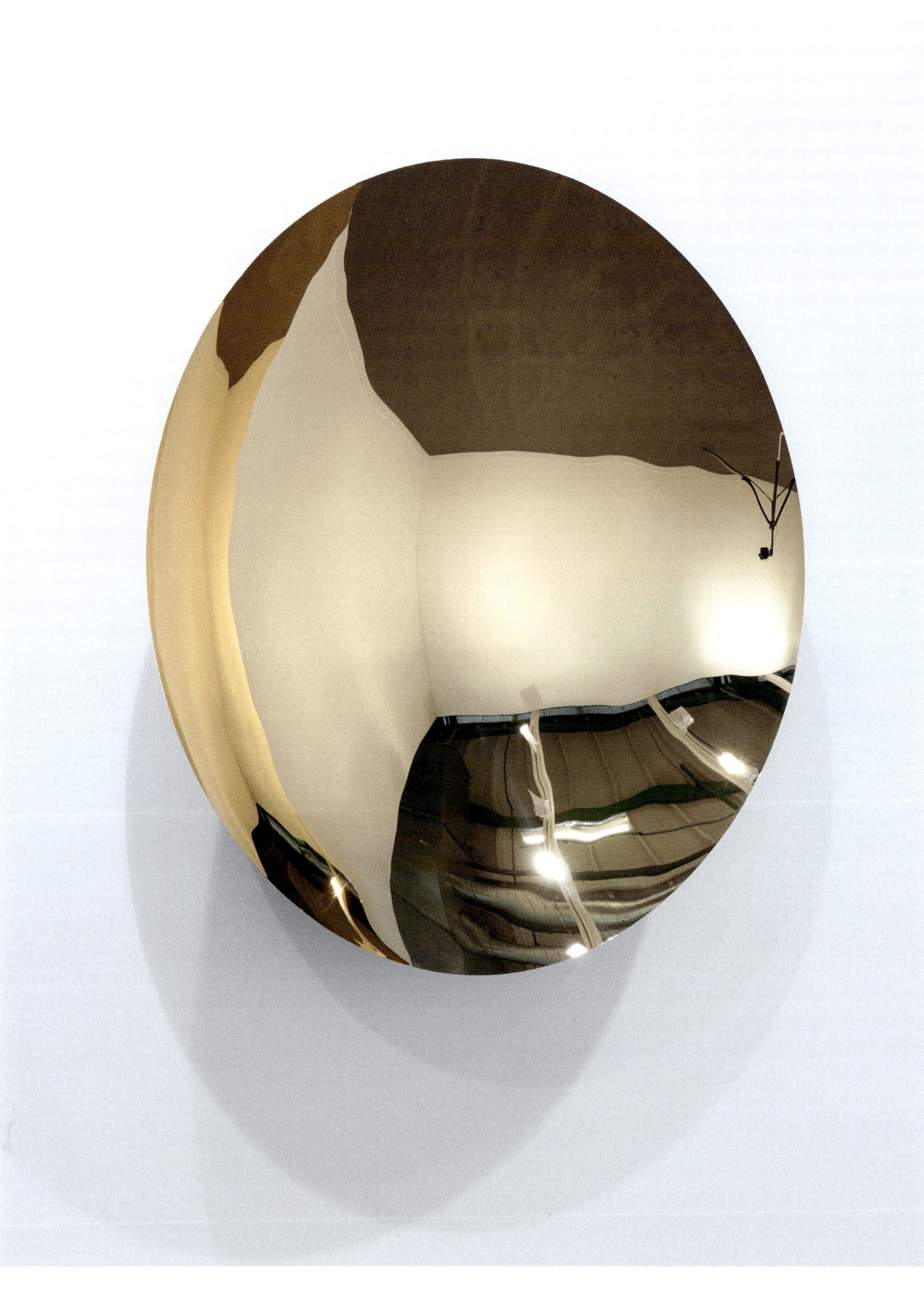

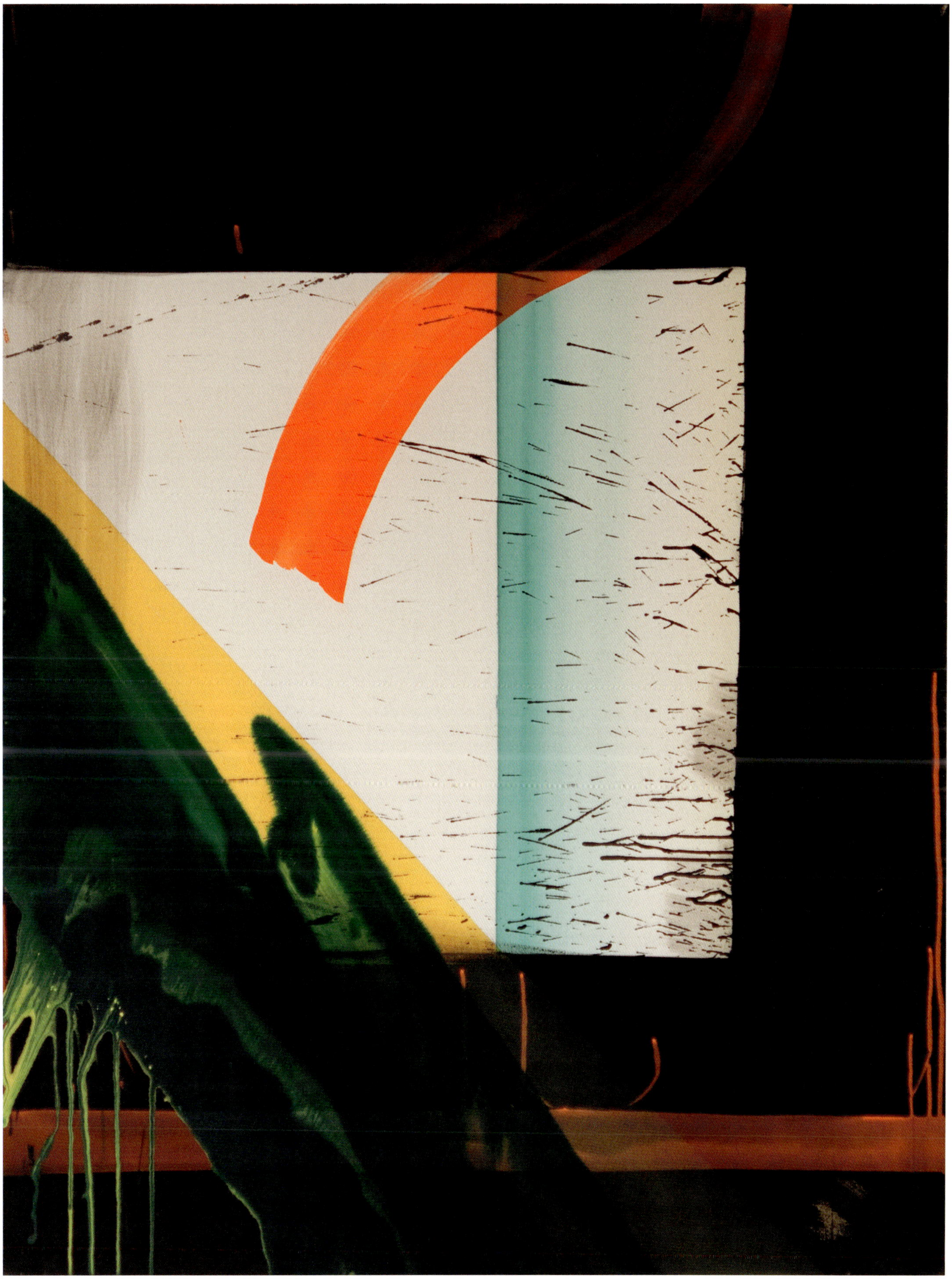

R. B. KITAJ
STUDY FOR THE WASTE LAND
1987–90

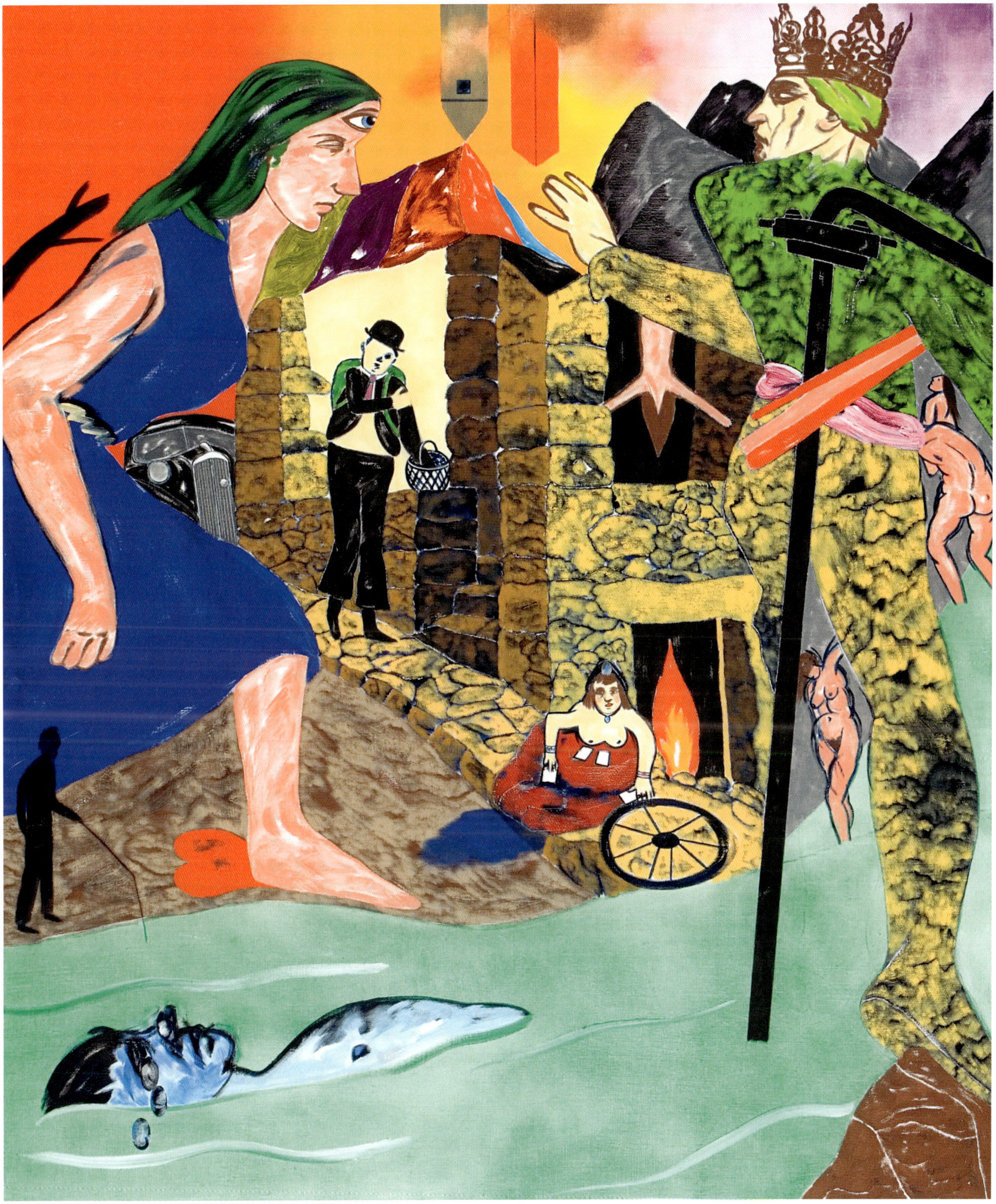

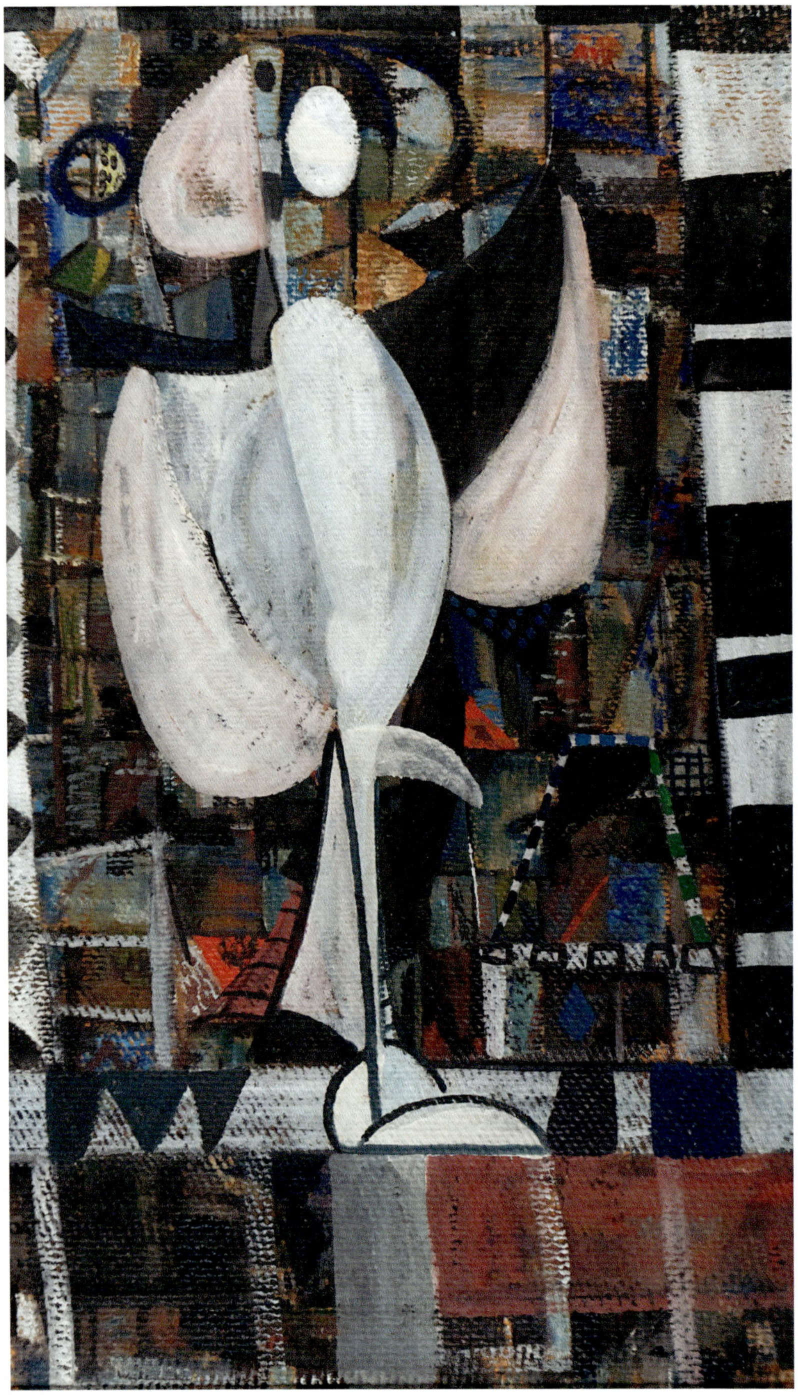

JAKOB WEIDEMANN
FUGL, 1945

P.31
LUIZ ZERBINI
PICA-PAU, 2016

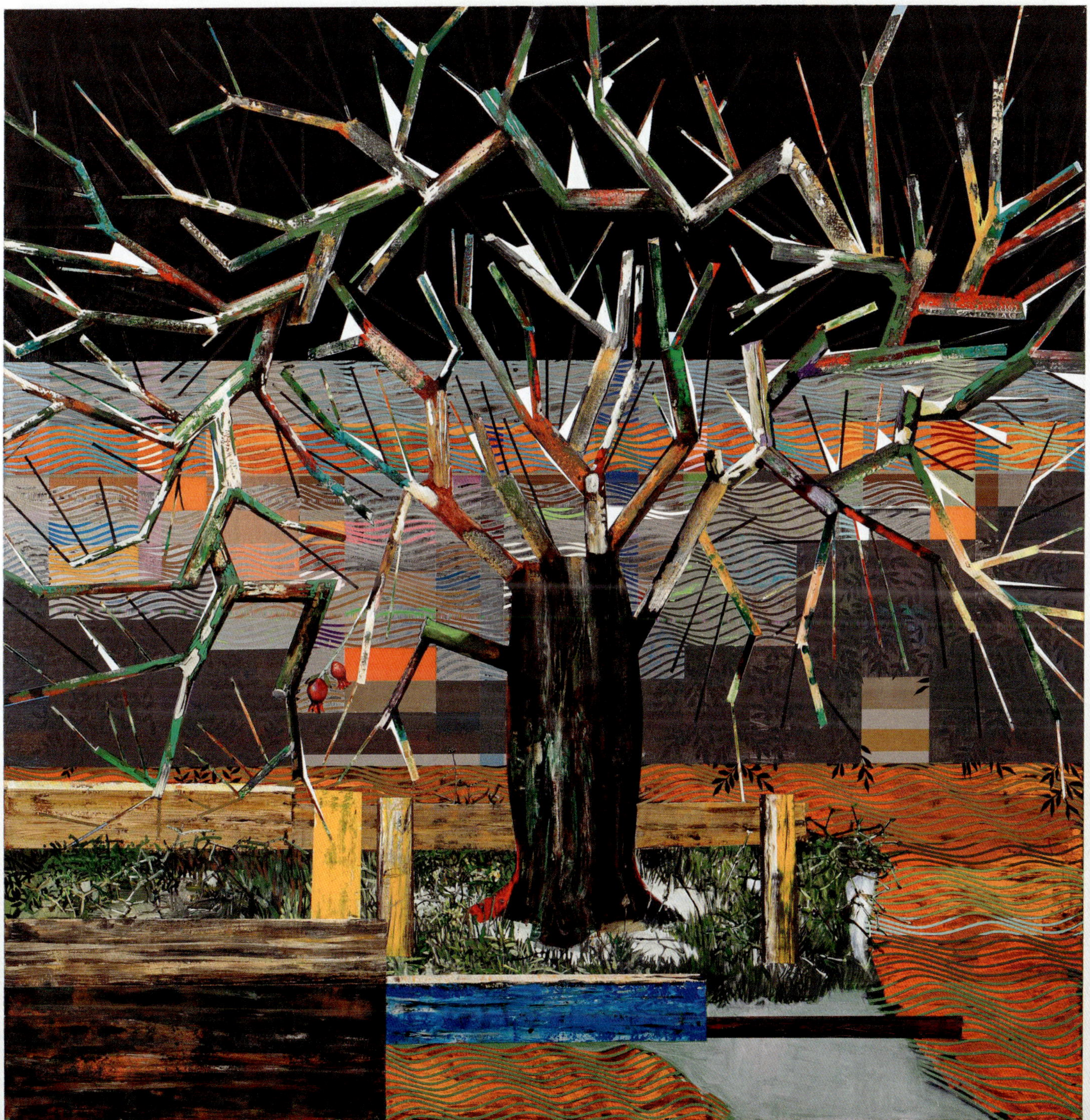

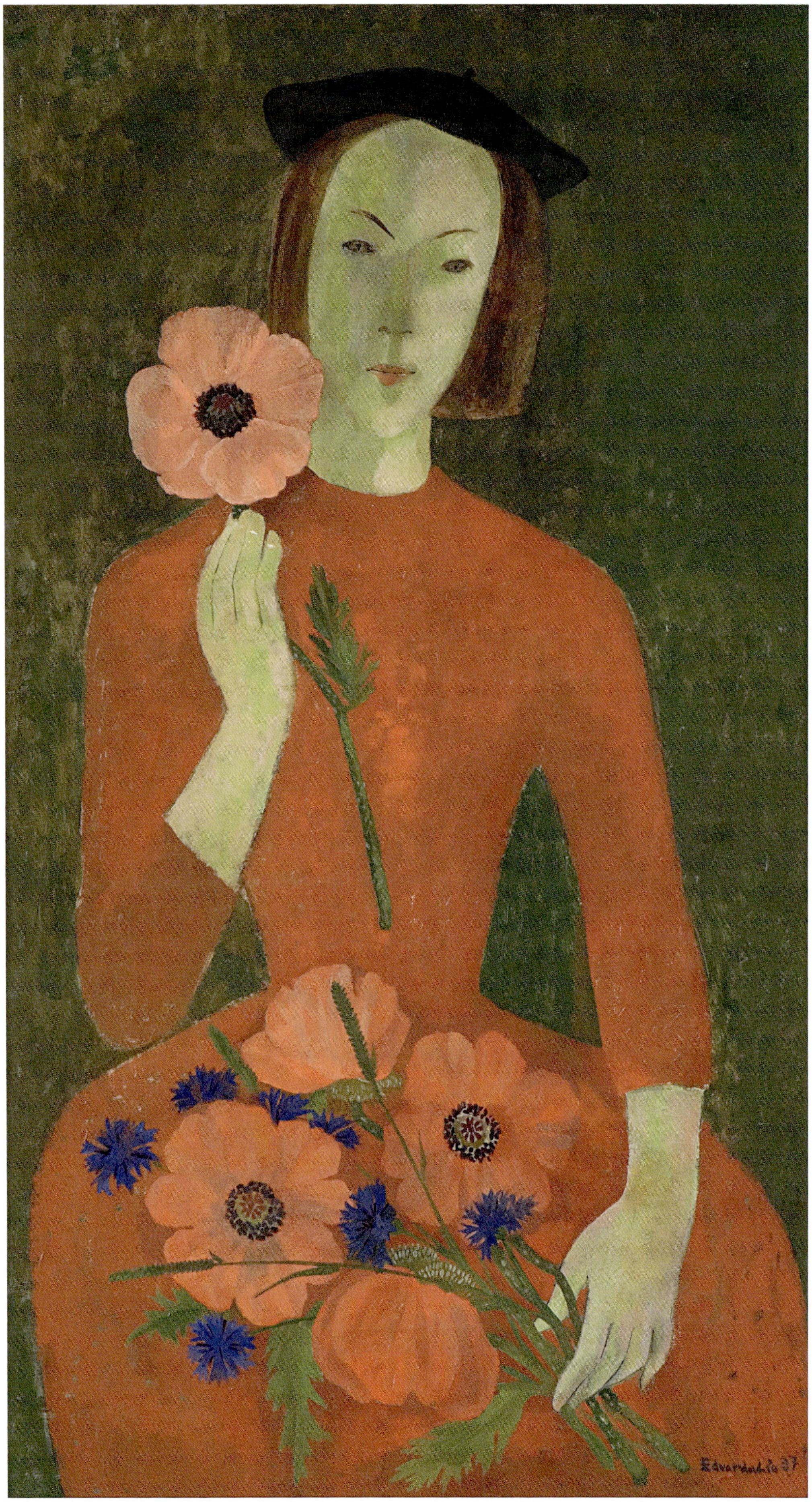

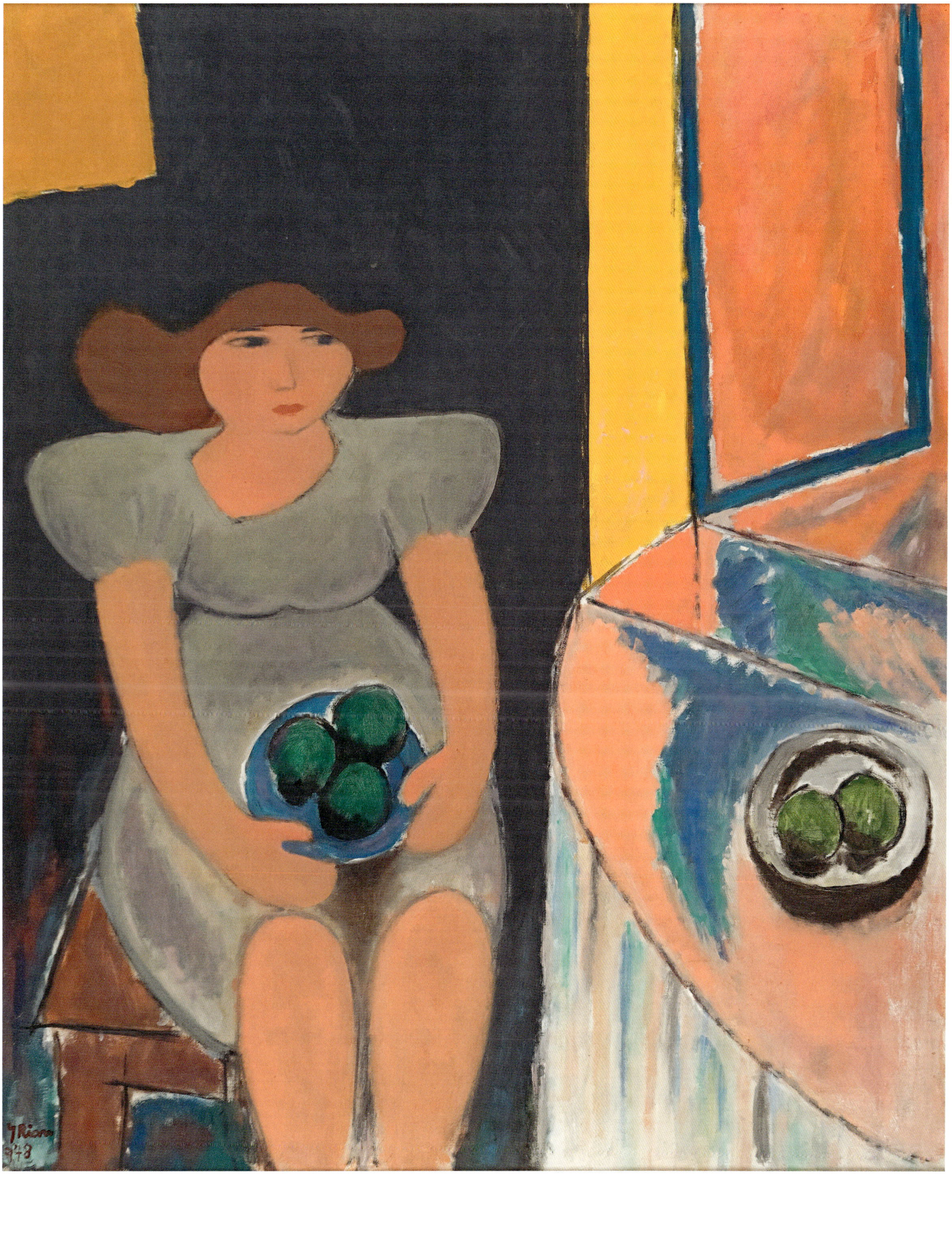

LARS TILLER
PIKE MED BLOMST, 1952

P.32
EDVARDA KLAUDINE LIE
PIKE MED BLOMSTER, 1937

P.33
JOHS. RIAN
PIKE MED GRØNNE EPLER, 1948

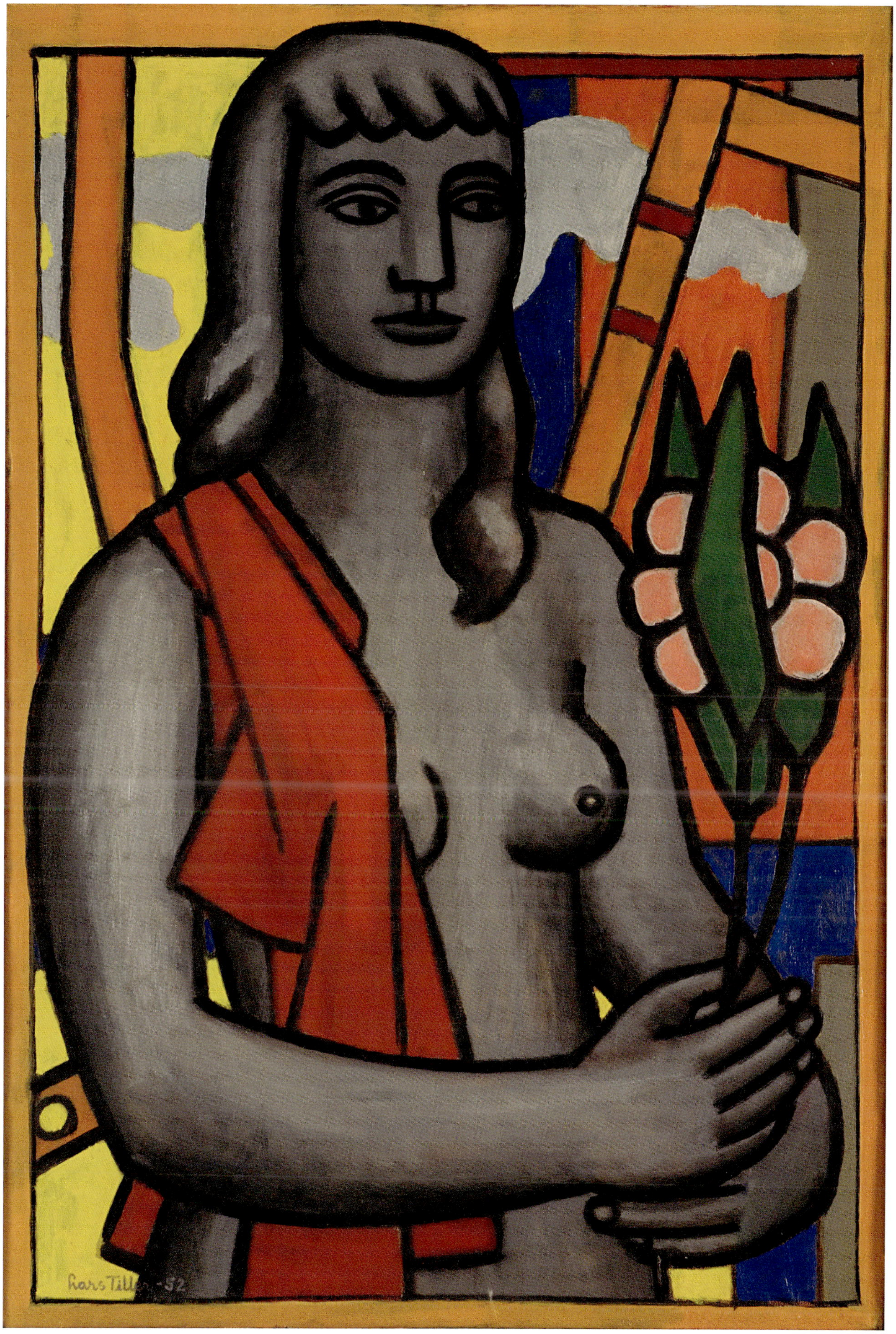
Lars Tiller -52

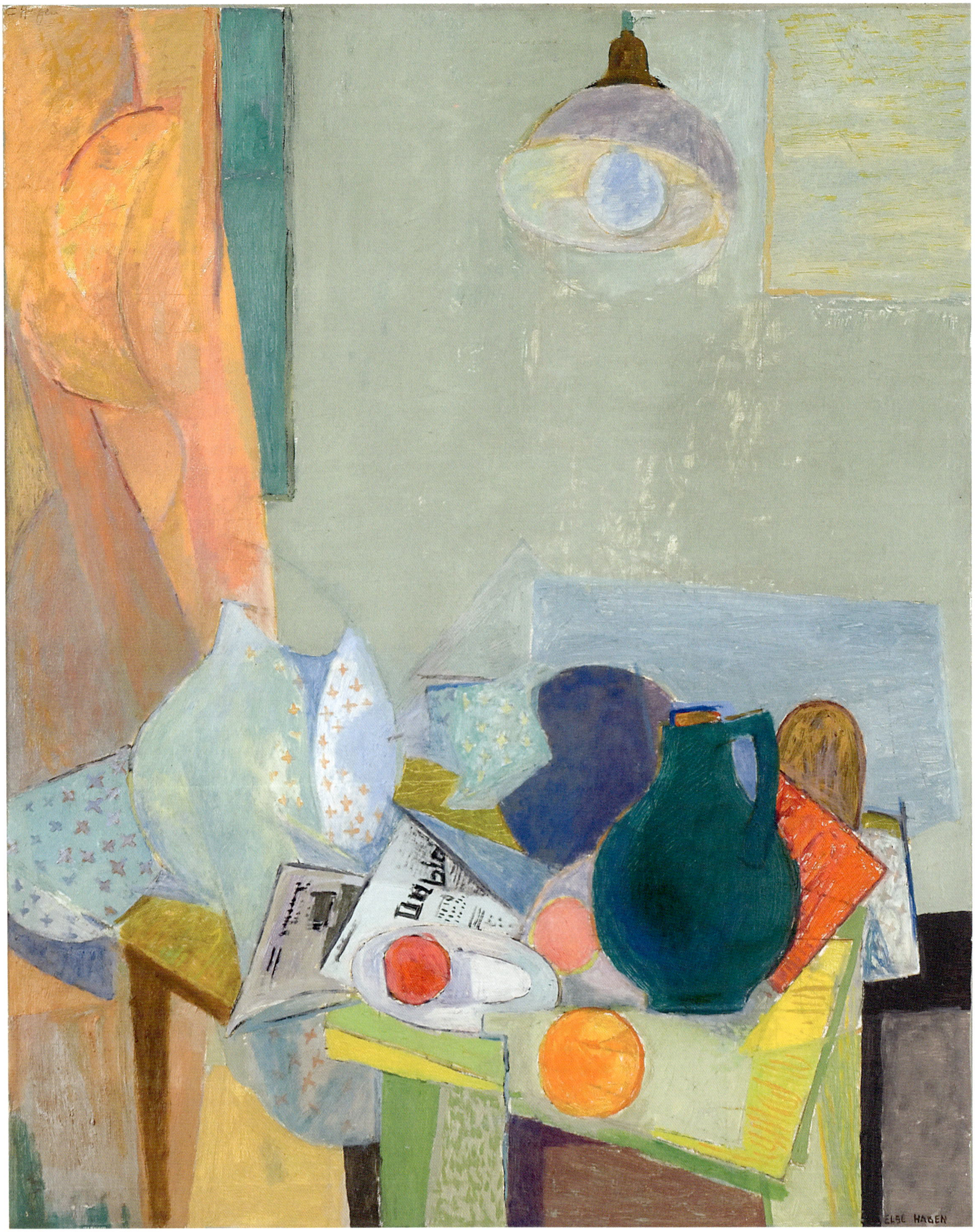
ELSE HAGEN

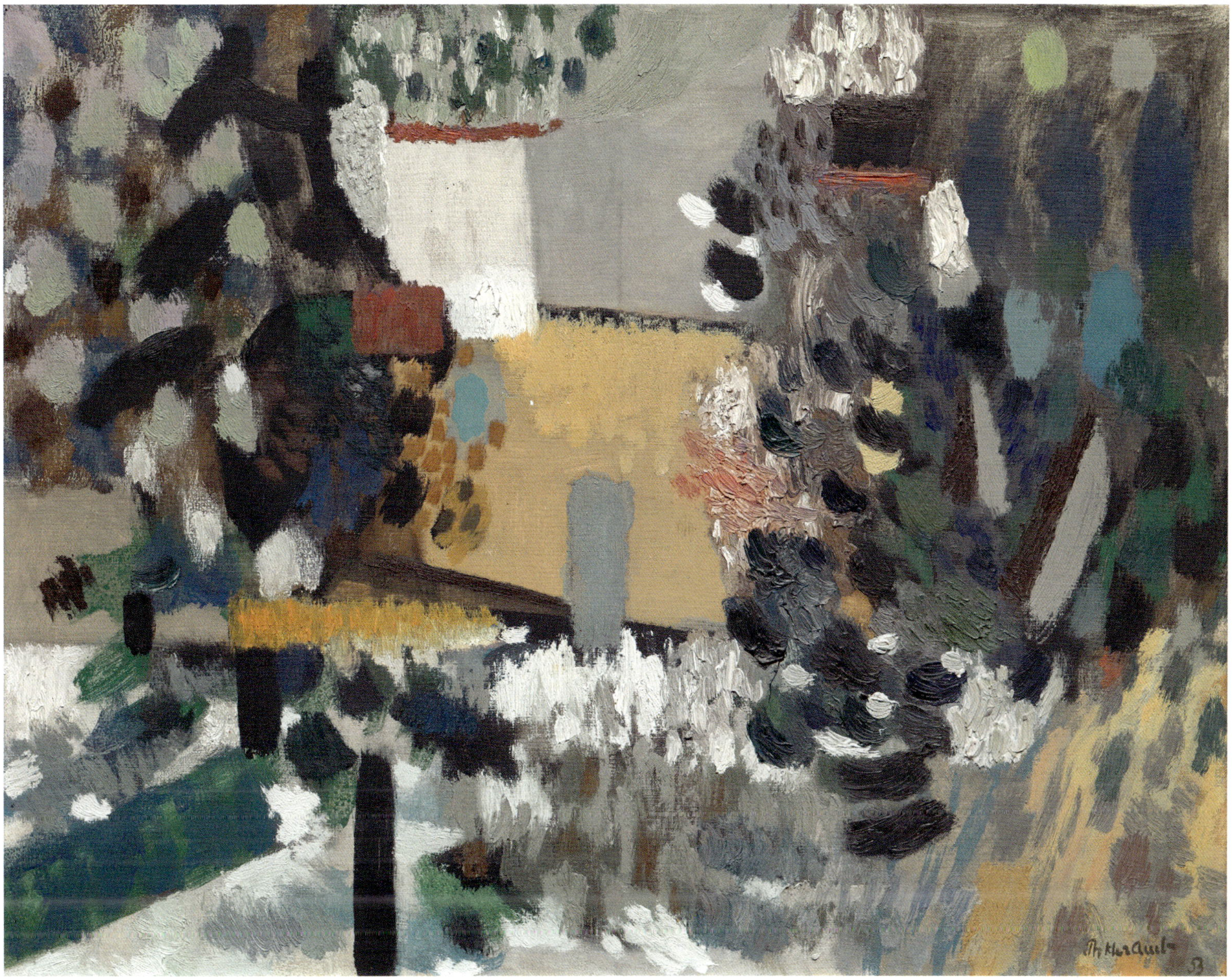

THORE HERAMB
HAGE, 1953

P.36
ELSE HAGEN
OPPSTILLING, 1939

ROBIN RHODE
EMPTIES (GREEN), 2007

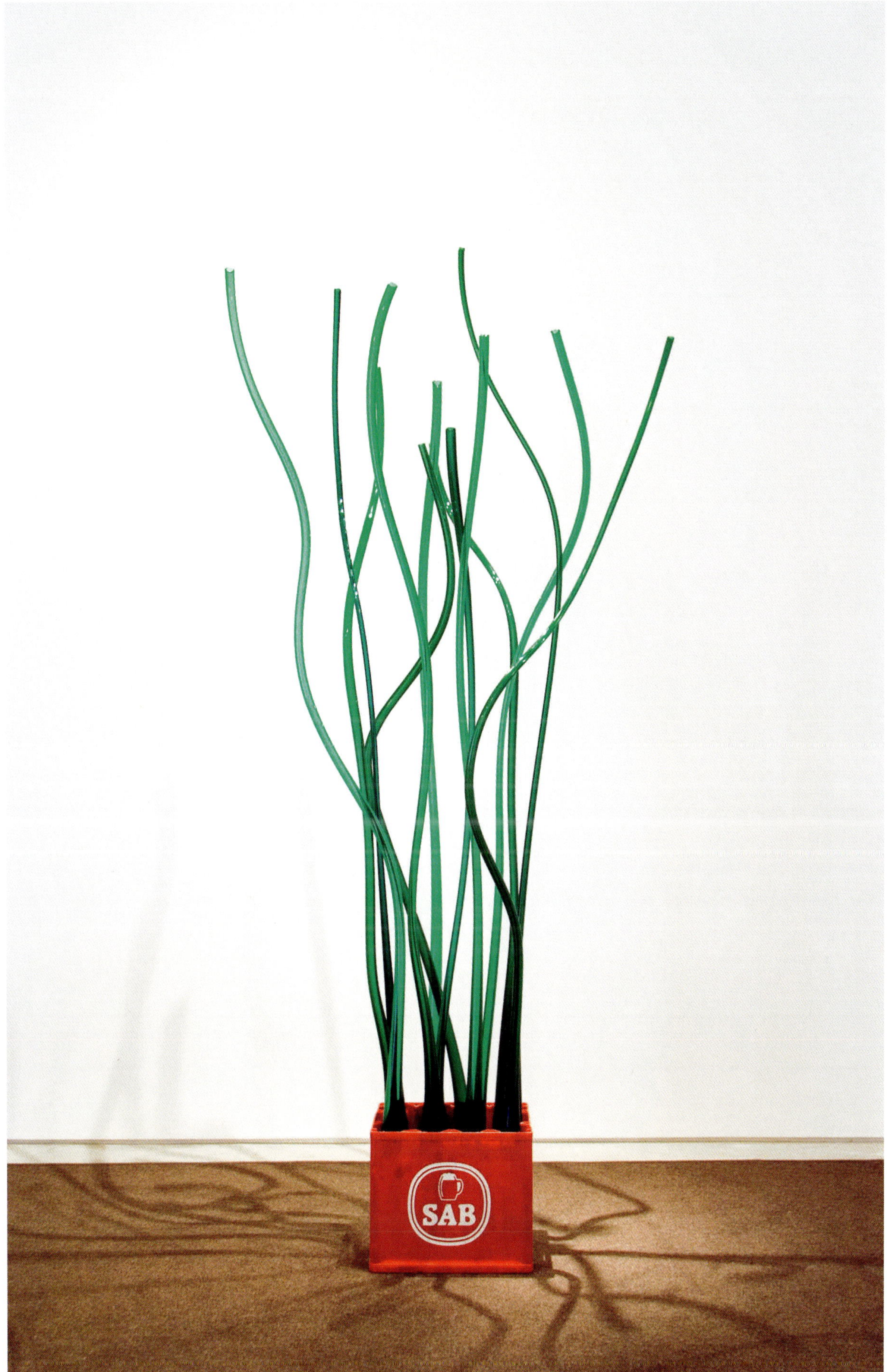
SAB

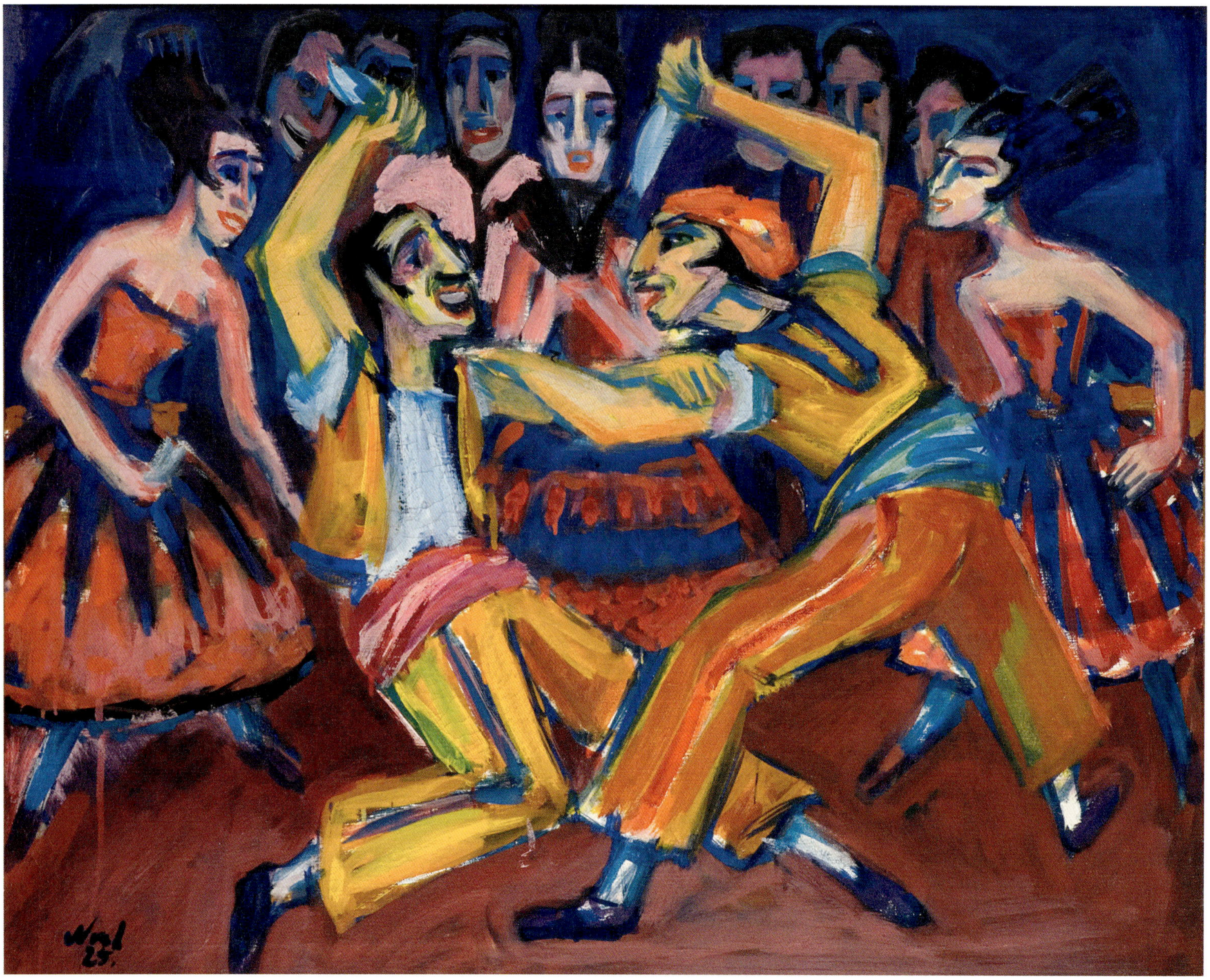

ROLF NESCH
RUSSISK BALLETT, STUTTGART, 1925

P. 41
THORVALD HELLESEN
DANS, 1921

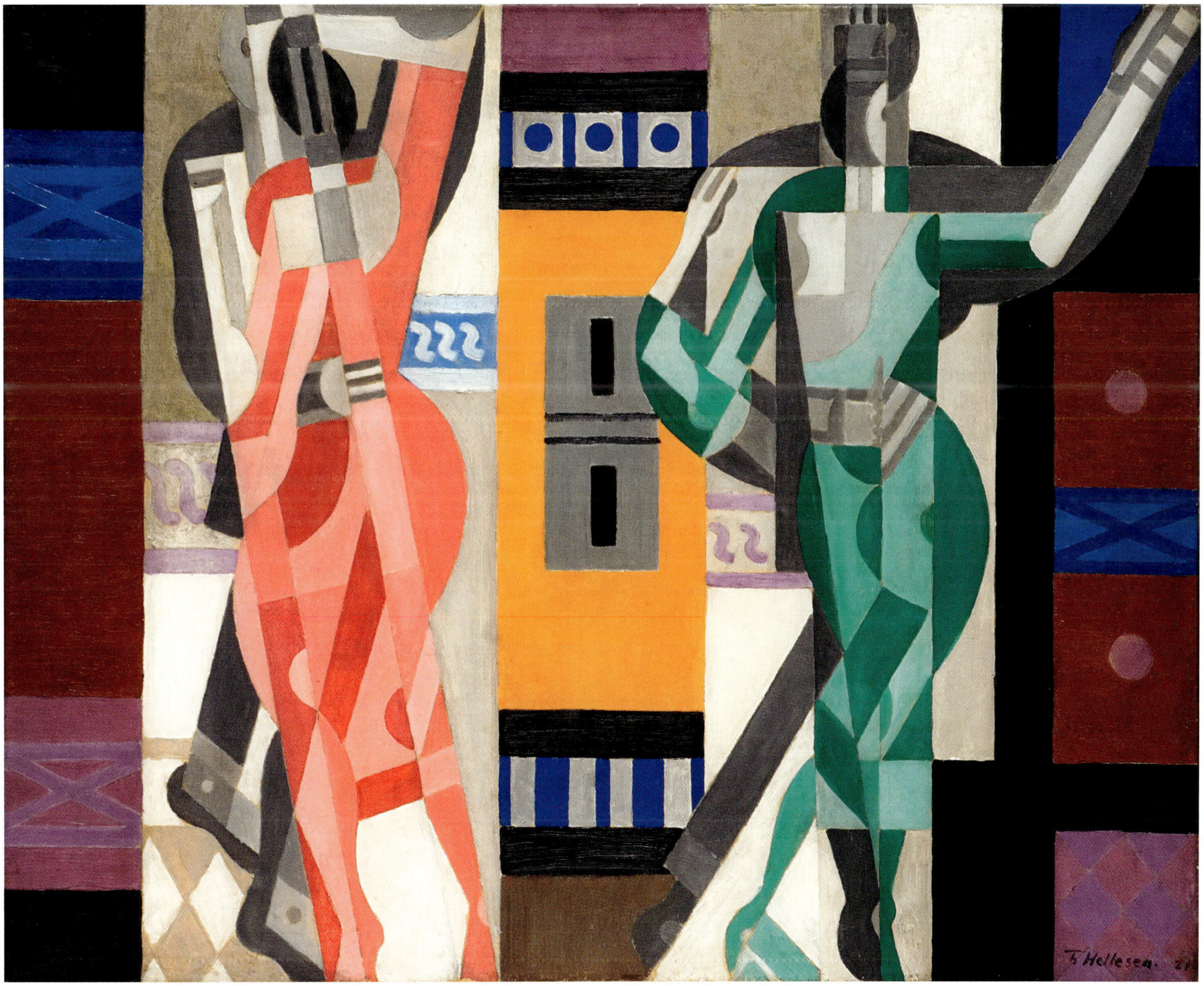

JULIE CURTISS
LE SERPENT QUI DANSE 2020

P. 44–45
WANGARI MATHENGE
AFTER EIGHT (THERE IS A MOMENT, FLEETING, WHEN ONE RETURNS TO SELF AND FEELS, AS IF FOR THE FIRST TIME, ALIVE), 2022

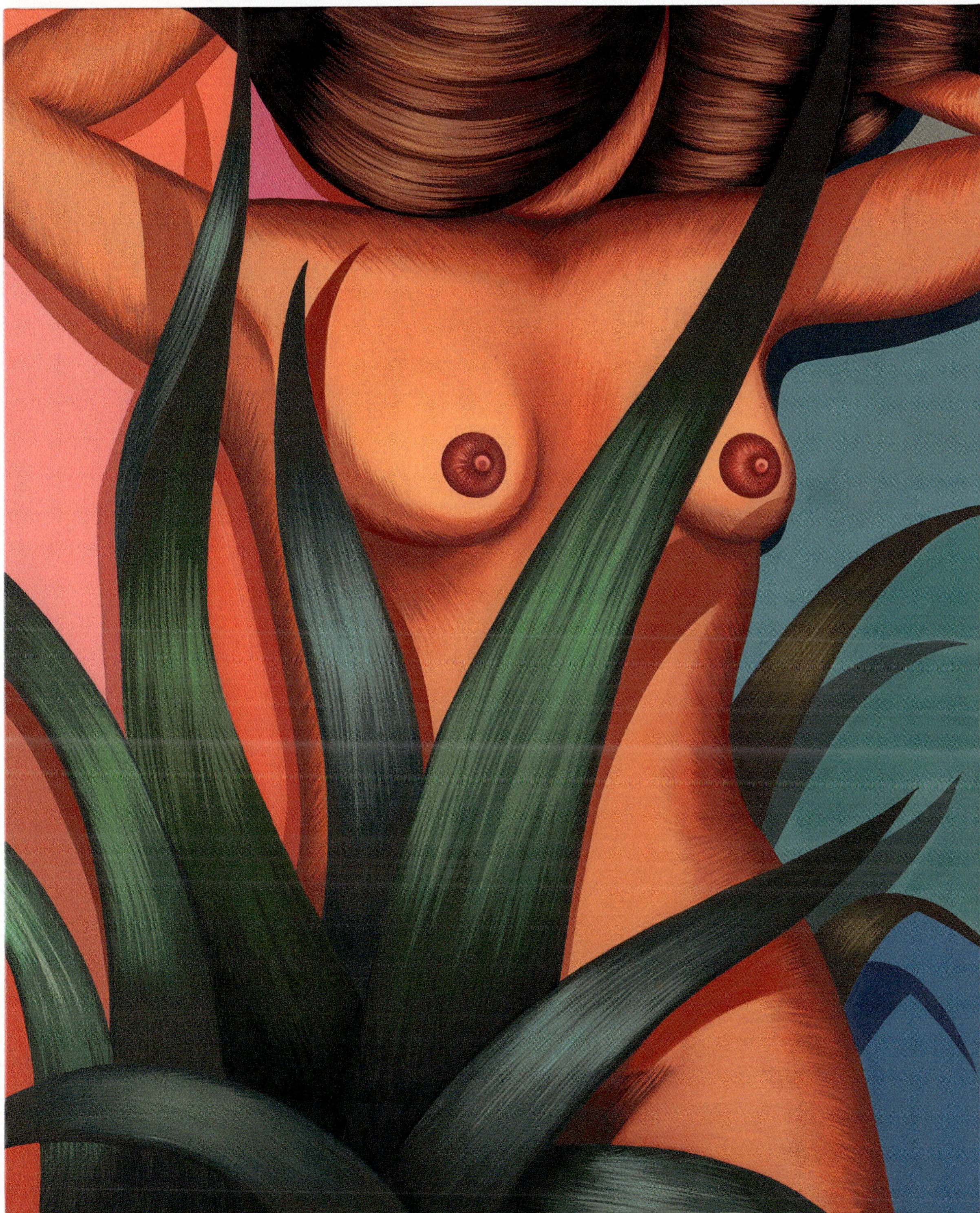

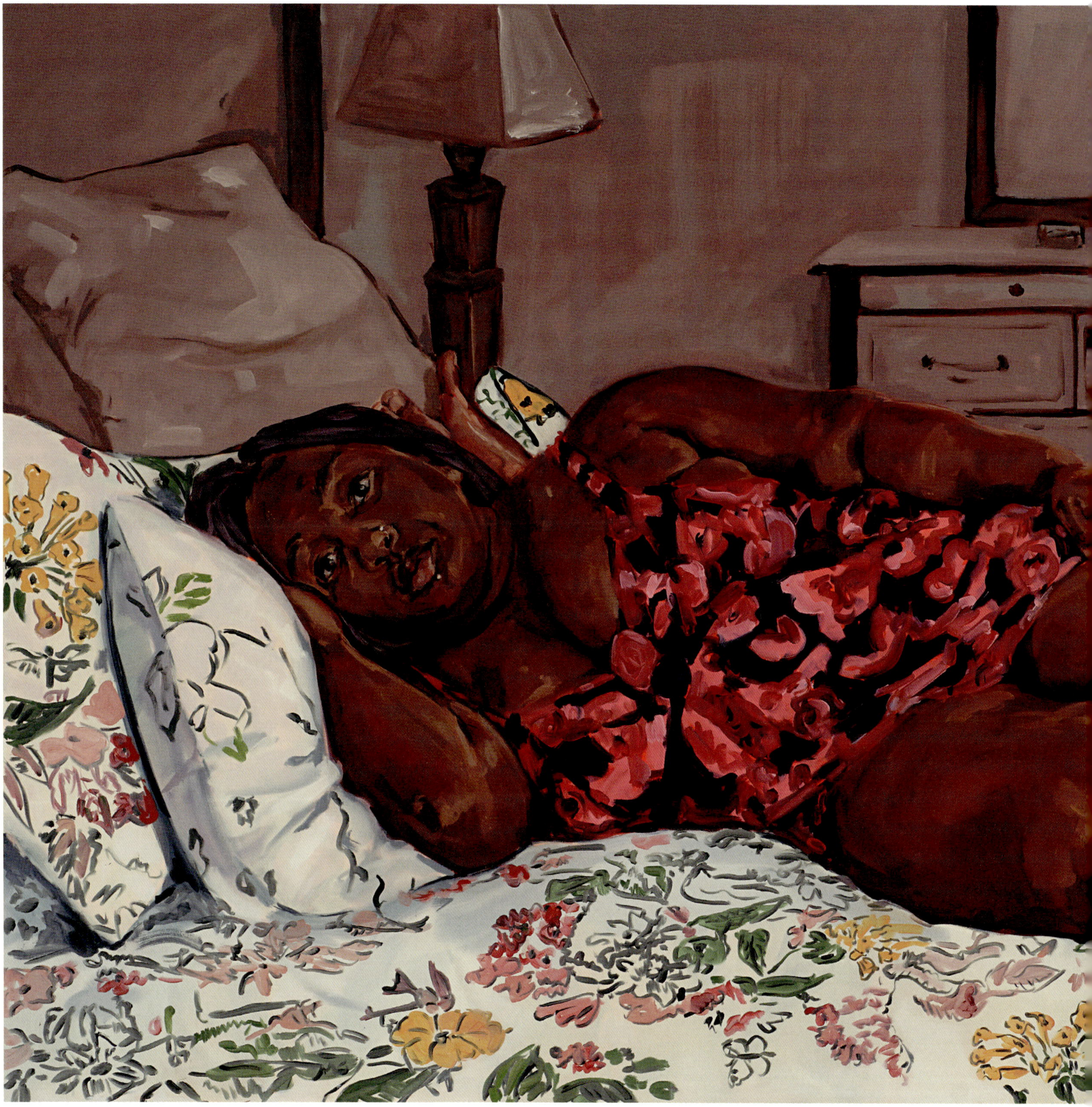

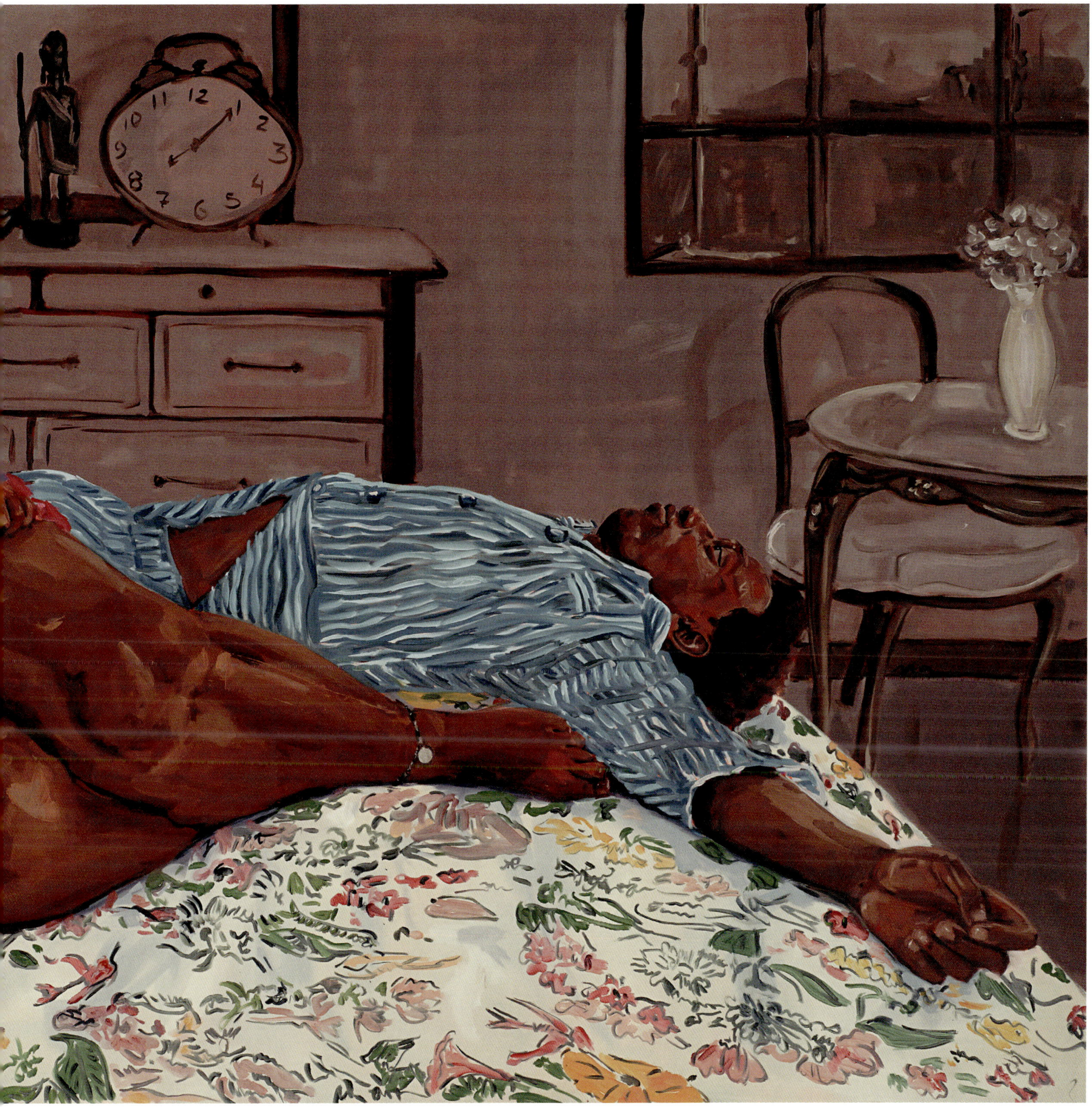

DANIEL SCHWARZ
WALPURGI, 2016

P. 48–49
ANDREAS GURSKY
MAYDAY IV, 2000

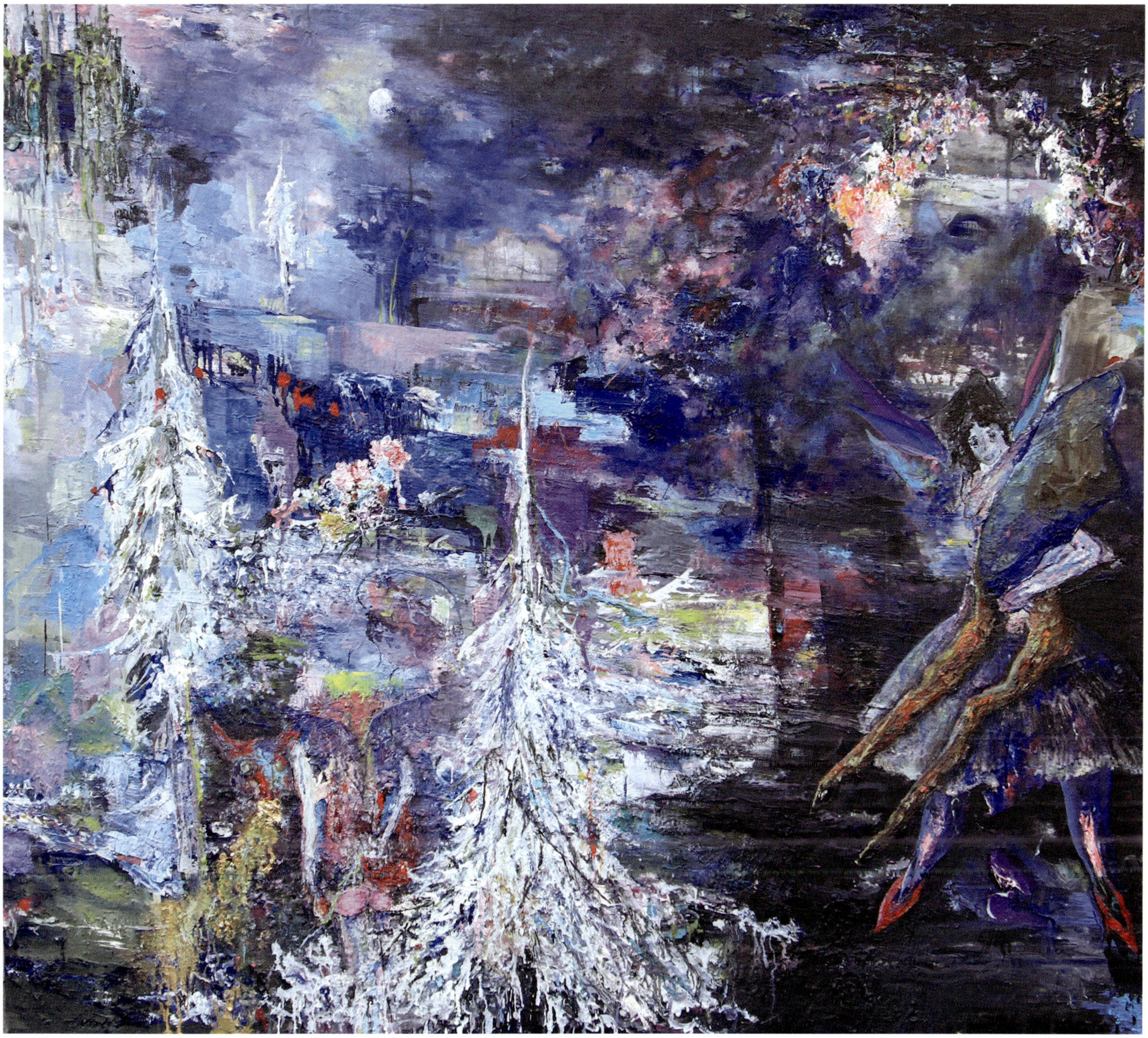

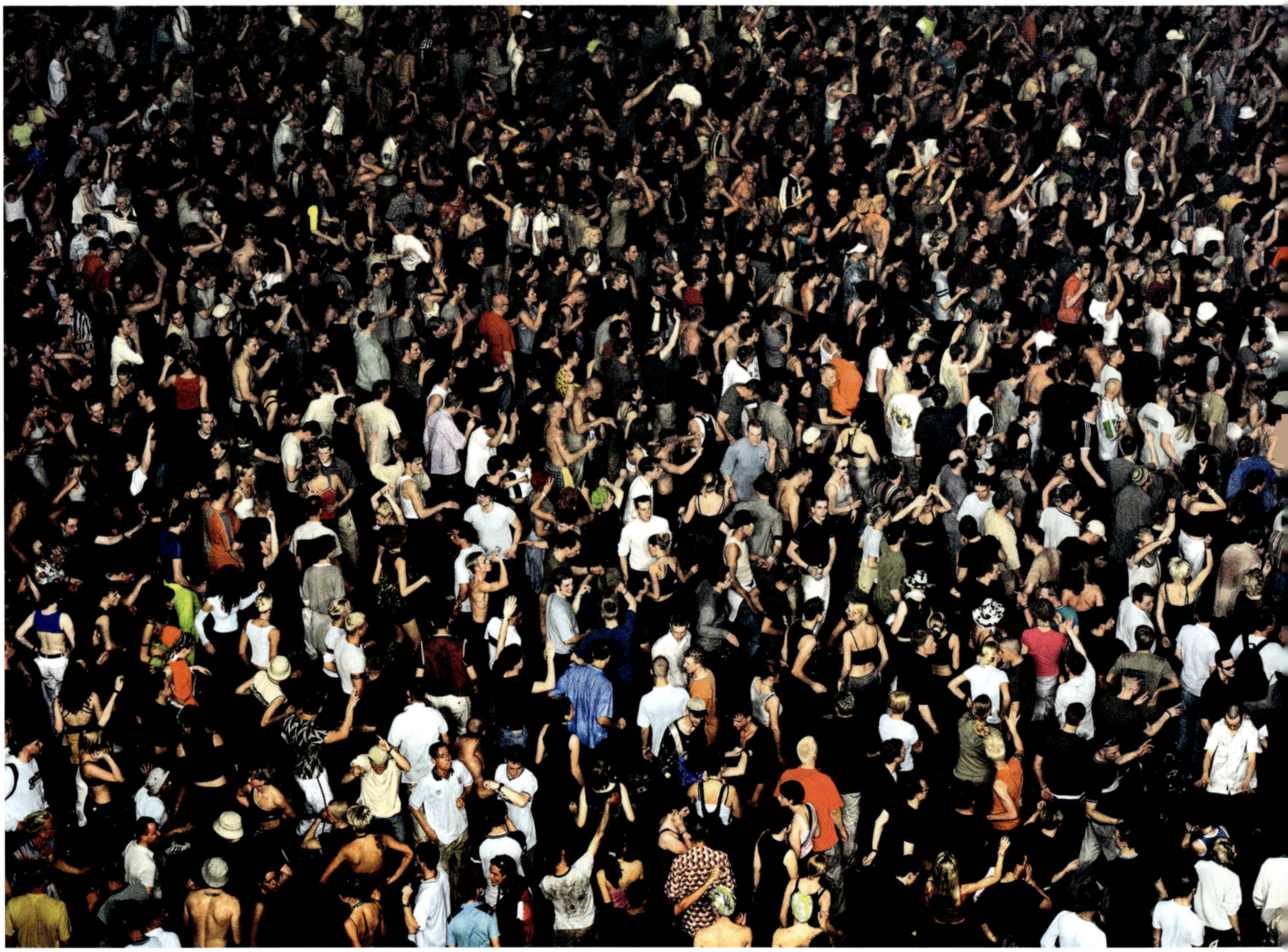

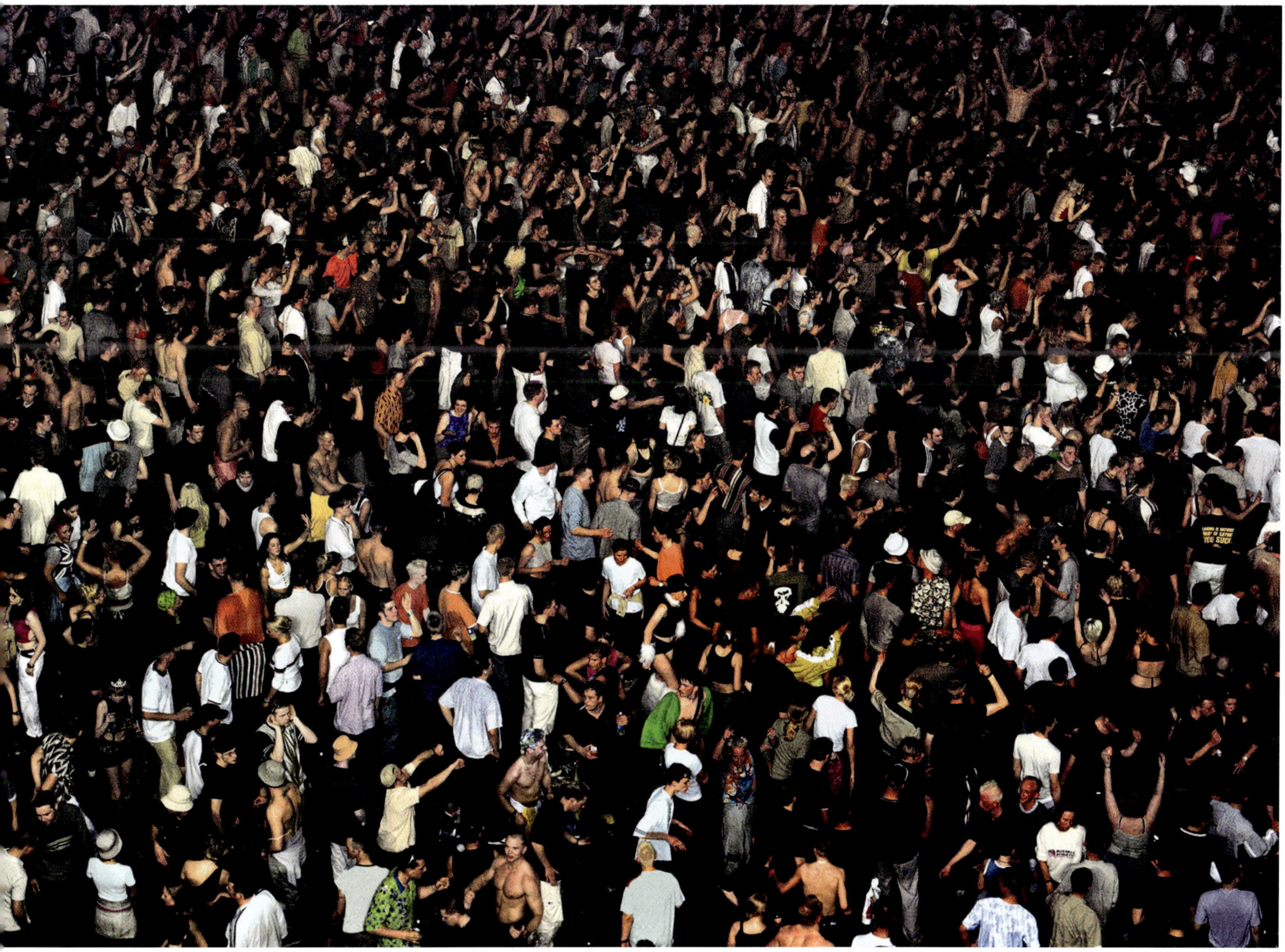

Summer

II.
SUMMER

As the Earth's axis tilts more closely towards the sun in the Northern Hemisphere, spring turns into summer, the days grow longer, the nights shorter, and the temperature rises. In the Southern Hemisphere, however, the opposite occurs; it is winter. Summertime scenes in art have historically been linked to agricultural life, such as haymaking and harvesting wheat, and originate in part from the 'labours of the months' depicted in medieval books of hours and illuminated calendars. In modern times, summer has come to be associated with sun, sky, water, sand and leisure-time activities. Assembled from moulded transparent PVC and acrylic glass in fluorescent yellow, orange, red and green, Berta Fischer's sculpture *Xurla* (2016) (→ p.55) reflects beams of light and colour like joyous summer solstice sunshine. A densely layered canvas in dayglow colours by Rosson Crow (→ p.56) features an overabundance of roses mixed with nostalgic references to the 1960s, from the Beach Boys' 'The Warmth of the Sun', to Harvey Ross Ball's Smiley graphic and Don Draper's Lucky Strike campaign. Perhaps inspired by a boat trip along the Norwegian coast, Anna-Eva Bergman combines translucent layers of tempera with metal foil to create an abstract image of the hull or square sail of a boat gleaming against the dark water or sky in *No 4—1960 Un bateau* (*No 4—1960 A Boat*, 1960) (→ p.59).

Warmer temperatures raise the level of moisture in the atmosphere, resulting in higher humidity and rain in summer. For *Drizzle* (1999) (→ p.61), from the series *Anagram (A Pun)*, Robert Rauschenberg used his own photographs in new configurations, making inkjet prints from images of umbrellas and transferring them to a polylaminate substrate with water and hand-burnishing tools. Hurvin Anderson's *Blue and gold umbrella* (1994) (→ p.62—63) combines collage, pencil and paint to rhythmically repeat and overlap the motif of the umbrella.

Since the Renaissance, bathers have been a recurring subject for artists who sought to depict idealised figures, particularly female bodies, in harmony with nature. No longer concerned with naturalism, modern artists have reimagined the motif of the bather by taking diverse, at times deliberately disjunctive, approaches to the unclothed figure. Aage Storstein's *Figurer på badestrand* (*Figures on the Beach*, 1930) (→ p.65) reveals an interest in Picasso's Cubist figuration, albeit tempered by the classicising return to order (*rappel à l'ordre*) that followed the First World War. *Die Badenden* (*The Bathers*, 1999) by Albert Oehlen (→ p.66—67) is a breakdown and remix of elements from a painting by John Graham titled *Tramonto Spaventoso* (*Terrifying Sunset*, 1940—49), including a stylised self-portrait and a mermaid. Engaged in acts of violence and sexual assault, Carroll Dunham's nude wrestlers offer a male counterpart to his predominantly female bathers (→ p.68). Referencing Cezanne's bathers, George Condo transforms the group of nudes into a grotesque orgy in his *Nocturnal Figure Composition* (2004) (→ p.69).

A painting featuring a group of figures enjoying an afternoon on the beach, *Charles Rosenthal: On the Beach, 1929* (1996) (→ p.70), is part of the oeuvre of a fictional artist invented by Ilya Kabakov. The bather in Vibeke Bärbel Slyngstad's *The Nordic Pavilion I* (2009) (→ p.71) is the corpse of a fictitious art collector floating face down in the swimming pool from Elmgreen & Dragset's Nordic Pavilion for the 2009 Venice Biennale. Mette Tronvoll's *Boy #5* (1998) (→ p.73) is from a series of photographs of Greenlanders bathing in the natural hot springs of the island of Uunartoq. Nan Goldin's *Jimmy Paulette and Tabboo! in the Bathroom, NYC, 1991* (1991) (→ p.74) captures two drag queens in an intimate moment in the bathroom of their New York apartment, getting ready for a night out.

Summer is paradoxically a time for both labour and leisure, toil and travel. Many people take on extra work and save up to be able to take a summer holiday abroad. In the summer of 1951, American writer James Baldwin travelled to Leukerbad, Switzerland to restore his mental health, at the invitation of his partner Lucien Happersberger whose family owned a chalet there. His essay ‘Stranger in the Village’ (1953) describes the racism and alienation he experienced in the small alpine village and in the United States. In *Stranger #65* (2012) (→ p.75), Glenn Ligon silkscreened excerpts from Baldwin’s essay and, in contrast with other works from this series, obscured them beneath a thick dusting of coal, a protective layer encasing the scars of racism in abstraction. Theaster Gates also references the author and activist in *Resolution 2: The Only Lasting Resolutions Have Something To Do With James Baldwin* (2013) (→ p.76). Made from a decommissioned fire hose, the work can be understood as an abstraction, a red monochrome. But high-pressure hoses like these were also used against protesters to break up demonstrations during the US civil rights movement. Gates’s sculpture *Migration Rickshaw for Sleeping, Building and Playing* (2013) (→ p.77) is comprised of a wooden handcart laden with bedding, planks of wood and colourful blocks. Ibrahim Mahama shares with Gates a deep concern with the poetics and meaning of materials. His work *UB40 Kofi* (2016) (→ p.79) features torn jute sacks—used to store and transport goods such as cocoa, coffee and charcoal—stitched together and embellished with metal authentication tags from the Ghana Cocoa Board. Mahama is also interested in the words and names written on some of the sacks by the labourers who reused them, and in their inadvertent references to Ghanaian and other cultural figures.

The humble fish seller is reimagined in richly-coloured dress and full-length aristocratic pose in a recent painting by Lubaina Himid (→ p.81), but she also reminds us that safety and danger coexist. *Journey (32)* (2021) (→ p.83) by Tewodros Hagos is a portrait of a group of young, brown-skinned migrants wrapped in silver foil blankets, an all-too-familiar summertime image. *Stryder* (1985) (→ p.84–85) is an early work by Denzil Forrester depicting a scene in a dance hall. The vibrant canvas captures the colourful outfits of the musicians and expressive rhythms of the reggae or dub music. At the centre of the canvas, a Black figure is pushed up against a wall by a police officer, underscoring the discrimination and police brutality experienced in Caribbean communities at the time.

Ida Ekblad flips the notion of ‘day for night’, a cinematic technique for filming a night scene during daylight hours, and imagines having ‘twilight vision and you see unseen pigments and double horizons’.[2] Thick patches of hot reds, pinks and oranges mix with cooler blues and greens in her *NIGHT FOR DAY* (2022) (→ p.87), perhaps evoking a shift in colour perception due to a solar eclipse. From the dark and murky centre of *Night* (2011–12) (→ p.88) by Howard Hodgkin, thick orange, yellow and green brushstrokes radiate heat and light. Caragh Thuring’s cryptic canvas *August 2014* (2014) (→ p.89) is constructed from recurring motifs from her oeuvre, including brick work, a volcano and an inverted pyramid, set against a pitch-black night sky. While the title of the work may refer to the date of a volcanic eruption in Iceland or one of several other places, it is open-ended. Steinar Jakobsen’s *Street Eclipse* (2004) (→ p.90) captures the descent into darkness during a total eclipse. Based on a movie played back on videotape and photographed on a television screen, Judith Eisler’s *Car Door I (The 10th Victim)* (1999) (→ p.91) suggests the plot of a 1970s summer crime drama.

The warm weather and longer hours of light in summer result in more social gatherings and outdoor events. Drawing on the influence of Matisse’s interiors, Norwegian painter Johs. Rian depicts a female figure seated at a table in the relaxed atmosphere of a Spanish restaurant (→ p.93). Latifa Echakhch paints nighttime scenes based on photographs taken

2. Quoted in press release for ‘Ida Ekblad: FLYABLE, RIDEABLE’, *Karma International,* Zurich 2022. https://karmainternational.ch/usr/documents/exhibitions/press_release_url/95/press_release-ida-ekblad-flyablerideable.pdf

by her friend Sim Ouch and then translates them into paint, obscuring then partially revealing the imagery (→ p.94). The resulting painting is disjointed, yet details such as a wine glass, a smile and casual poses convey a lively night out with friends. Summer is also associated with increased drinking and drug use. Ed Ruscha's *Painkillers, Tranquilizers, Olive* (1969) (→ p.96) is from a series of works depicting spherical objects hovering against a monochromic gradient background. Painted with precision, the arrangement of pills and olive suggest both a nighttime constellation and a cocktail of drugs and alcohol. Wilhelm Sasnal's image of a dingy toilet (→ p.97), the type one encounters while in a woozy state in a bar, oscillates between the photographic realism of the porcelain surfaces and the painterly landscape of stains and grime.

Summer draws to an end with the start of the harvest season. Commissioned to make photographs for patient rooms in a hospital in Winterthur, Switzerland, Thomas Struth captured the local landscape, including farmland, forests and gardens as well as flowers and other plants. *Mais-Acker, Winterthur* (*Cornfield, Winterthur* 1992) (→ p.98) documents rows of brown stubble that echo the curve of a road by an empty field after a late-summer harvest.

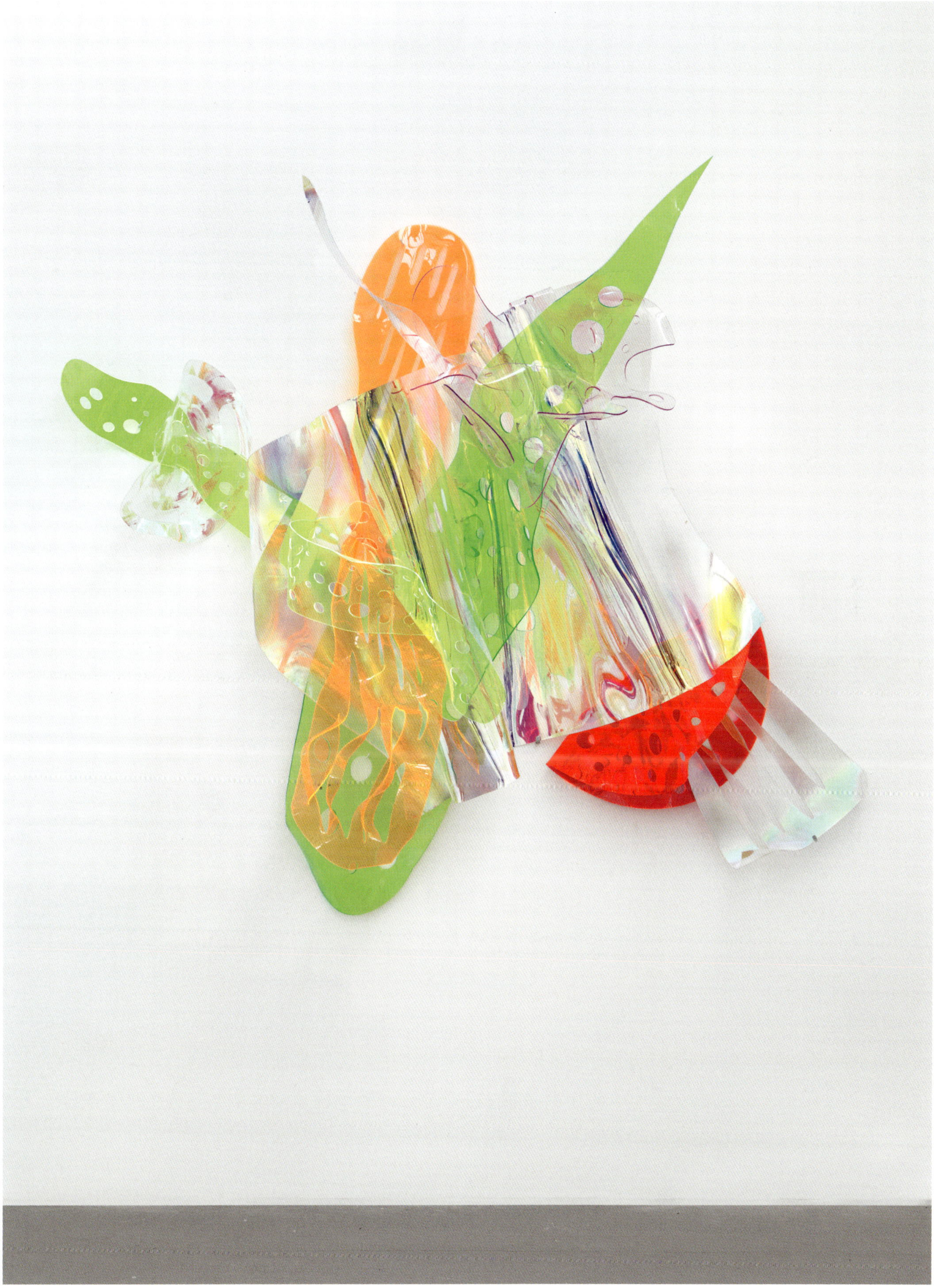

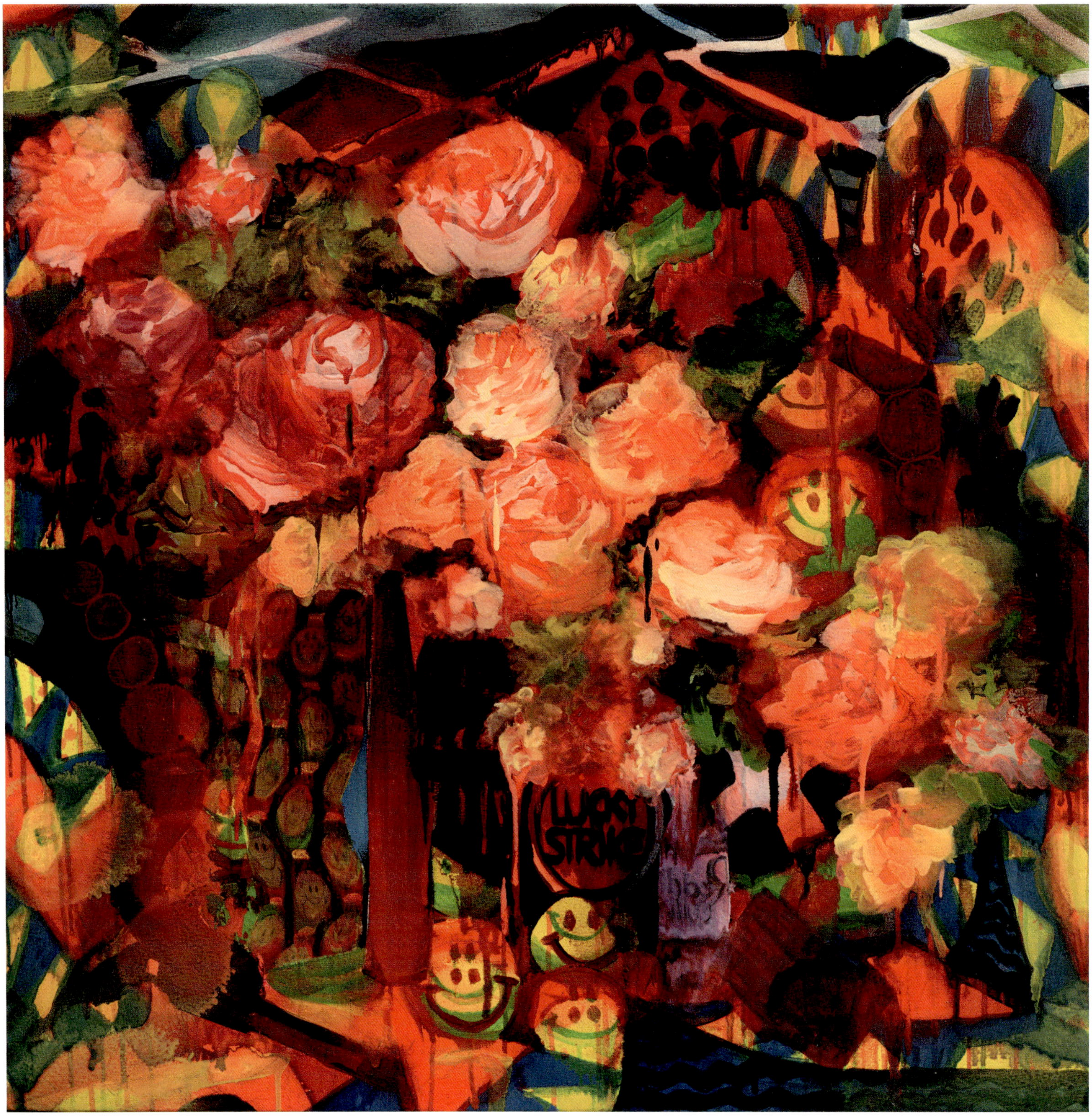

P.55
BERTA FISCHER
XURLA, 2016

ROSSON CROW
THE WARMTH OF THE SUN, 2014

ANNA-EVA BERGMAN
NO 4–1960 UN BATEAU, 1960

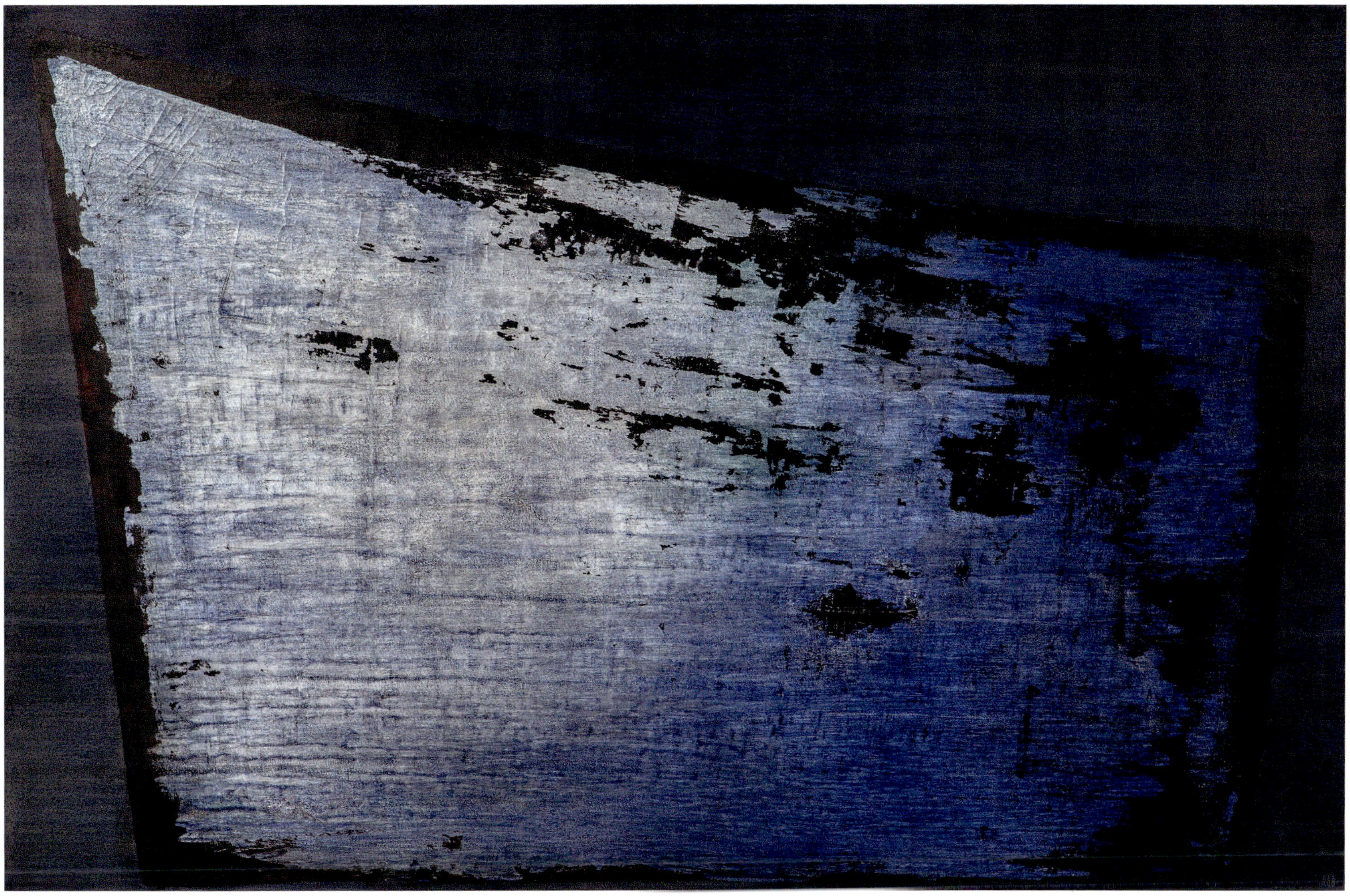

ROBERT RAUSCHENBERG
DRIZZLE, 1999

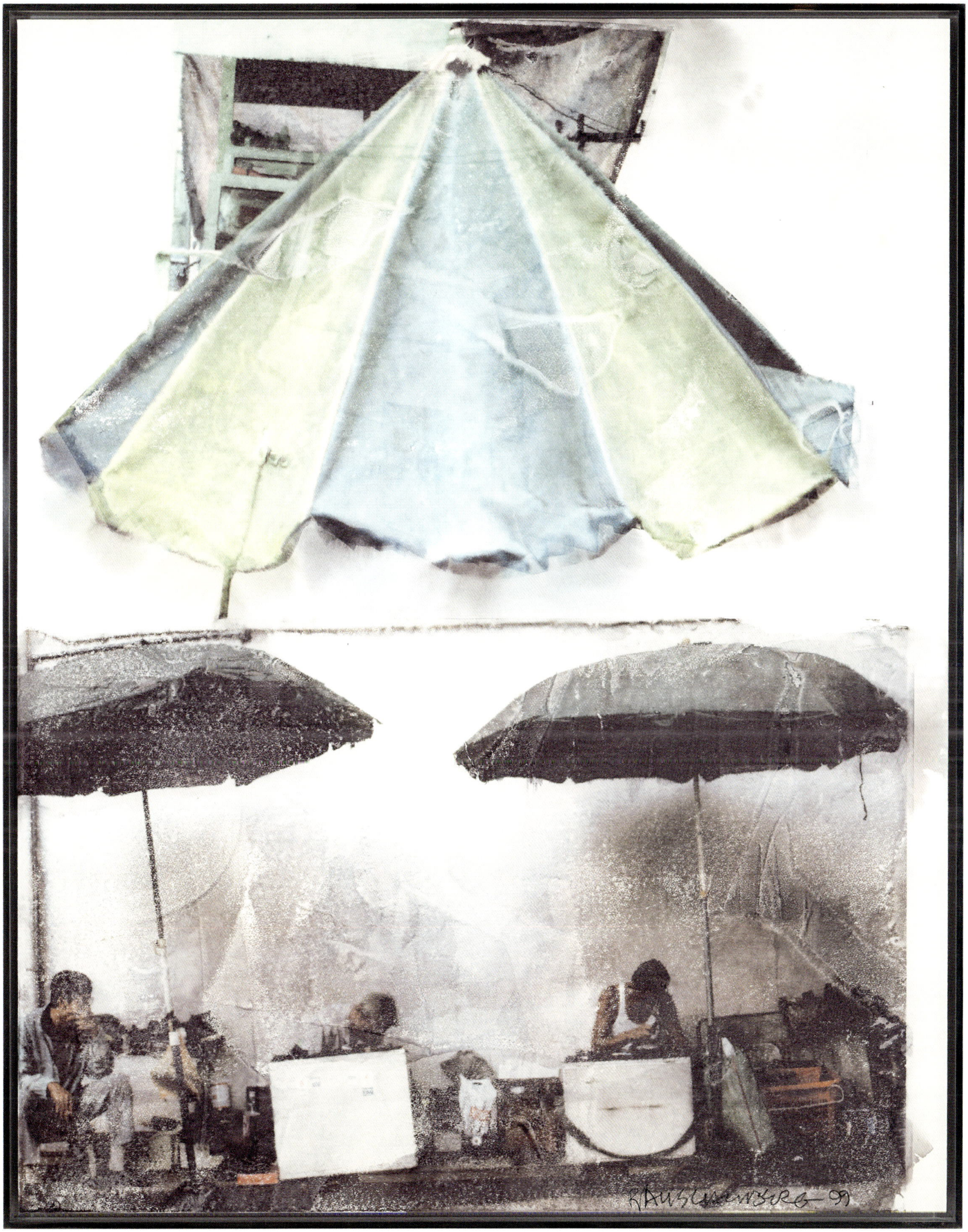

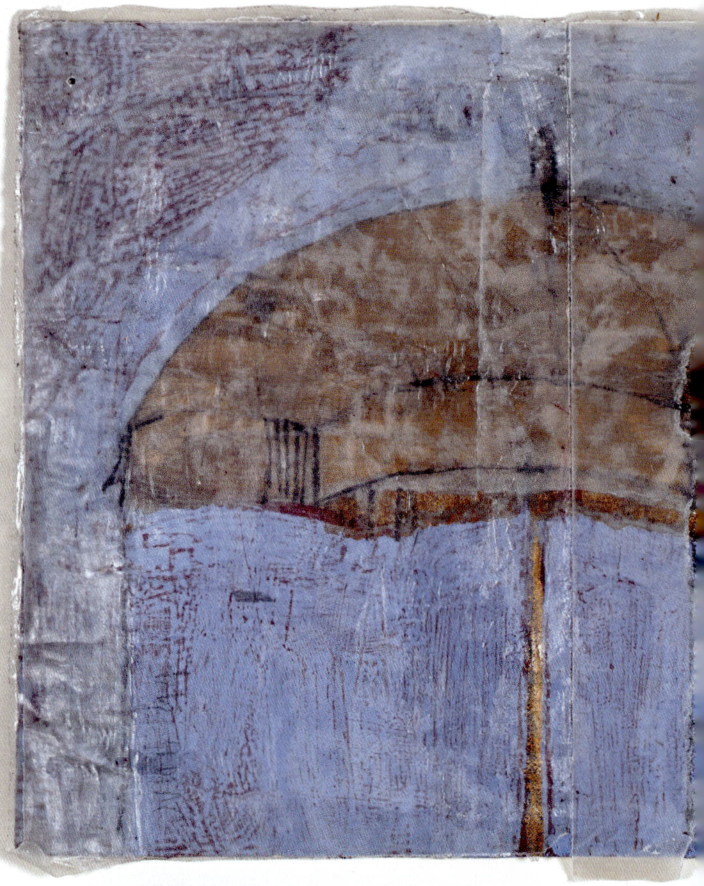

HURVIN ANDERSON
BLUE AND GOLD UMBRELLA, 1994

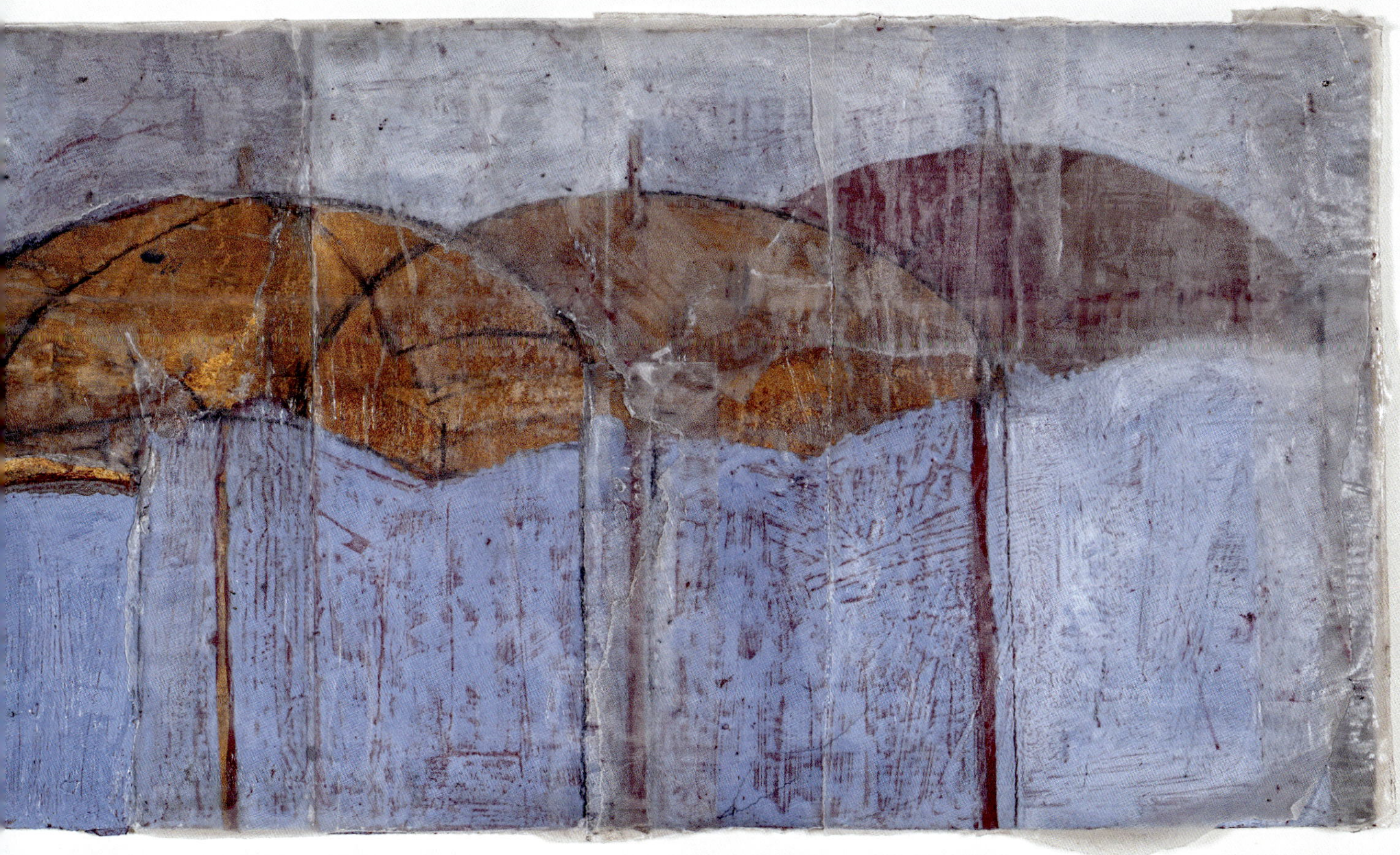

AAGE STORSTEIN
FIGURER PÅ BADESTRAND, 1930

P. 66–67
ALBERT OEHLEN
DIE BADENDEN, 1999

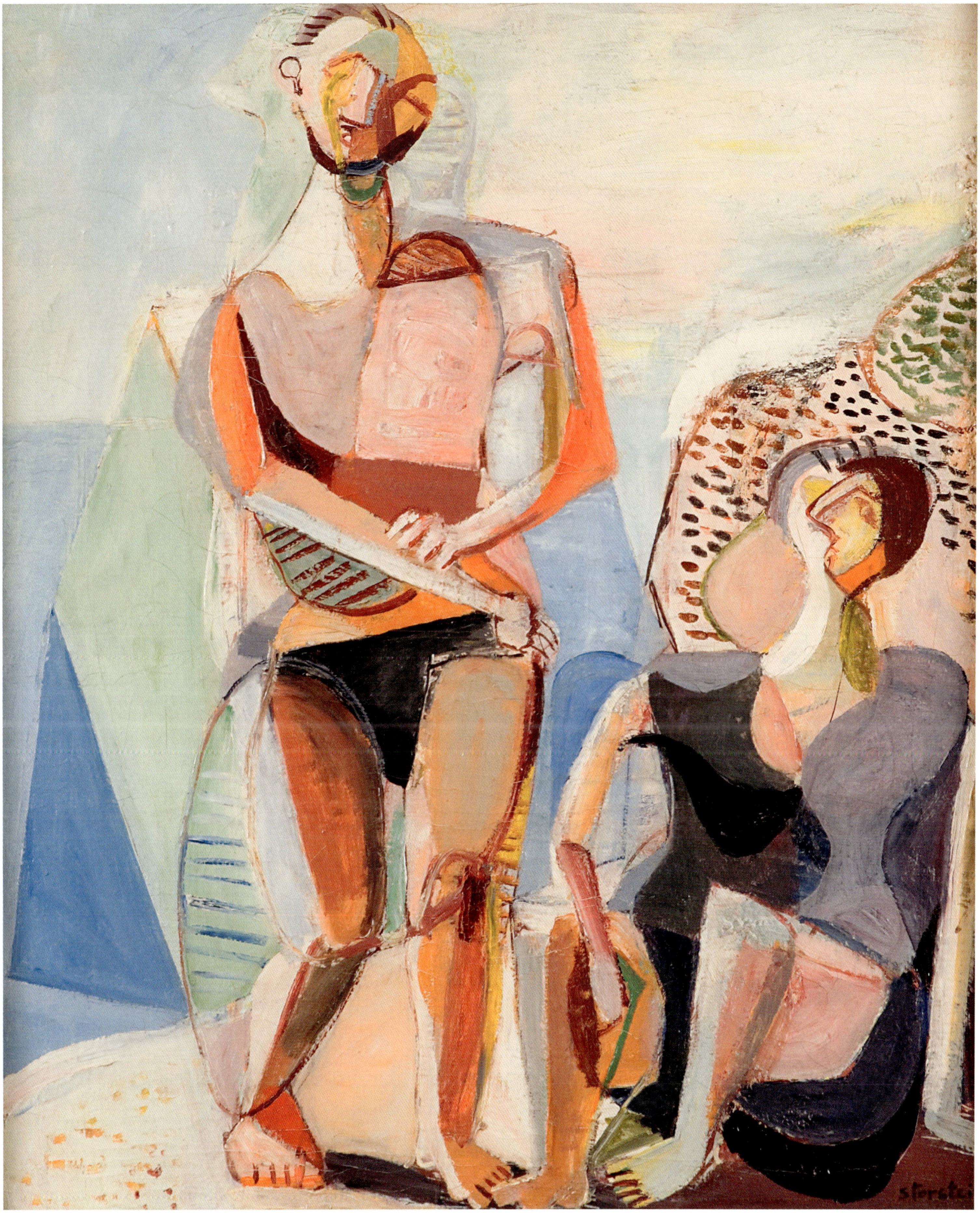

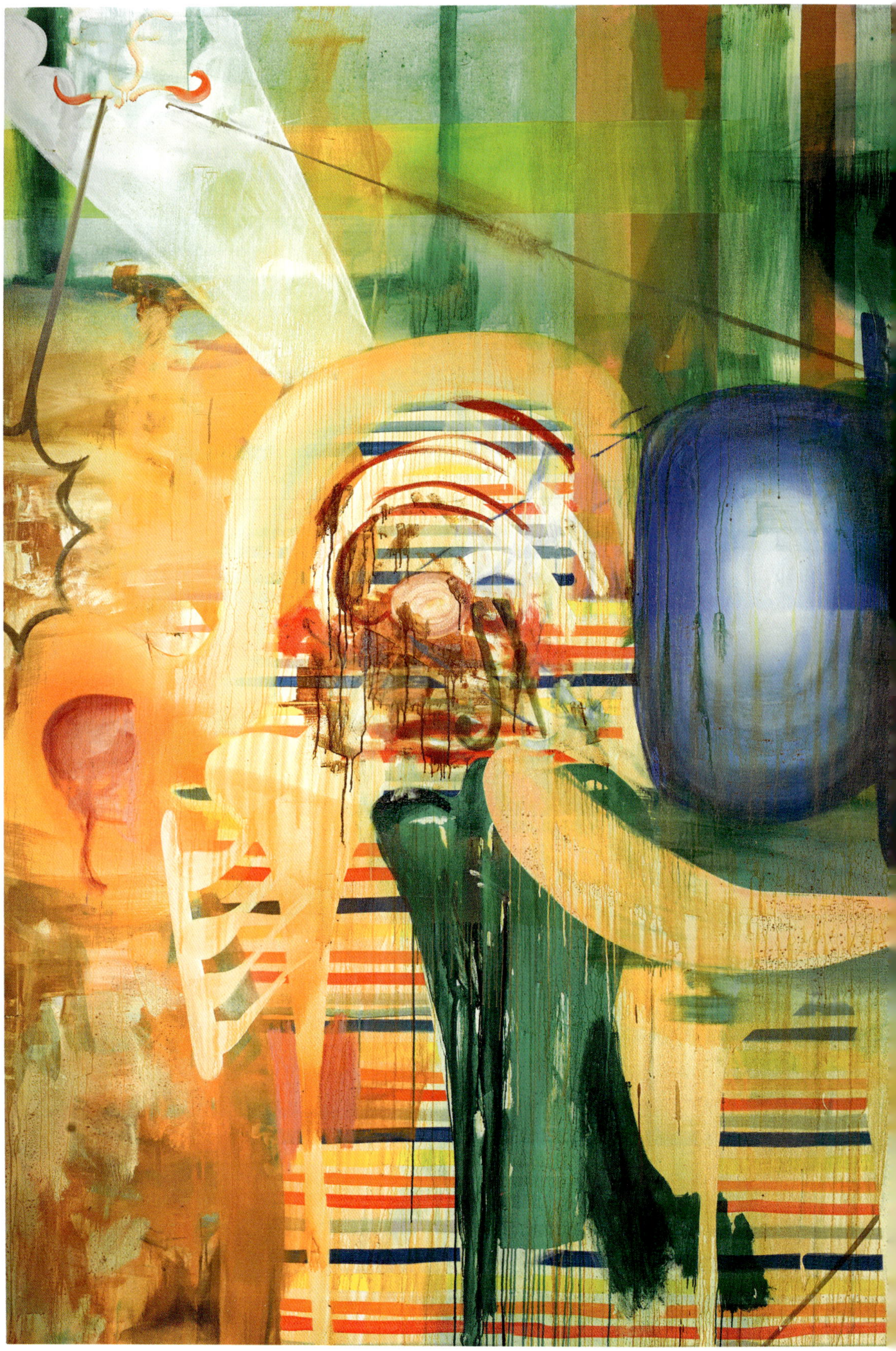

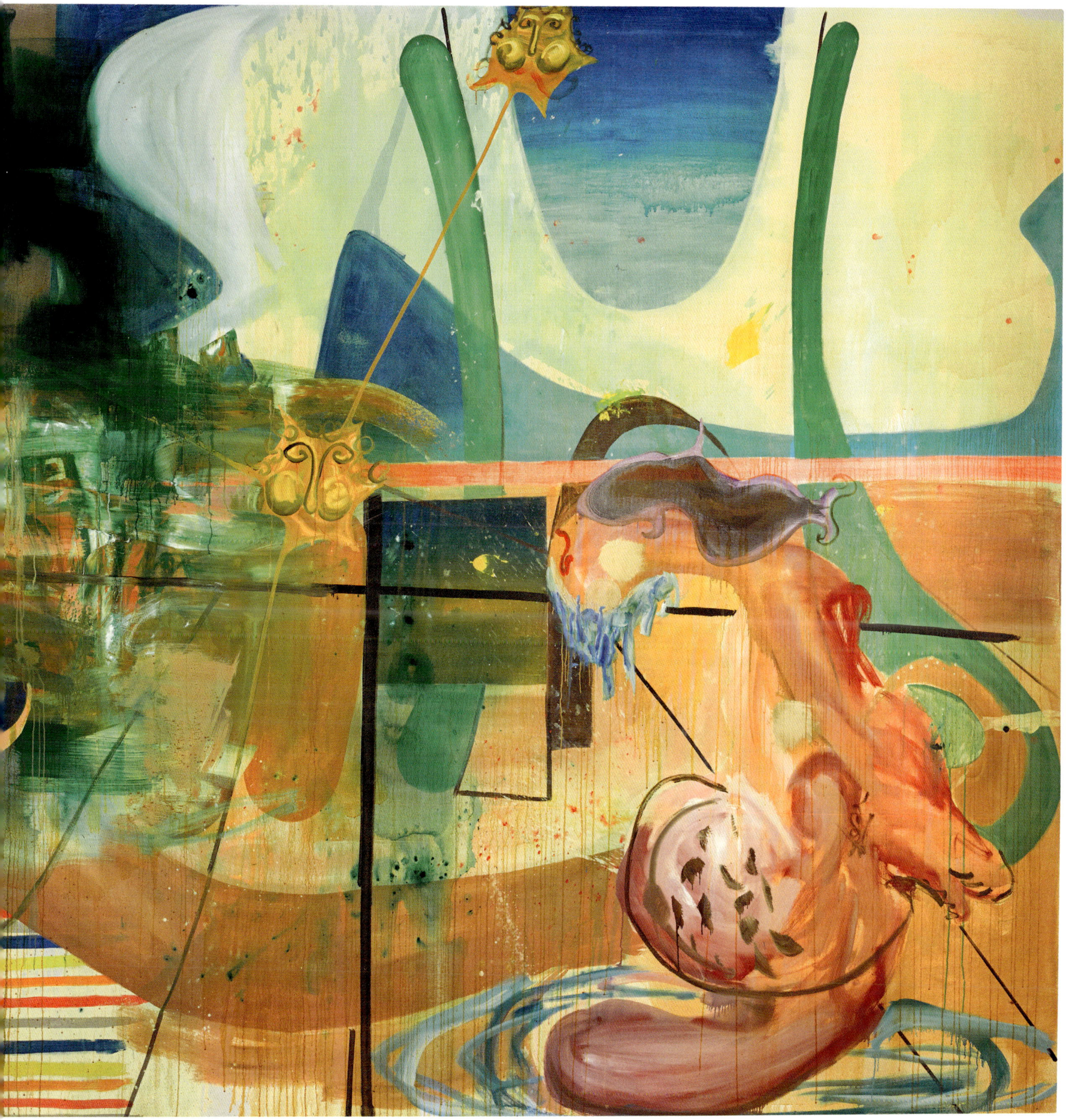

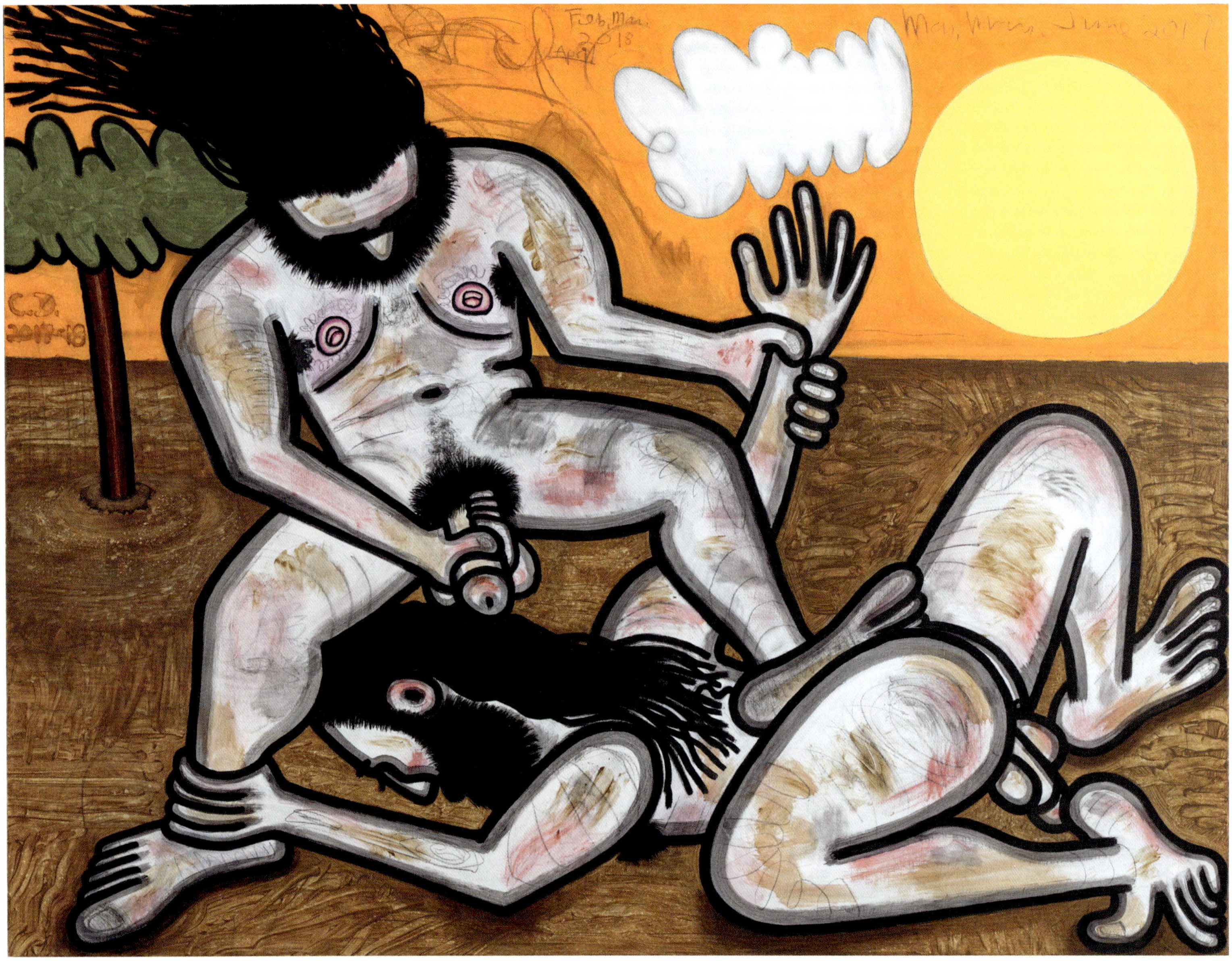

CARROLL DUNHAM
WRESTLERS/ ORANGE SKY, 2017

P. 69
GEORGE CONDO
NOCTURNAL FIGURE COMPOSITION, 2004

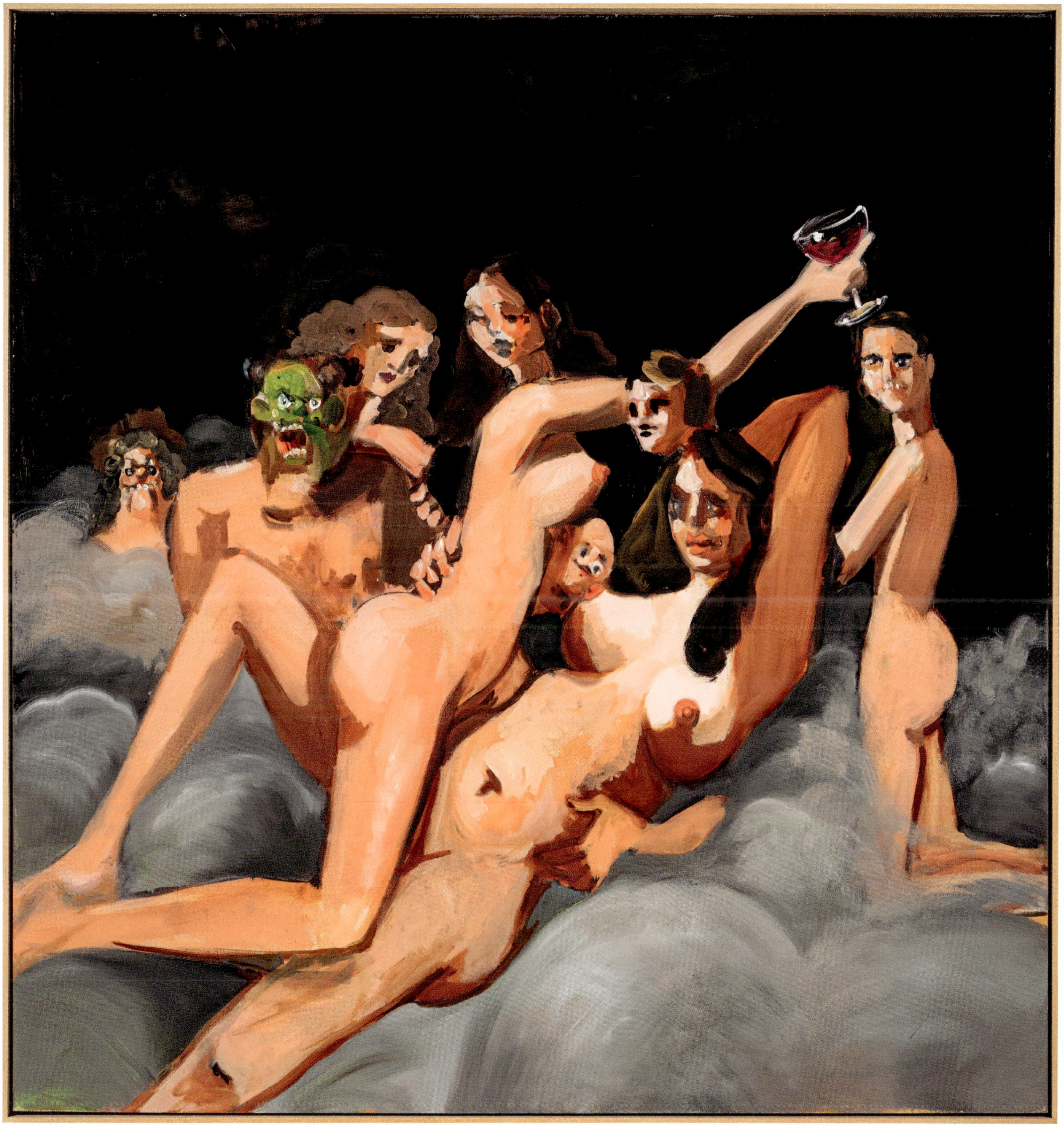

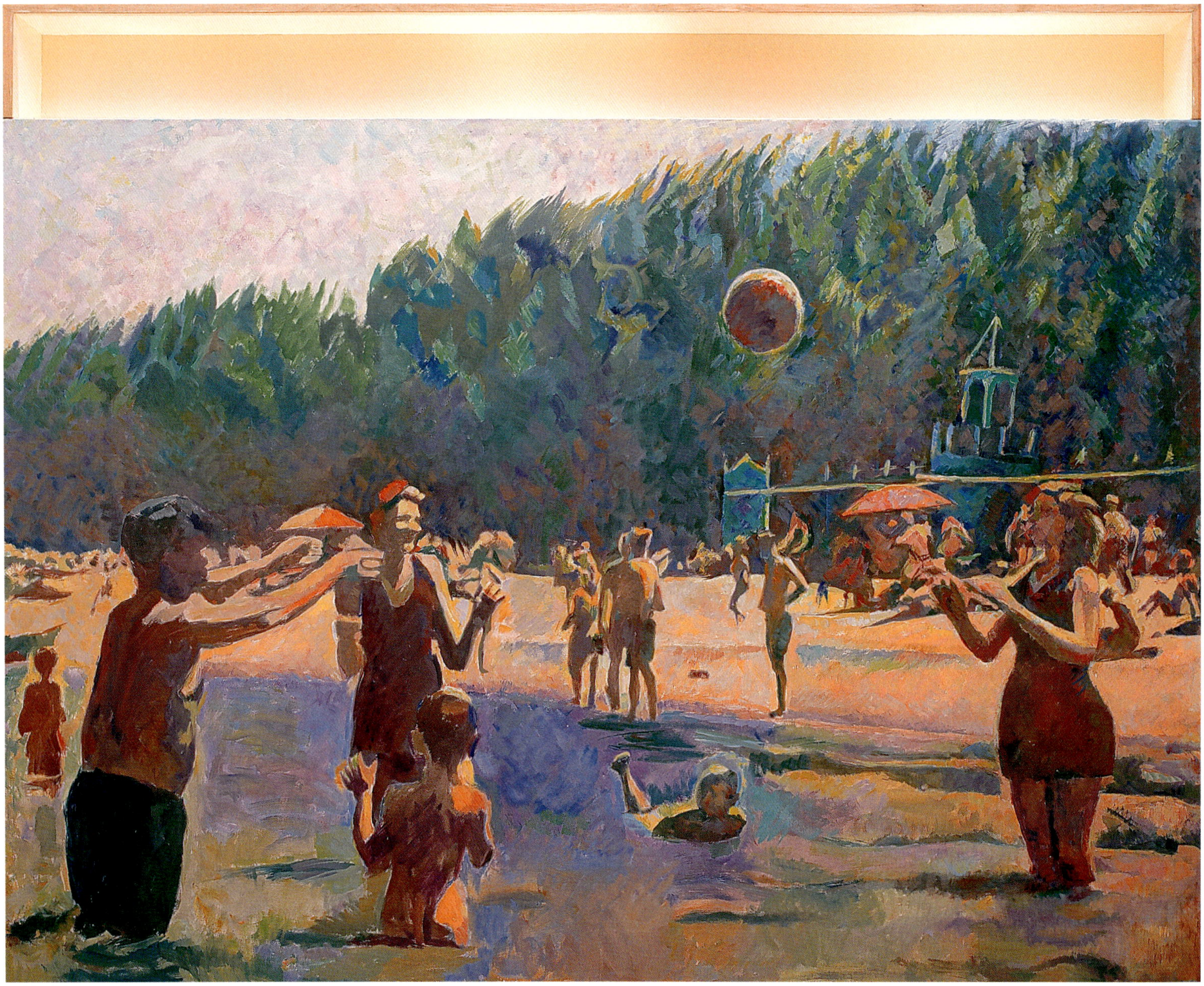

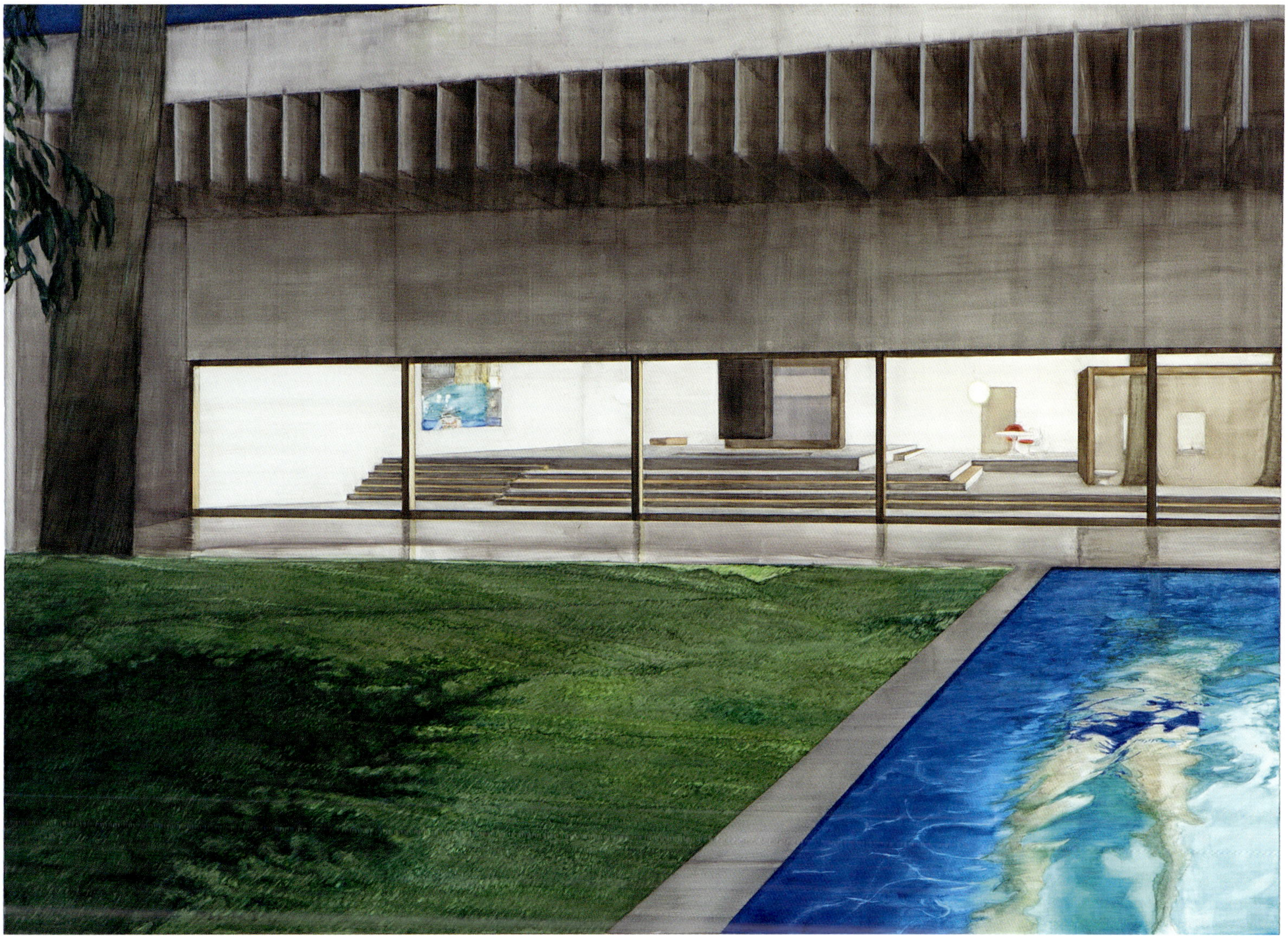

VIBEKE BÄRBEL SLYNGSTAD
THE NORDIC PAVILION I, 2009

P. 70
ILYA KABAKOV
CHARLES ROSENTHAL: ON THE BEACH, 1929, 1996

METTE TRONVOLL
BOY #5, 1998

P. 74
NAN GOLDIN
JIMMY PAULETTE AND TABBOO!
IN THE BATHROOM, NYC 1991, 1991

P. 75
GLENN LIGON
STRANGER #65, 2012

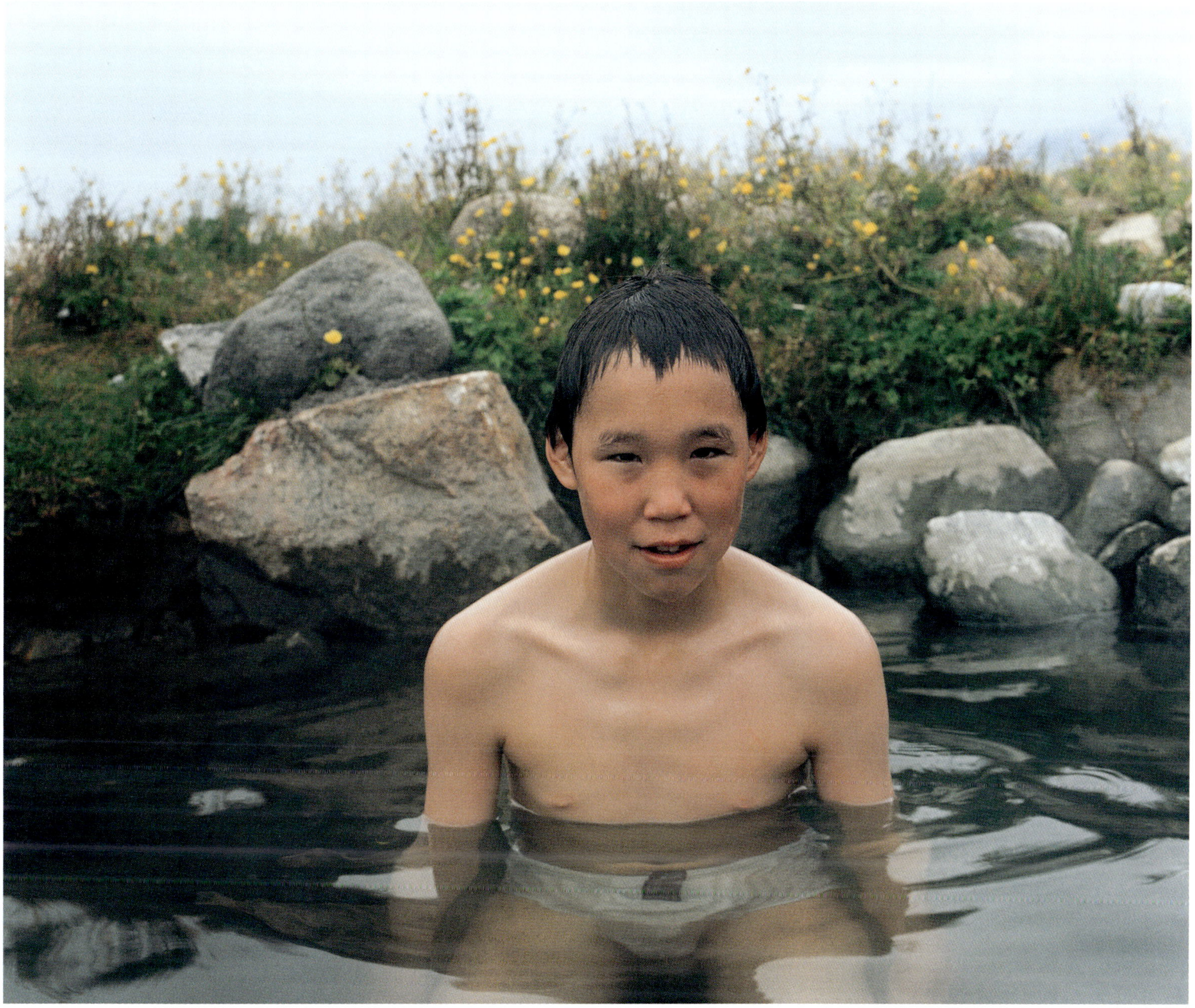

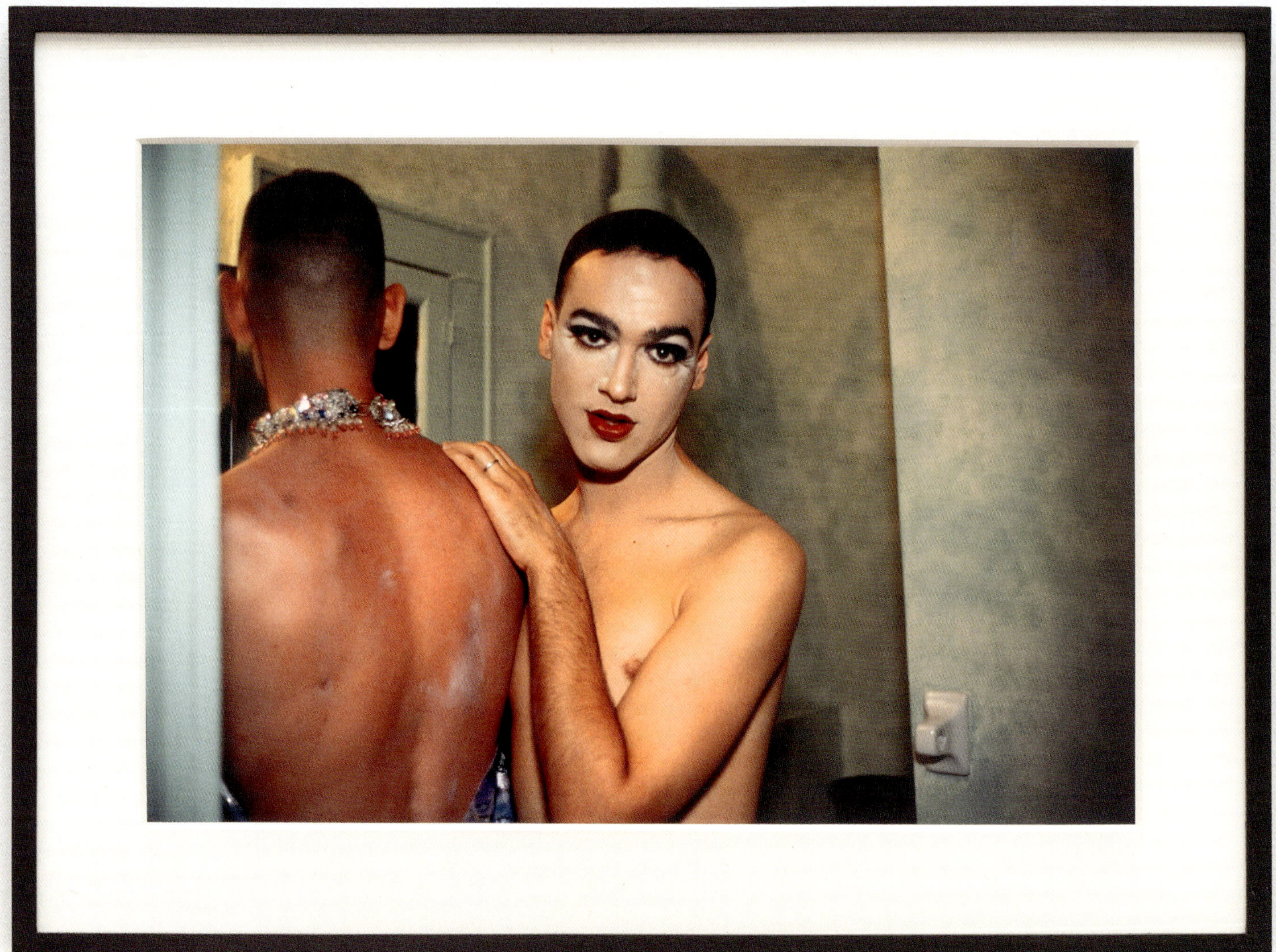

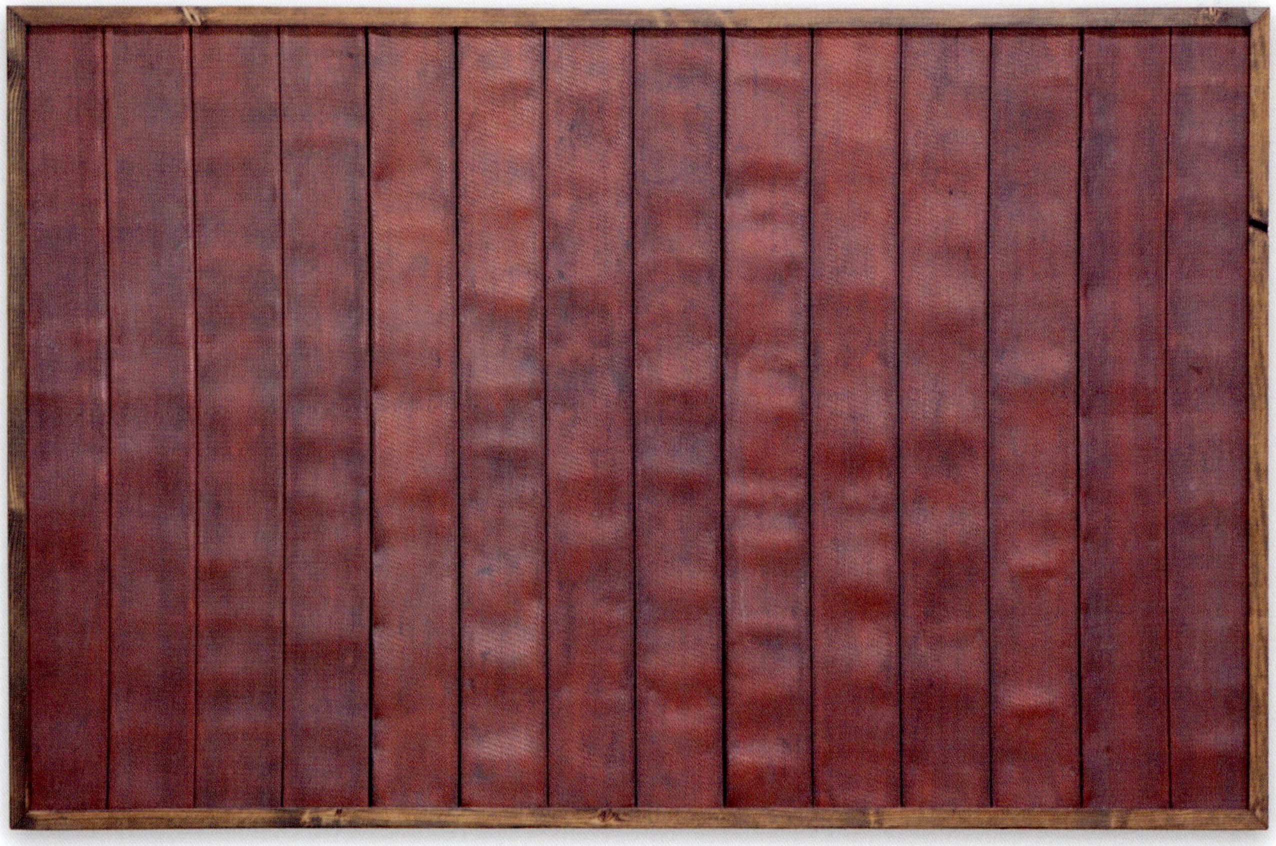

THEASTER GATES
RESOLUTION 2: THE ONLY LASTING RESOLUTIONS HAVE SOMETHING TO DO WITH JAMES BALDWIN, 2013

P. 77
THEASTER GATES
MIGRATION RICKSHAW FOR SLEEPING, BUILDING AND PLAYING, 2013

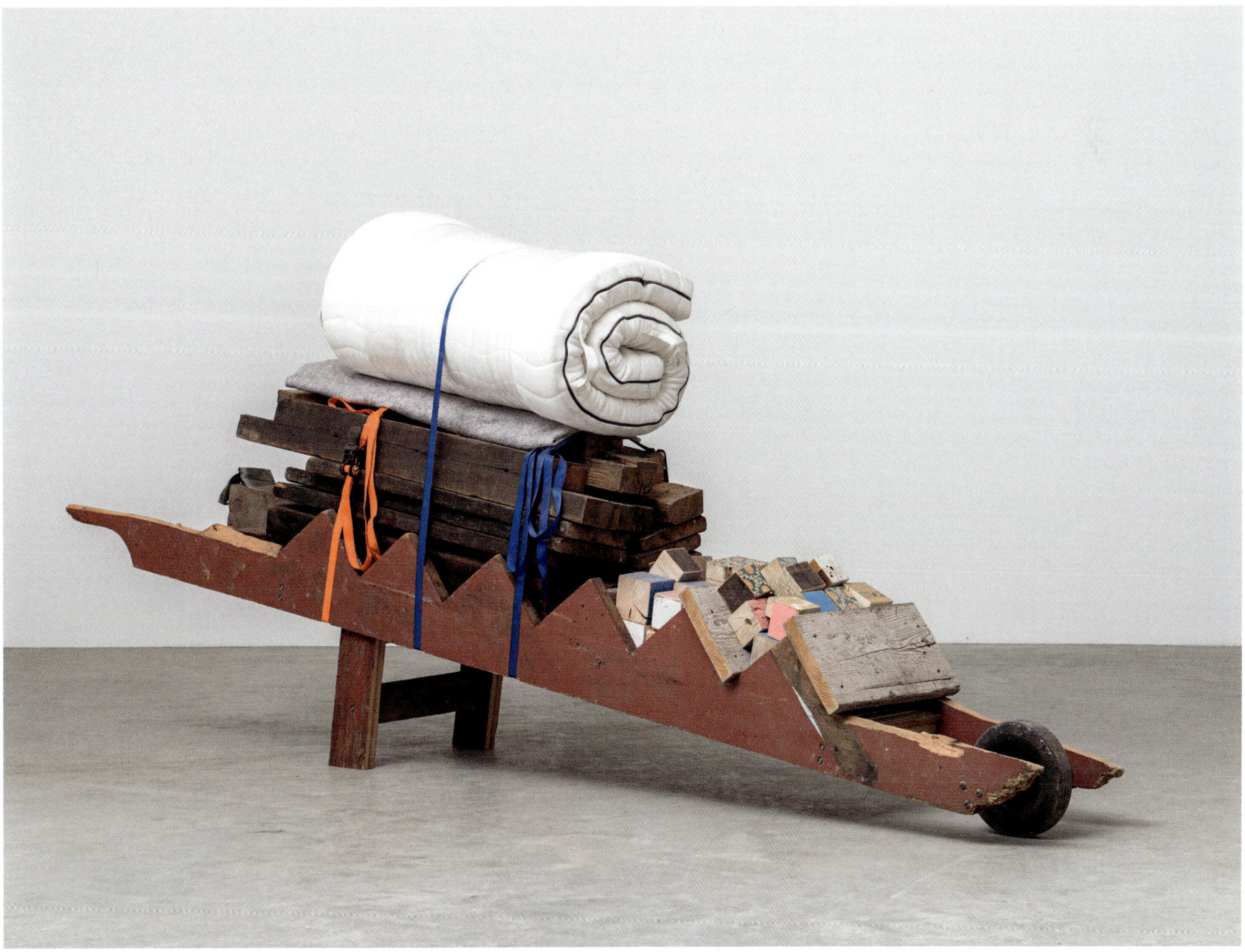

IBRAHIM MAHAMA
UB40 KOFI, 2016

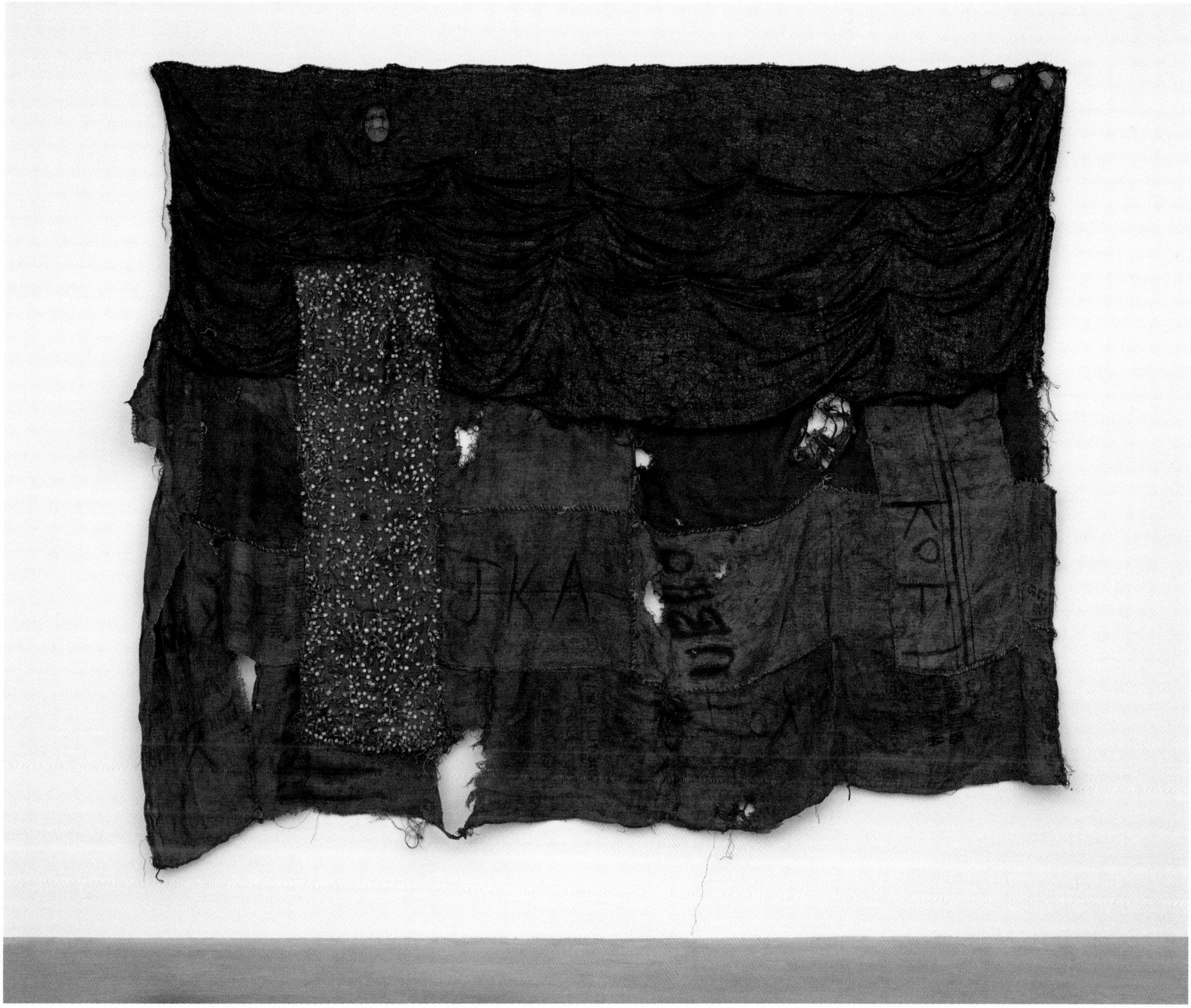
JKA
KOT

LUBAINA HIMID
*FISH SELLER:
SAFETY OR DANGER*, 2023

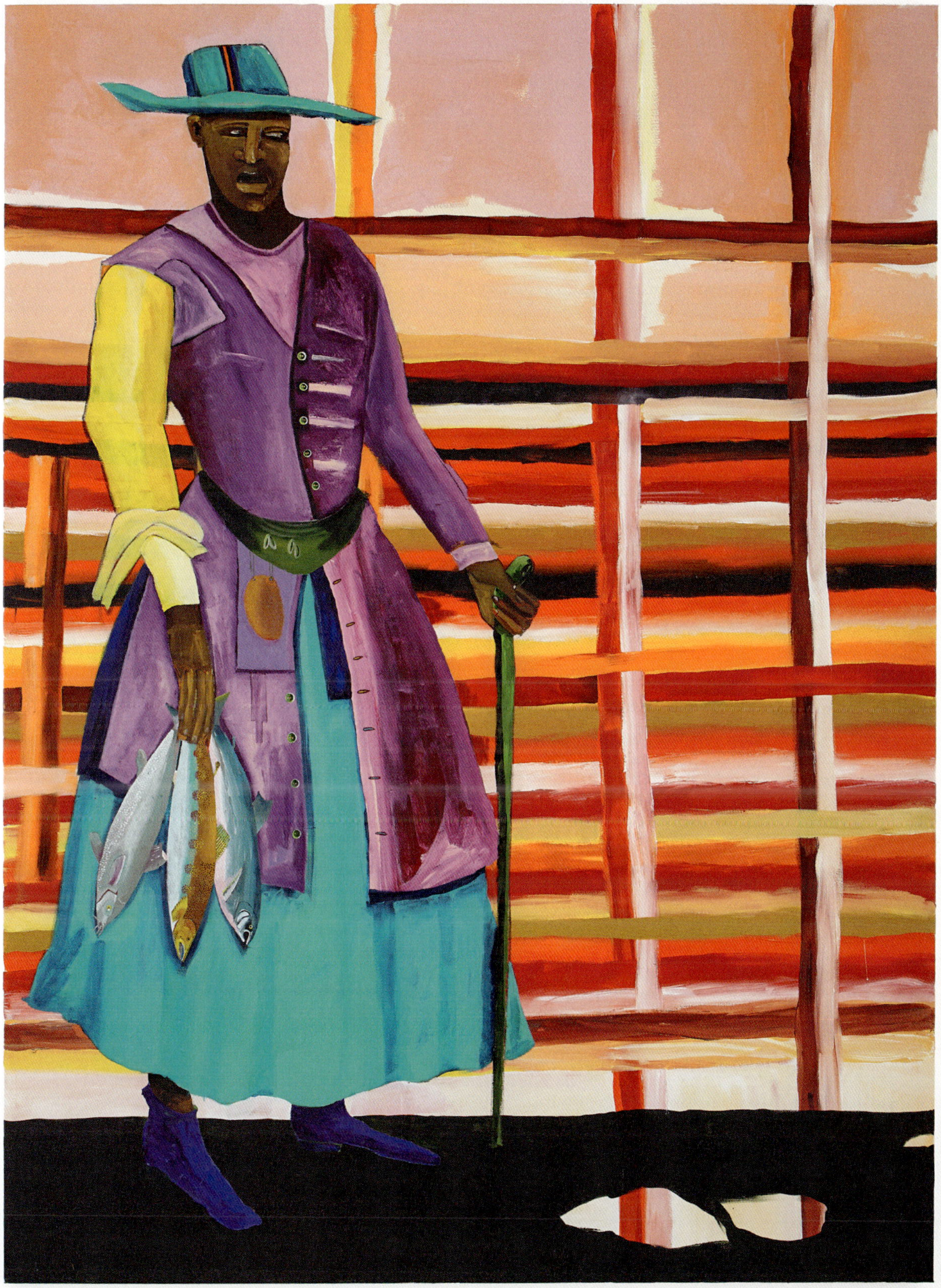

TEWODROS HAGOS
JOURNEY 32, 2021

P. 84–85
DENZIL FORRESTER
STRYDER, 1985

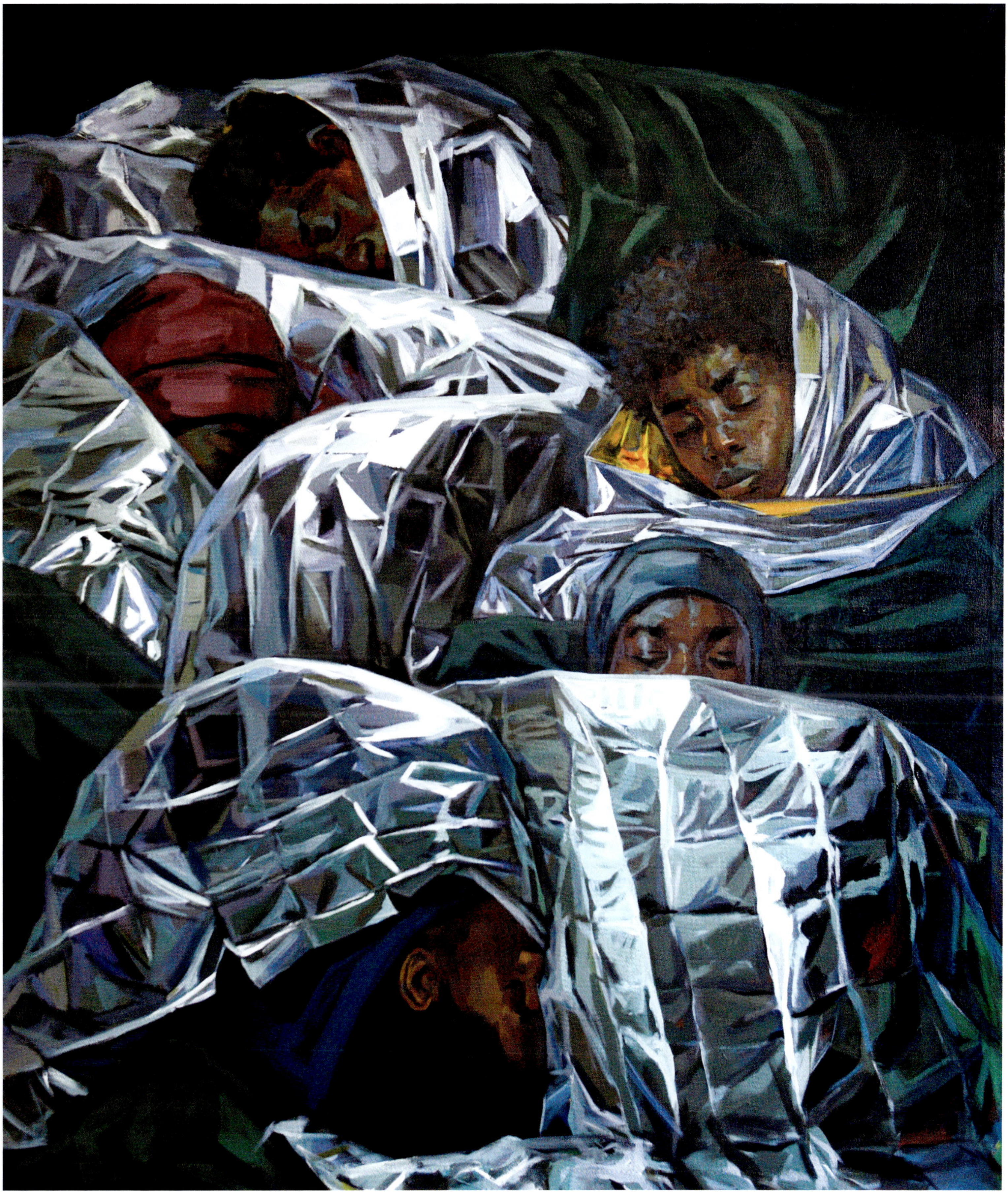

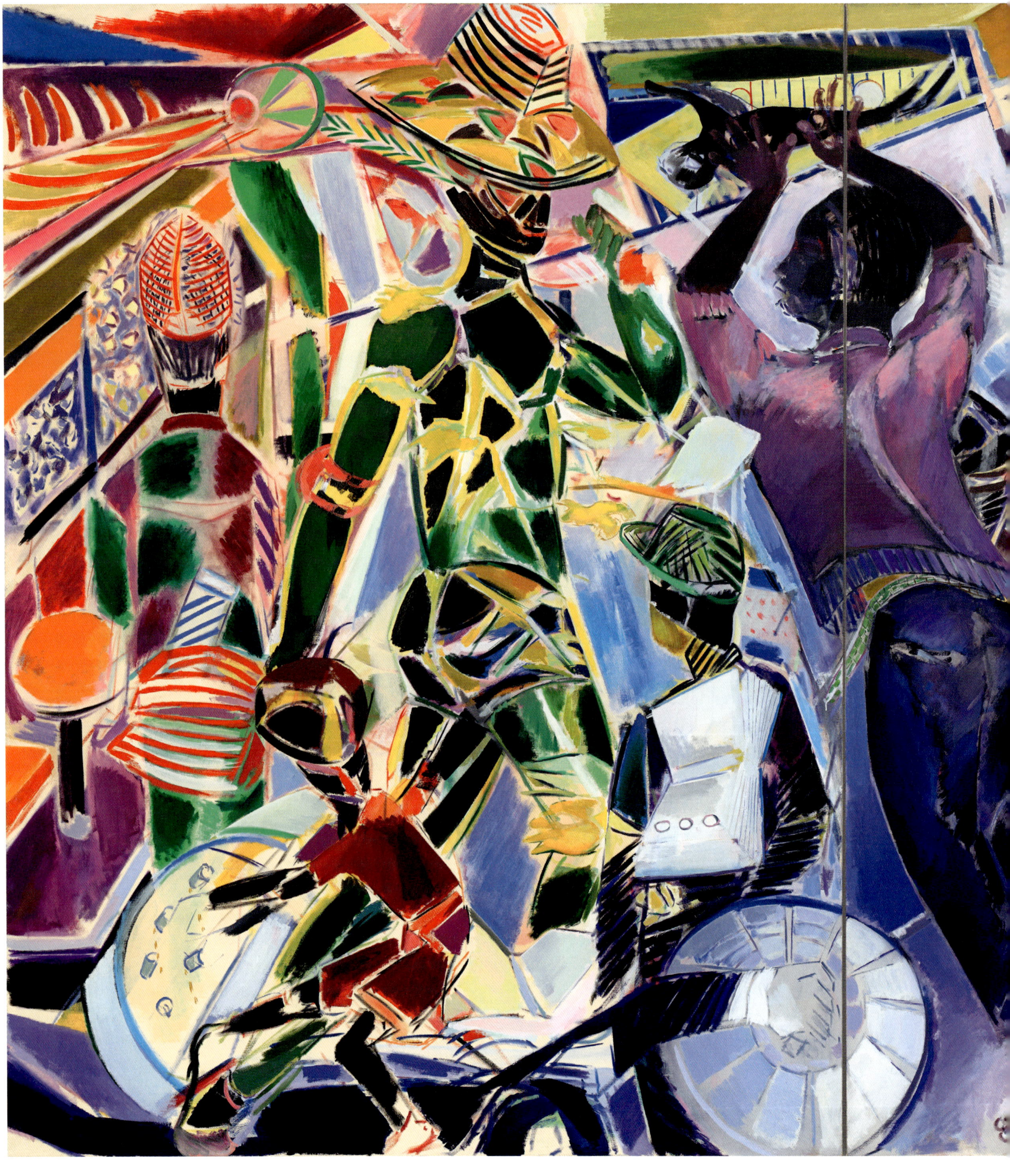

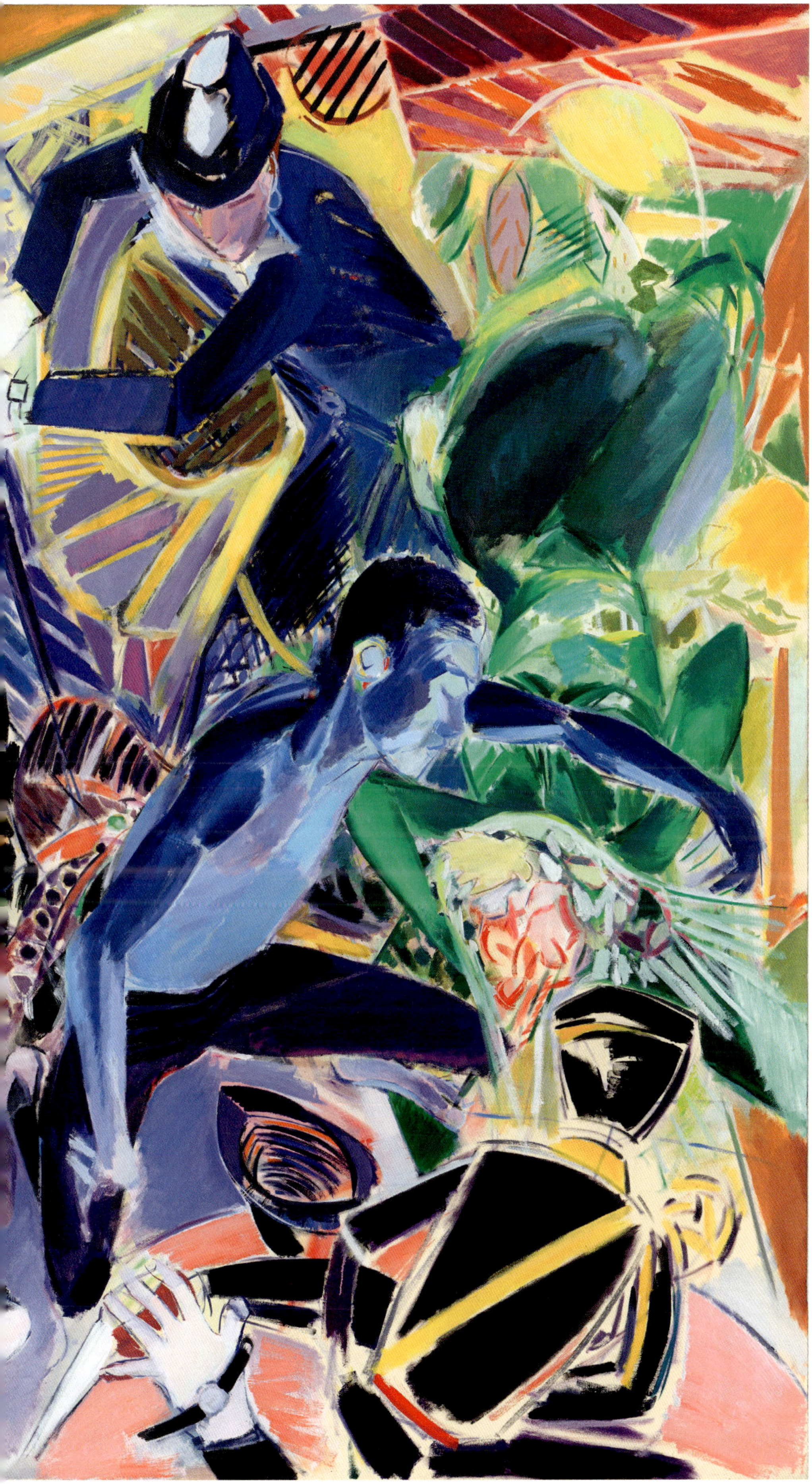

IDA EKBLAD
NIGHT FOR DAY, 2022

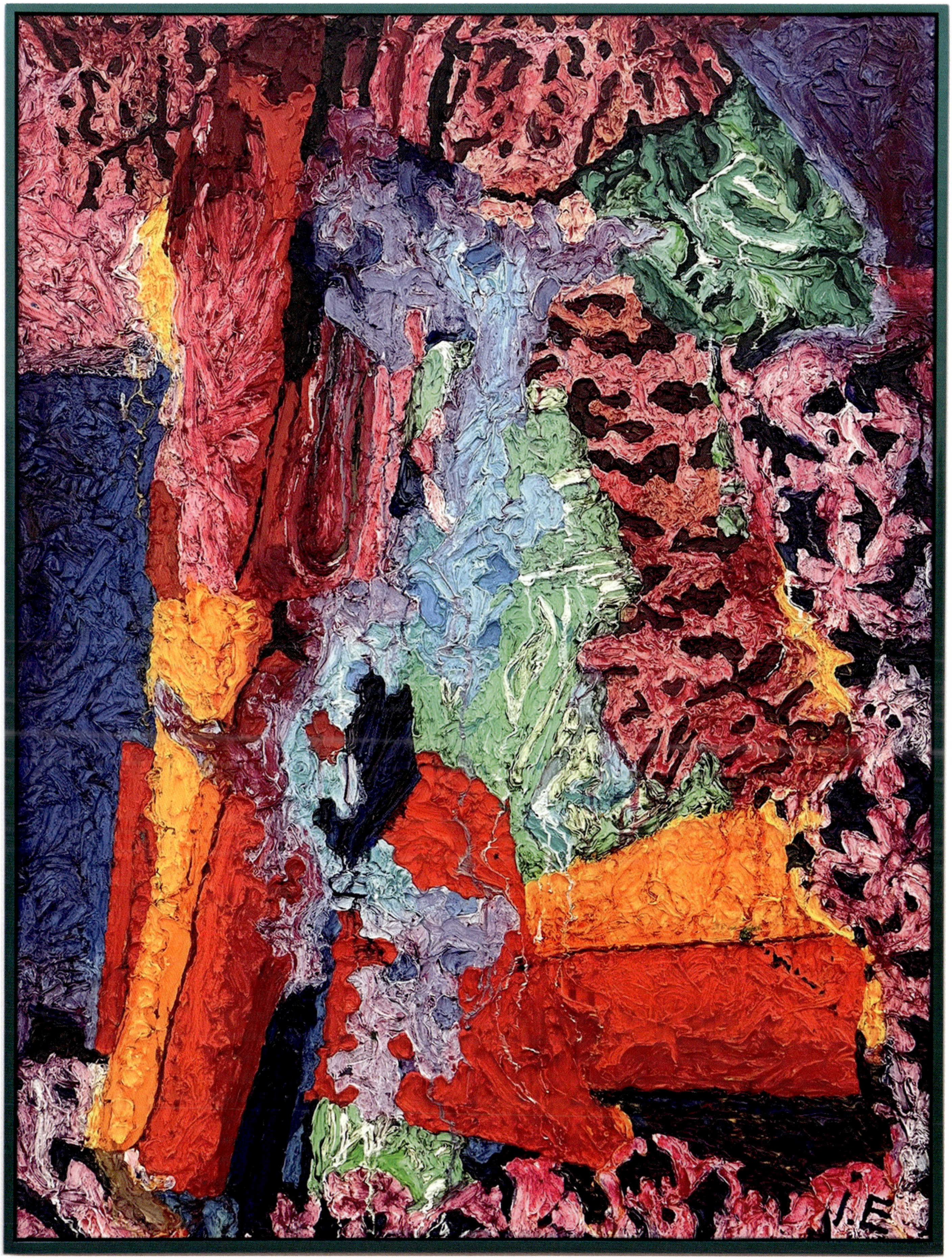
I.E

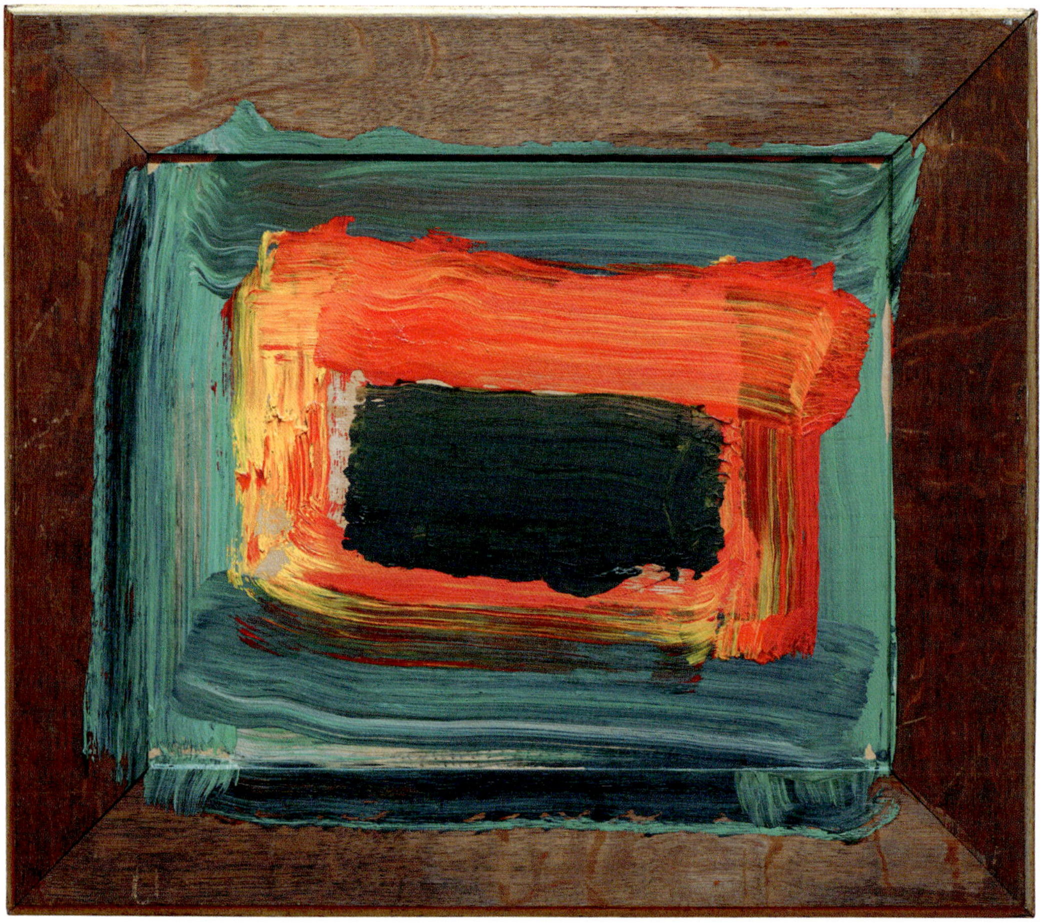

HOWARD HODGKIN
NIGHT, 2011

P. 89
CARAGH THURING
AUGUST 2014, 2014

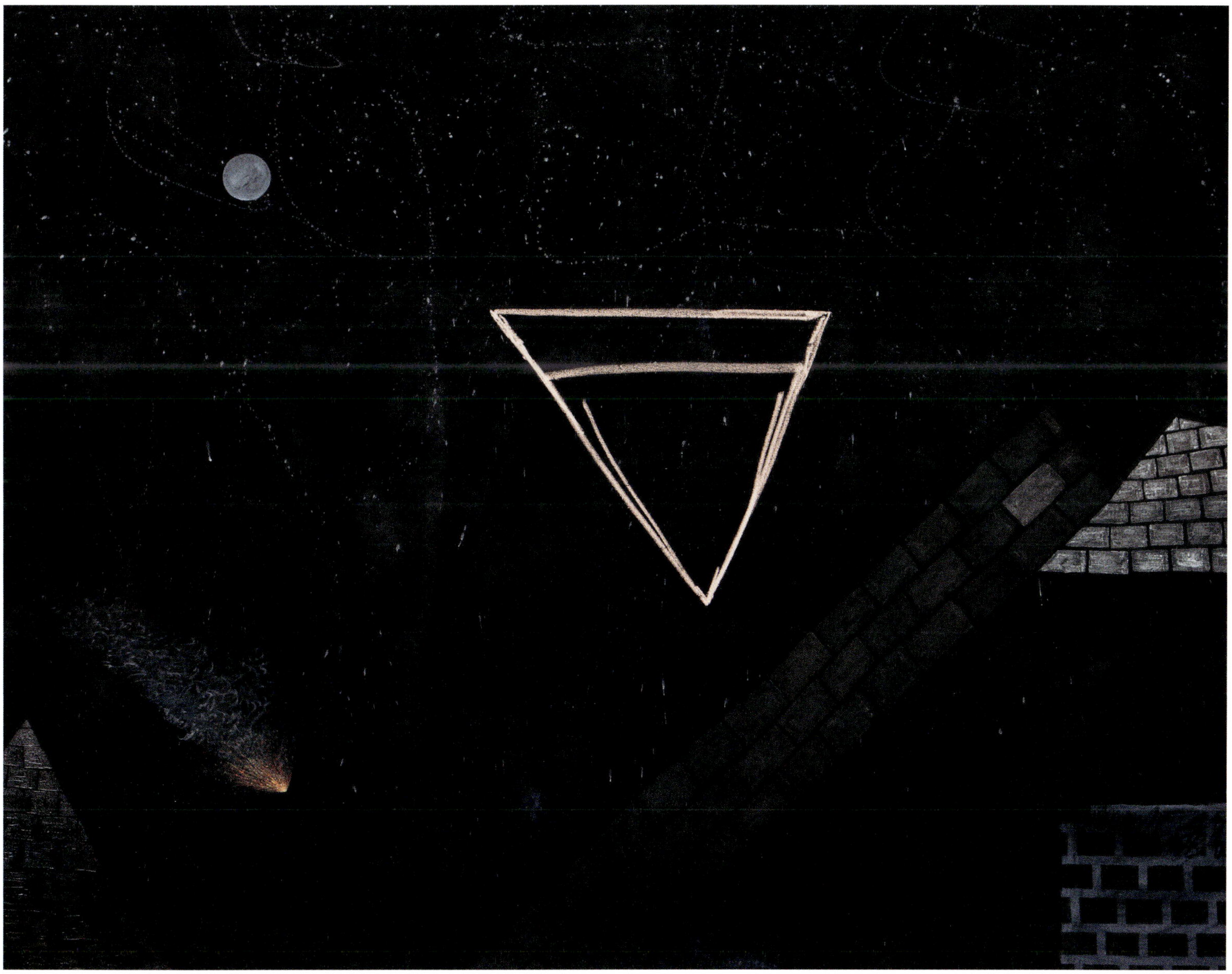

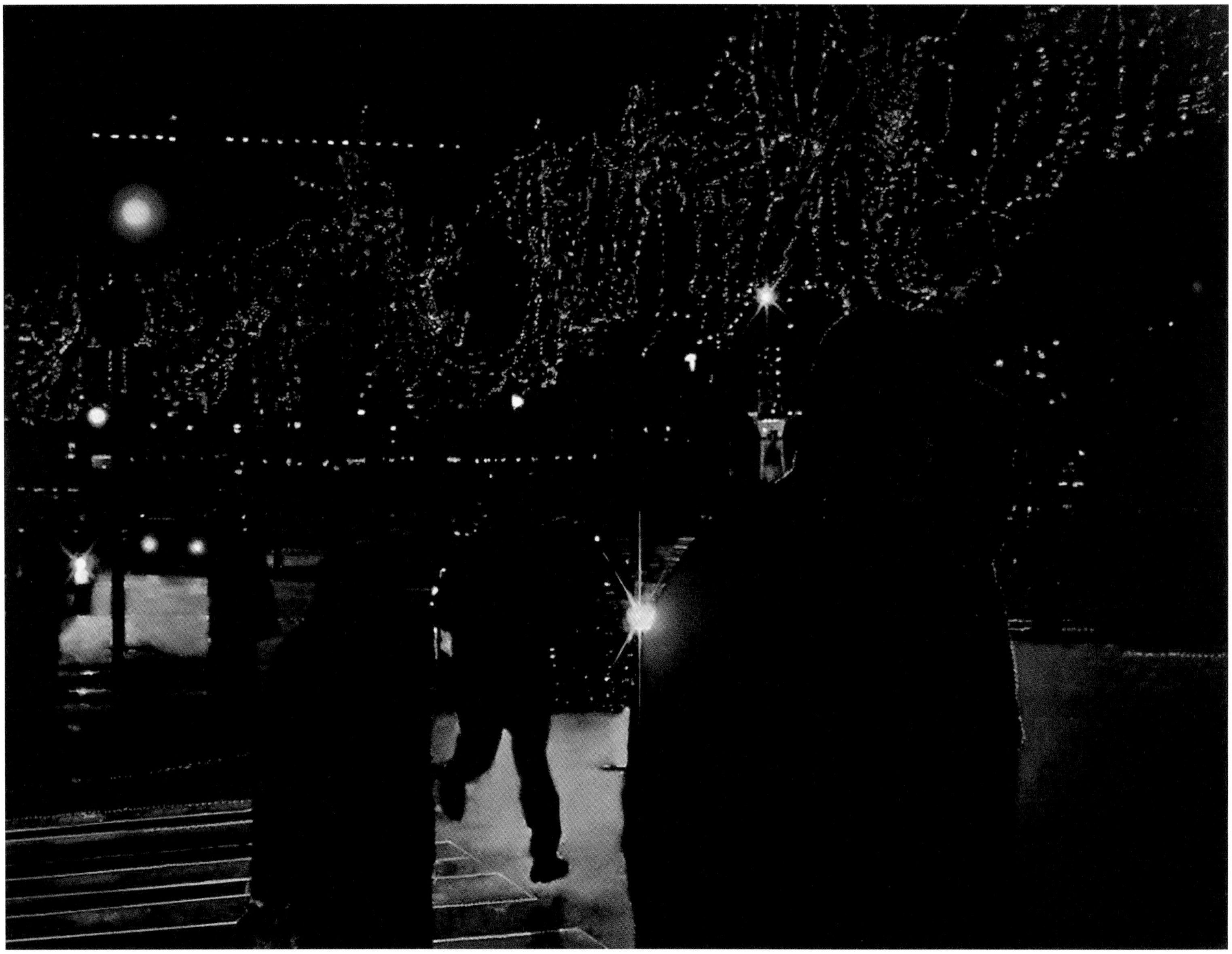

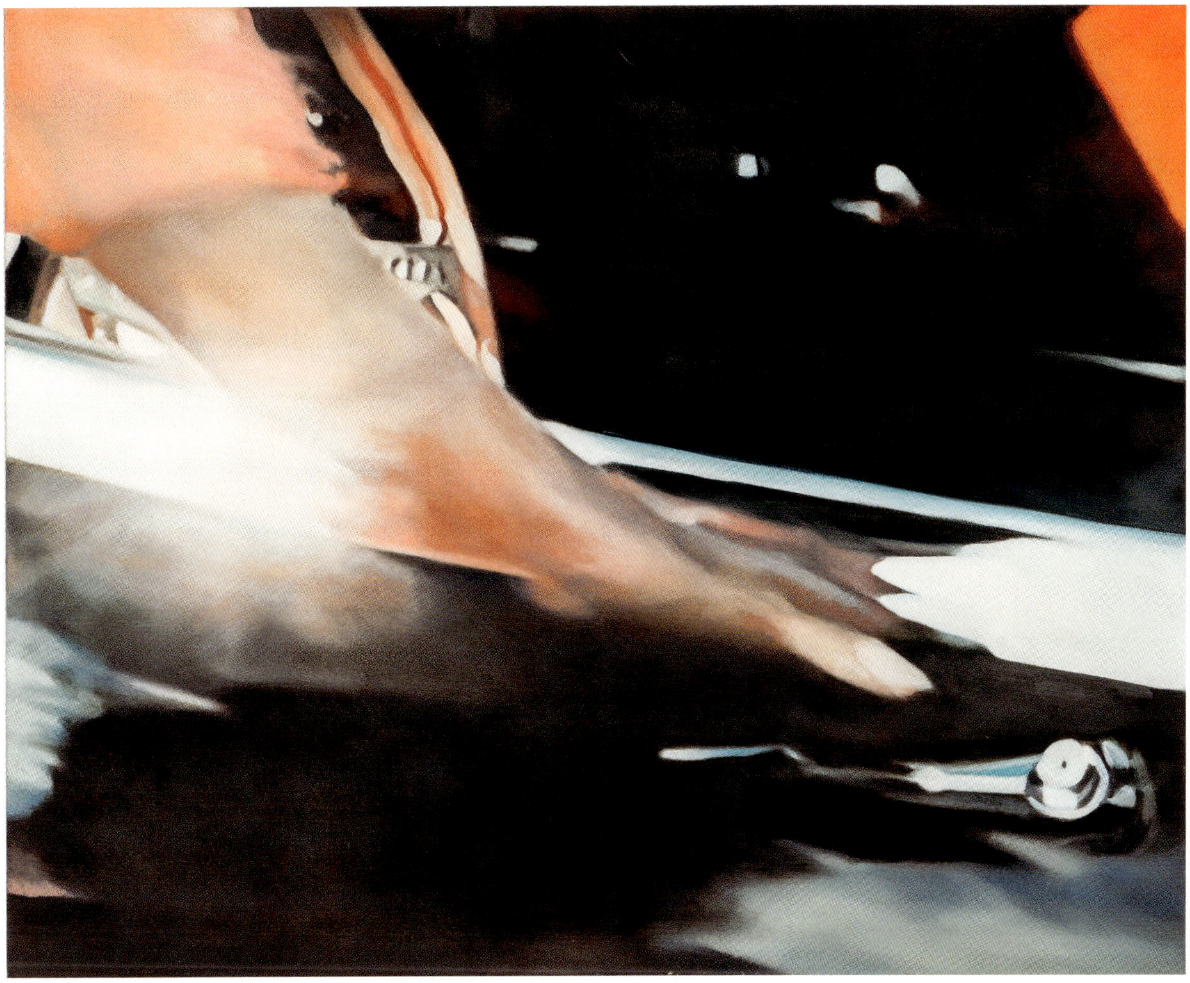

JUDITH EISLER
CAR DOOR I (THE 10TH VICTIM), 1999

P. 90
STEINAR JAKOBSEN
STREET ECLIPSE, 2004

JOHS. RIAN
SPANSK RESTAURANT, 1949

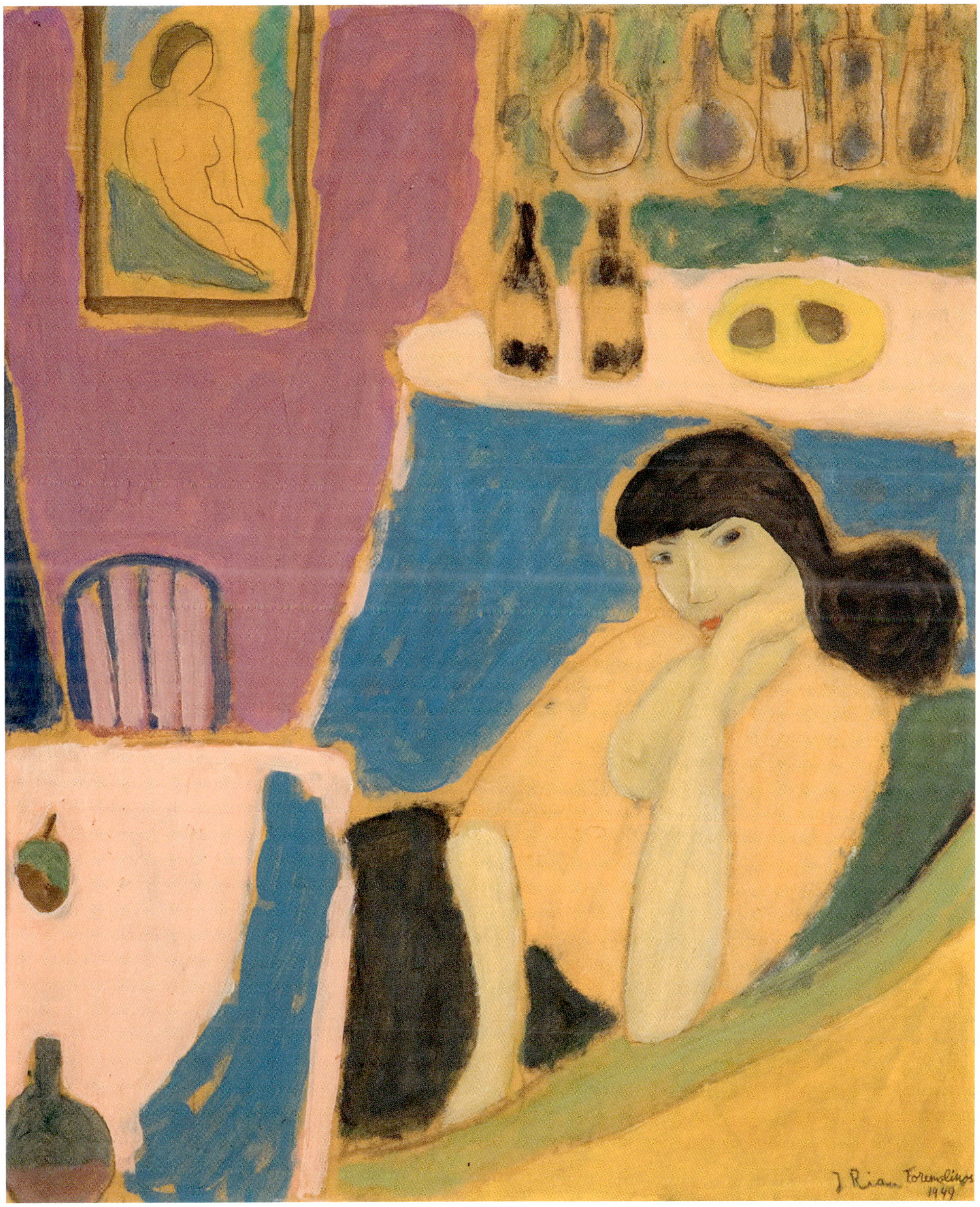

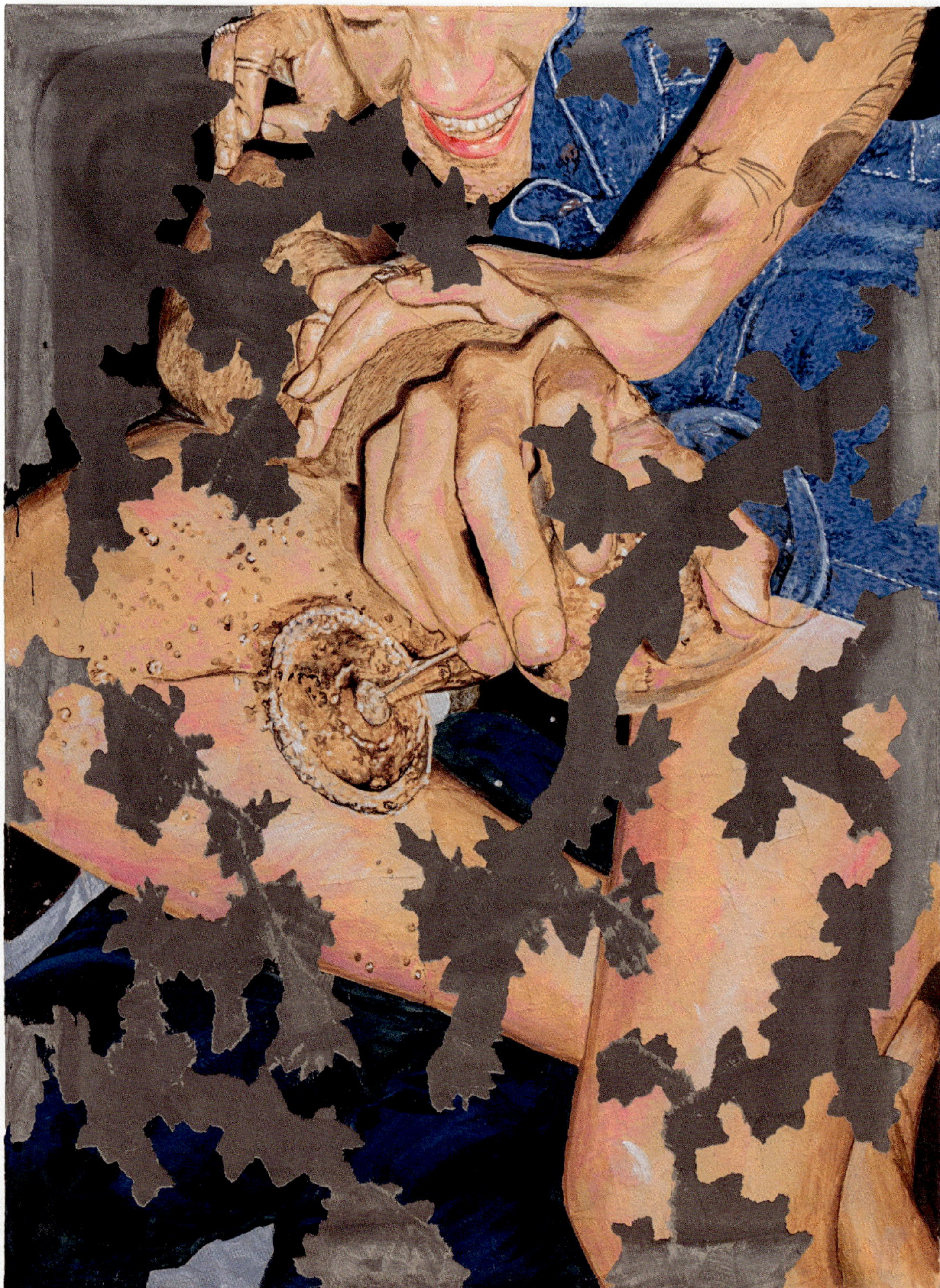

LATIFA ECHAKHCH
NIGHT TIME (AS SEEN BY OUCH), 2022

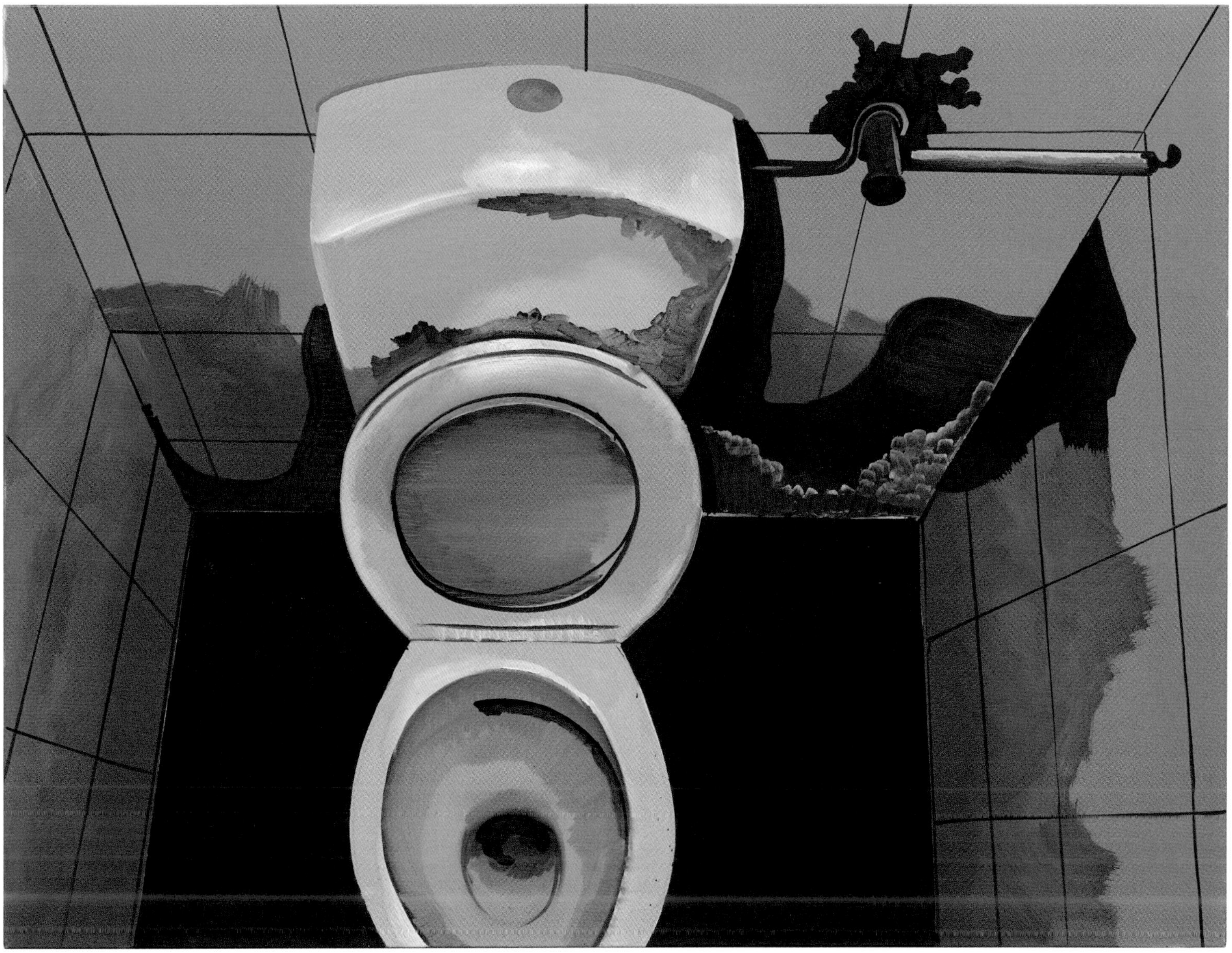

WILHELM SASNAL
BAR 2, 2007

P.96
ED RUSCHA
PAINKILLERS, TRANQUILIZERS, OLIVE, 1969

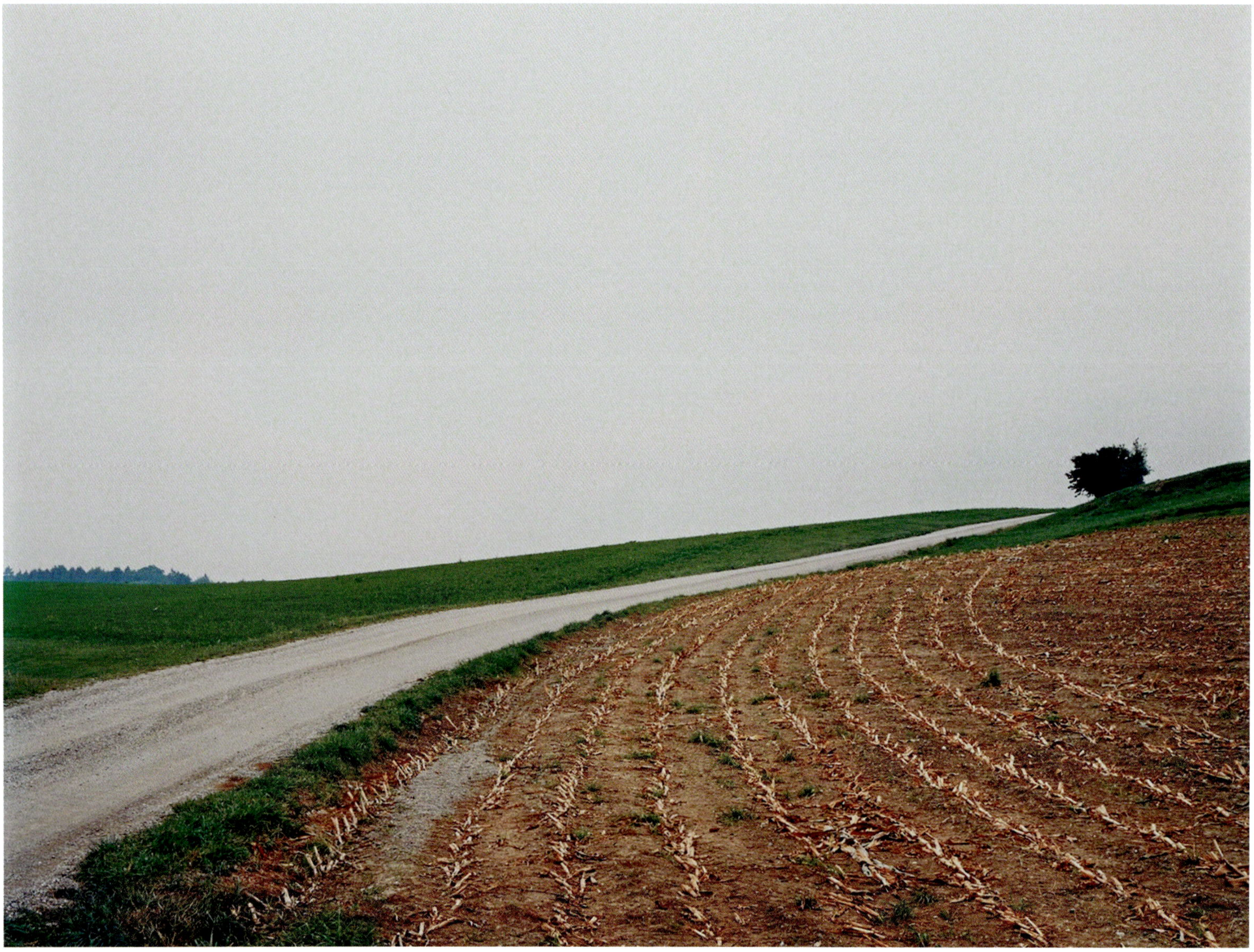

THOMAS STRUTH
MAIS-ACKER, WINTERTHUR, 1992

Autumn

III.
AUTUMN

Autumn is the rainy season in many parts of Europe. October is the rainiest month in northern Norway. Black cloud-like forms hover along the top edge of Thore Heramb's abstraction *Regnværs. Gaustad gård* (*Rainy Weather, Gaustad Farm*, 1951) (→ p.103), and the farmhouses are enveloped by a grey-green mist. In Howard Hodgkin's *Venice Rain* (1984—87) (→ p.105), bold strokes in autumnal colours of wine red and russet brown blot out the sky blue and inky water, and push the more vibrant hues onto the frame. Korakrit Arunanondchai literally and figuratively uses fire and water to burn and extinguish his materials and to represent the baptismal process of creation in *Rains in a tear 1* (2017) (→ p.106). He makes reference to the 'tears in rain' monologue of the dying replicant in Ridley Scott's film *Blade Runner* (1982), conjuring up the dualities of life and death, bodies and ghosts, the spiritual and the material. Known primarily as a poet, Stein Mehren has also made paintings inspired by meteorological phenomena in works such as *Borealis* (1993) (→ p.109).

At the autumnal equinox, day and night are of equal duration, and then the days start to grow shorter north of the equator and longer south of the equator. In the Northern Hemisphere, the equinox is often celebrated with harvest festivals. In some languages, the word for autumn—*høst* in Norwegian, for example—also means harvest. In his video *Untitled, Harvest* (2005) (→ p.110—111), Robin Rhode uses spray paint and animation to sow and grow a bed of crops, and then he reaps the harvest with a scythe. The remaining stalks become a bed, and the artist spreads a sheet and lies down to sleep.

Autumn is seen as the time to take reading seriously and to indulge in its pleasures. The short days and dark nights make it ideal to spend a lazy Sunday morning reading in bed or to curl up in the evening with a book. Rodney Graham's *Sunday Sun, 1937* (2012) (→ p.113), features a figure reading the 23 October 1937 edition of *The Sunday Sun*, obscured behind the colourful comics and surrounded by patterned wallpaper and bedding. Mounted in a light box, the image is based on a scene from Alfred Hitchcock's *The Lady Vanishes* (1938), in which the two hands belong to two different people sharing the newspaper in a narrow bed. Laura Owens's painting *Untitled* (2015) (→ p.114) is also puzzling as it appears to be a reproduction of a full page from a newspaper called *The Echo*, published on October 22. Closer scrutiny, however, reveals an incongruous collection of articles and advertisements from different eras and locales. Digital and painted daubs and brushstrokes have been placed on the surface, raising further questions about what is real and what is constructed. The dark trees in a 2014 canvas by Sean Landers (→ p.115) resemble both a dense thicket of pine trunks and book spines, meticulously painted and covered with the artist's stream-of-consciousness ramblings carved into the bark. Dexter Dalwood reminds us of the origin of Mary Shelley's novel *Frankenstein* (1818) on the shores of Lake Geneva on a Munch-like moonlit night (→ p.117). 'It was on a dreary night of November', Shelley's protagonist Victor Frankenstein recalls, 'that I beheld the accomplishment of my toils.' Frankenstein's monster is now commonly associated with Halloween celebrations, which meld pagan celebrations of the harvest festival and the Christian Allhallowtide, a period for remembrance of the dead.

Autumn is a season of melancholy. Leaves change colour and fall from trees, the hours of daylight grow shorter, and the transition from the warmth and vibrancy of summer to the cold, dark winter all serve as reminders of death and decline. Adrian Ghenie's sombre painting *Duchamp's Funeral I* (2009) (→ p.118—119) imagines Marcel Duchamp's death on 2 October 1968 as if staged for a movie camera. By depicting the funeral of the father of conceptual art, Ghenie is also reaffirming the place of painting in a post-Duchampian world. This painting anticipated, in fact, the discovery of Man Ray's photograph *Duchamp on his Deathbed* (1968), which was acquired by the Getty Research Institute in 2011 but only made public in 2018.[3]

In *Land of Gloom* (2009) by Christer Karlstad (→ p.120), a young man sporting a tweed jacket and corduroy trousers has the appearance of a hunter, but he does not carry a gun and is entangled in the leads of his four dogs. Human and hounds are distracted, as if by an unseen presence in the gloomy forest. Only the nuthatch remains focused on its search for food. The deteriorating body of an abandoned car in Kjell Nupen's bleak *Hjemsted Nature Morte* (*Homestead Still Life*, 2010) (→ p.121) is shown in its final resting place, obscured behind a matrix of dots and verticals formed by stretcher bars and bare spindly tree trunks. Adrian Ghenie has reinterpreted the flaming tree (→ p.123) from Van Gogh's oeuvre, such as *The Mulberry Tree* (1889), as a burning bush, in which the burst of autumnal colour is supplied by the fire rather than the foliage.

The off-kilter table in Martin Kippenberger's *Nachttisch* (*Night Table*, 1985) (→ p.124) initially looks quite commonplace with a couple of books, a pitcher, a framed photograph and a wicker plant basket. The photo of an American soldier clutching a bust of Adolf Hitler, however, is a reminder of the uncomfortable post-war relationship between former adversaries. *Atelier* (2013) (→ p.127) by Sverre Bjertnæs represents an interior illuminated by melancholic evening light, revealing an artist's studio filled with Magrittean motifs: the window framing the sky, paintings within paintings, and the shrouded head of the figurative sculpture. Ross Bleckner's elegiac painting of birds (→ p.129) falling suddenly and in mass from the night sky is a memorial to the many who have died of AIDS. World AIDS Day has been observed on the 1st of December since 1988 to raise awareness of the epidemic, to promote prevention and to remember the lives lost to the illness.

3. See Donald Shambroom, *Duchamp's Last Day*, David Zwirner Books, New York, 2018.

THORE HERAMB
REGNVÆRS. GAUSTAD GÅRD, 1951

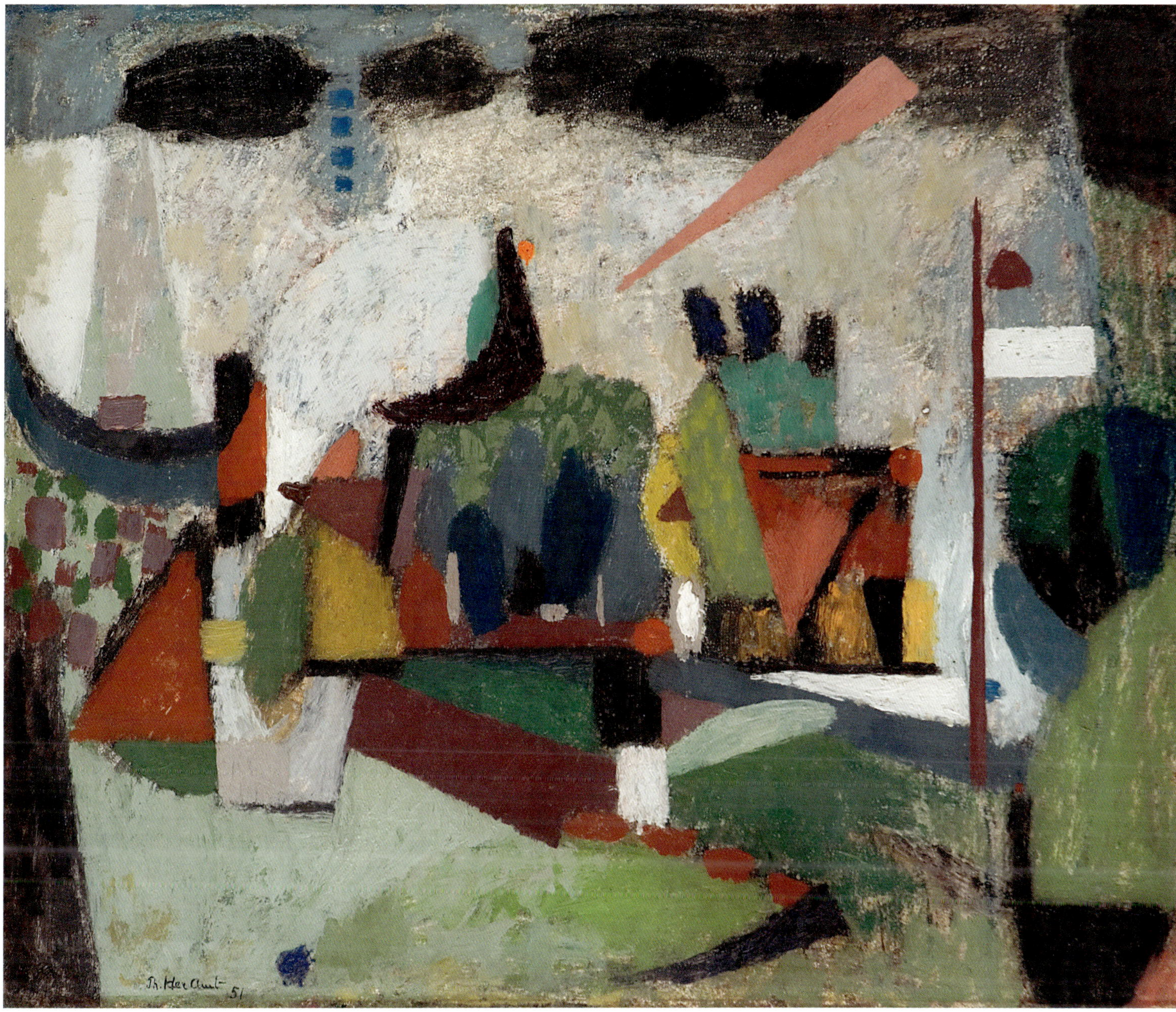

HOWARD HODGKIN
VENICE RAIN, 1984–87

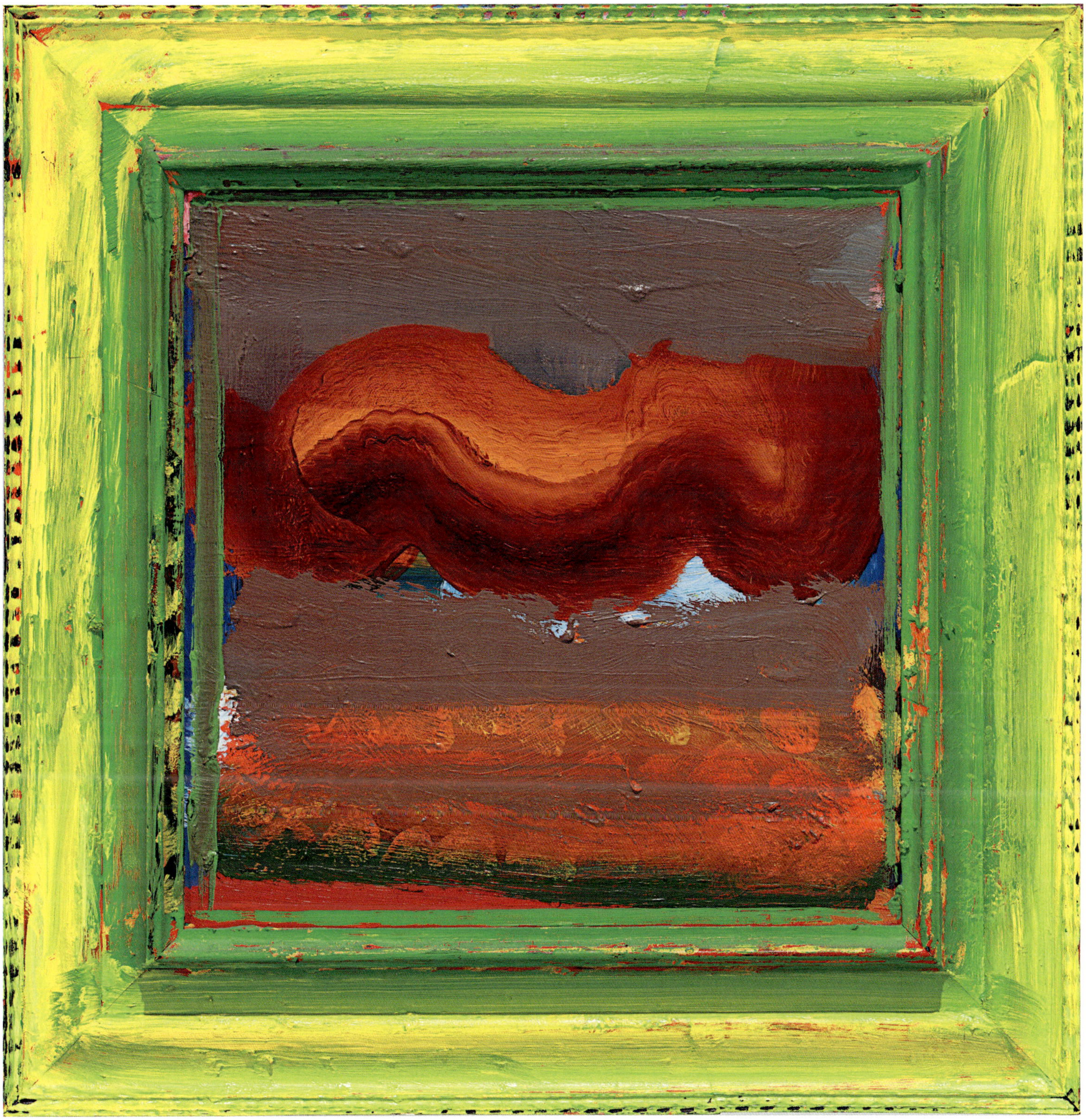

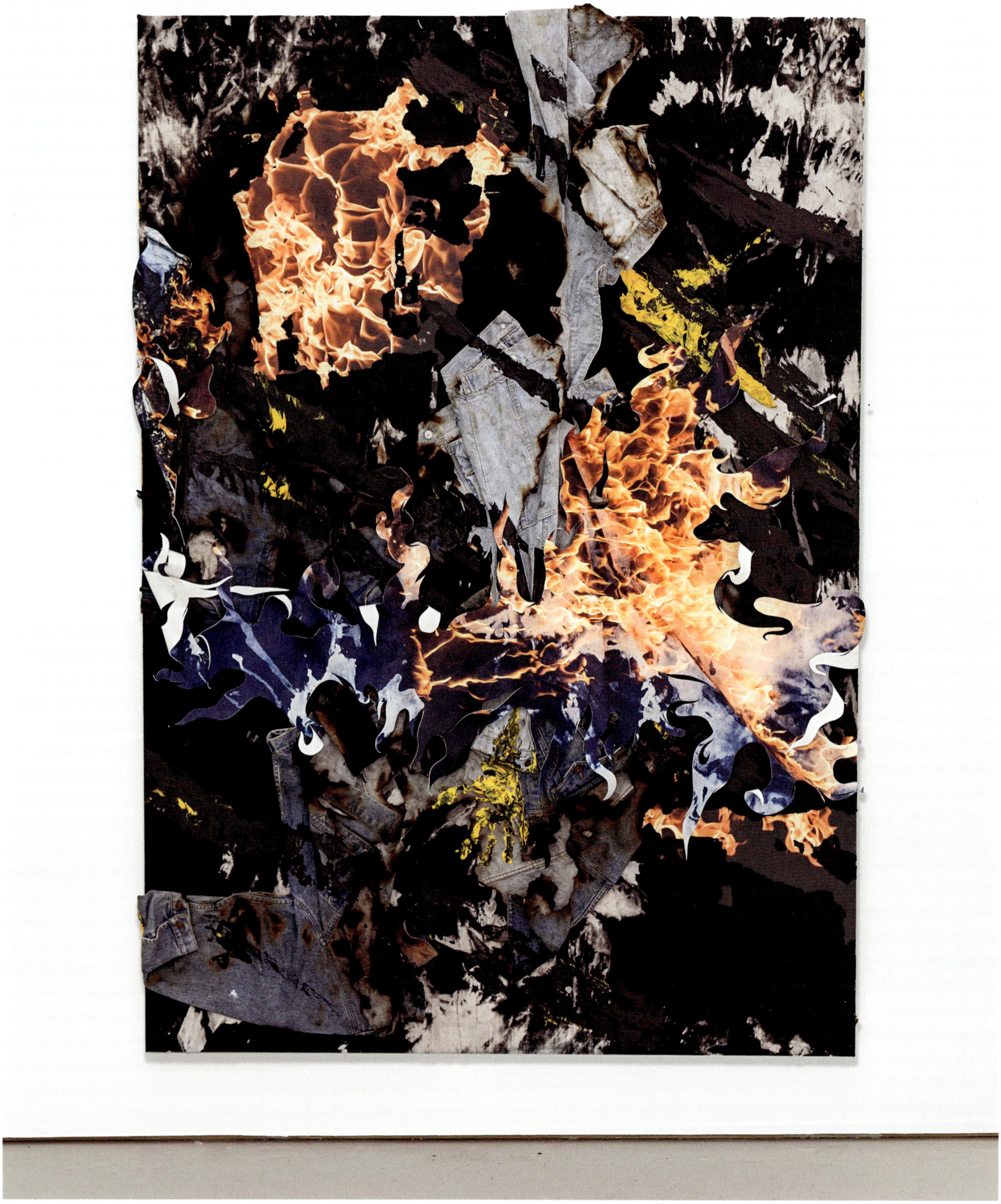

KORAKRIT ARUNANONDCHAI
RAINS IN A TEAR 1, 2017

STEIN MEHREN
BOREALIS,1993

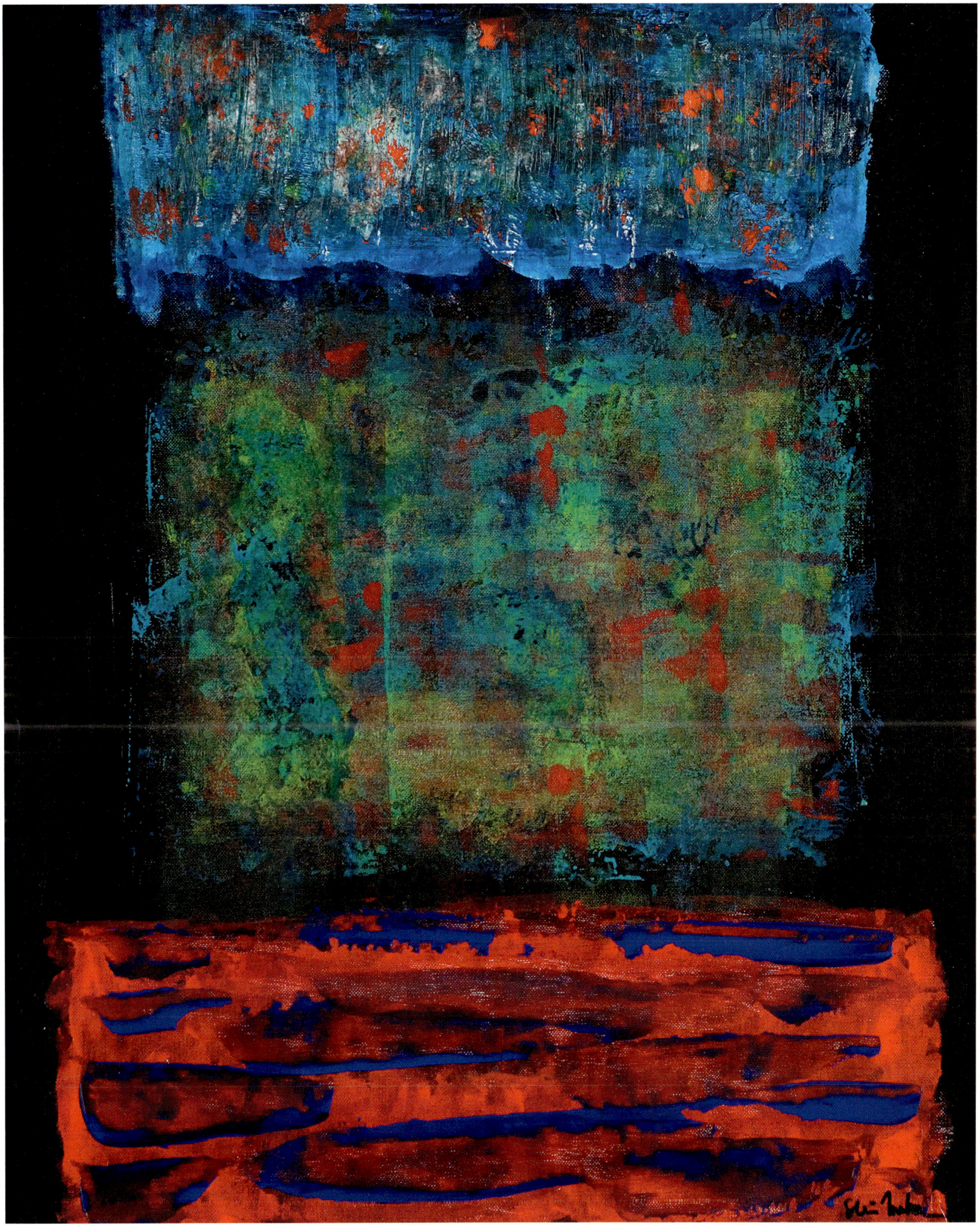

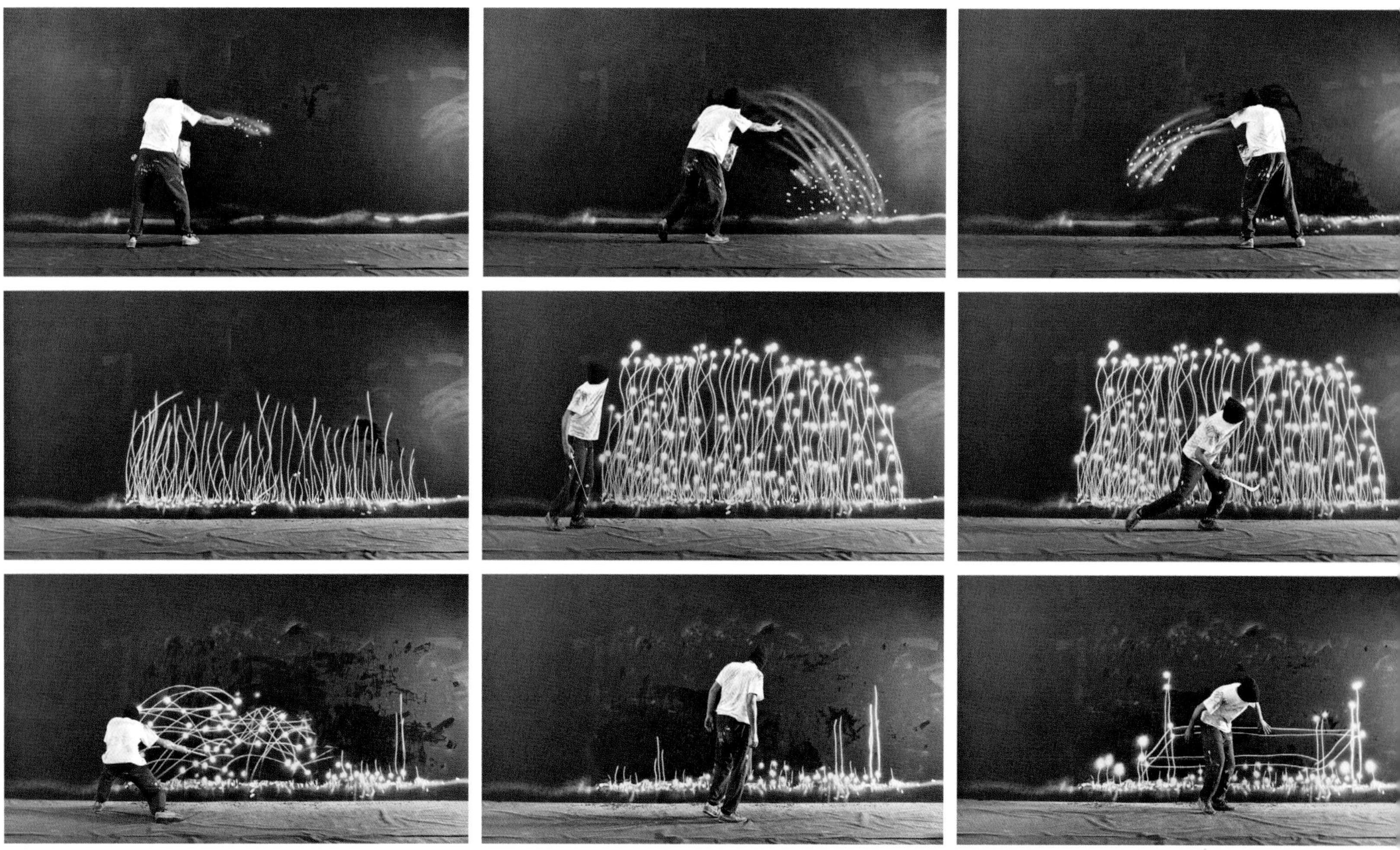

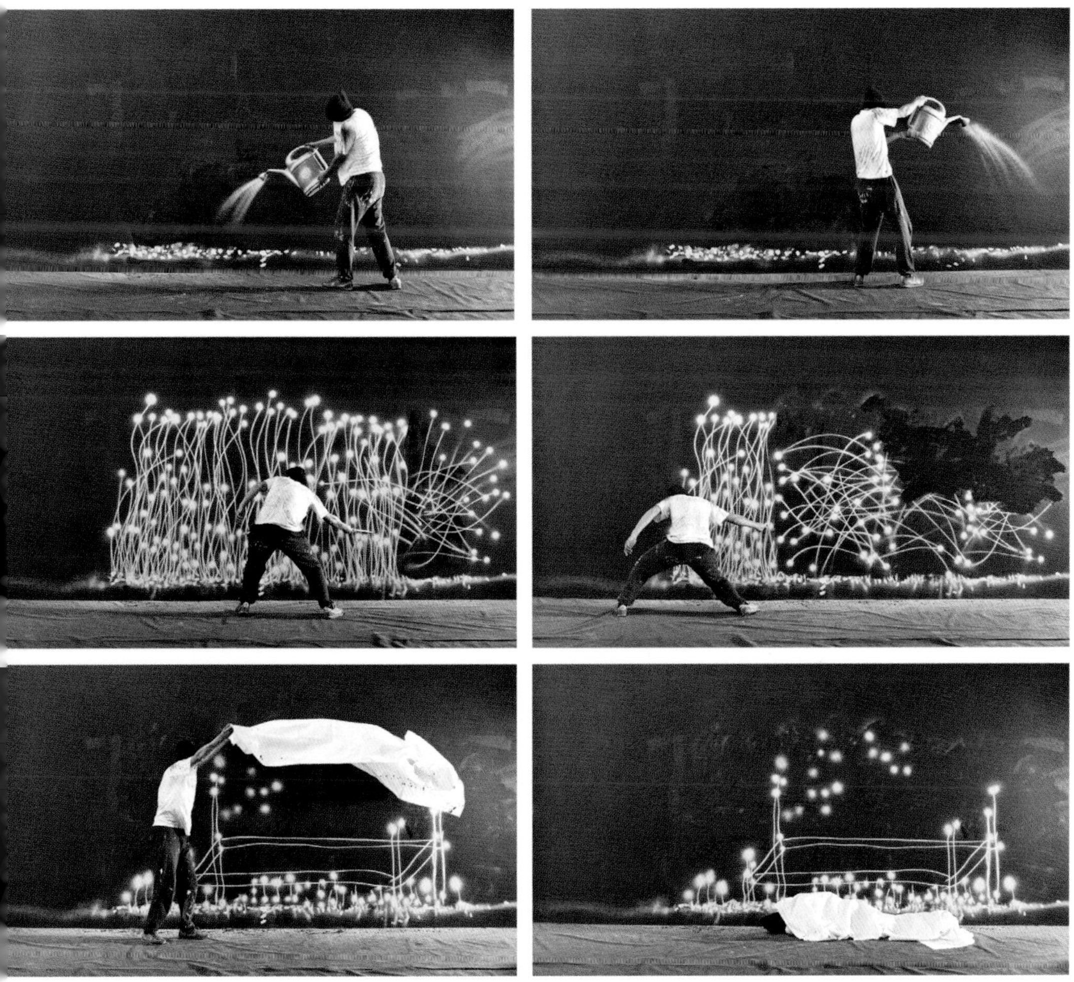

ROBIN RHODE
UNTITLED, HARVEST, 2005

RODNEY GRAHAM
SUNDAY SUN, 1937, 2012

P. 114
LAURA OWENS
UNTITLED, 2015

P. 115
SEAN LANDERS
DARK TREES (HELLO!), 2014

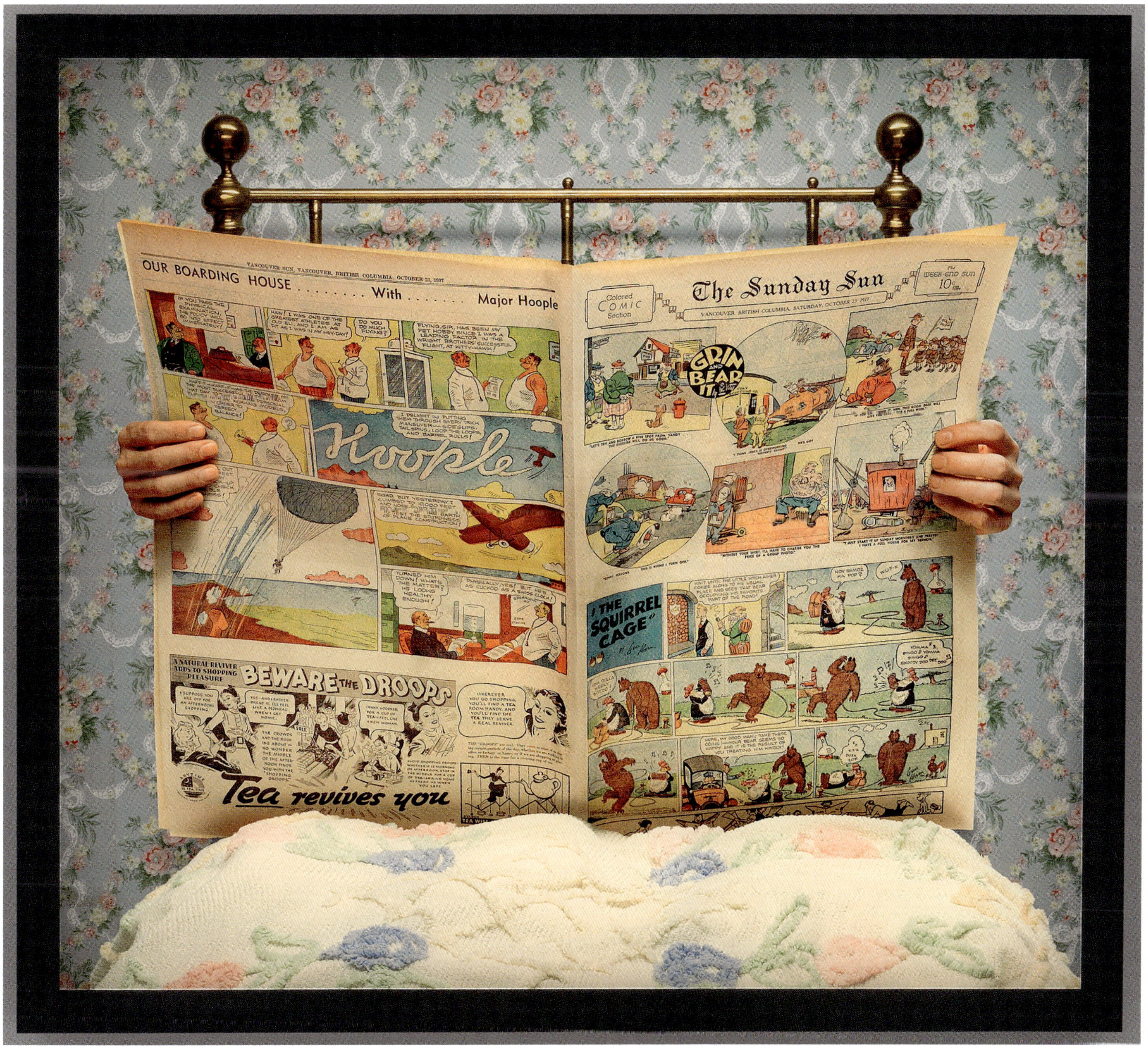
OUR BOARDING HOUSE . . . . With . . . . Major Hoople
Hoople
The Sunday Sun
Colored COMIC Section
WEEK-END SUN 10c
GRIN AND BEAR IT
THE SQUIRREL CAGE
A NATURAL REVIVER ADDS TO SHOPPING PLEASURE
BEWARE THE DROOPS
Tea revives you

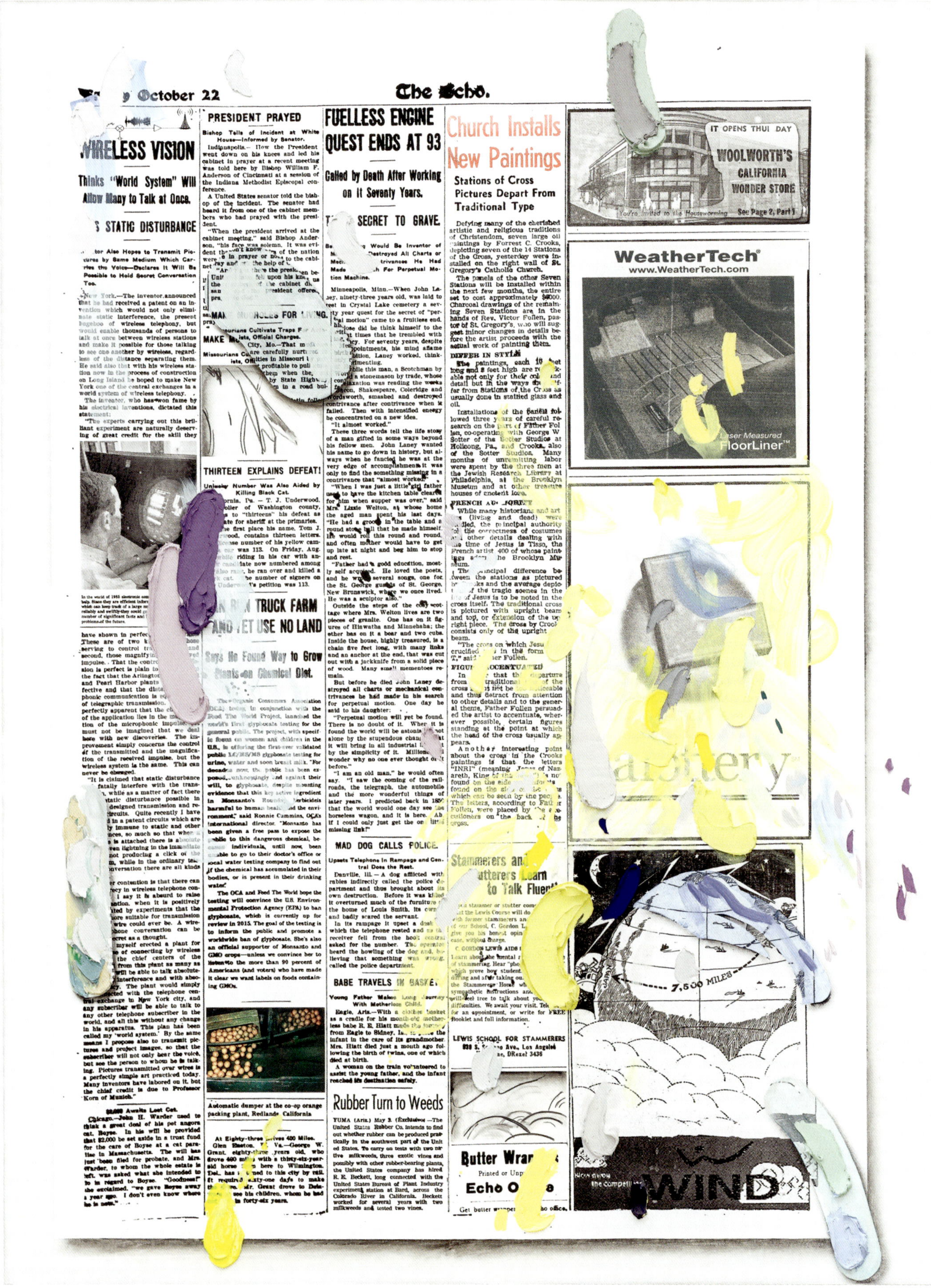
October 22
The Echo.
WIRELESS VISION
Thinks "World System" Will Allow Many to Talk at Once.
PRESIDENT PRAYED
FUELLESS ENGINE QUEST ENDS AT 93
Called by Death After Working on It Seventy Years.
Church Installs New Paintings
Stations of Cross Pictures Depart From Traditional Type
IT OPENS THURSDAY
WOOLWORTH'S CALIFORNIA WONDER STORE
WeatherTech
www.WeatherTech.com
Laser Measured FloorLiner™
THIRTEEN EXPLAINS DEFEAT!
MAD DOG CALLS POLICE
BABE TRAVELS IN BASKET
Rubber Turn to Weeds
Automatic dumper at the co-op orange packing plant, Redlands California
LEWIS SCHOOL FOR STAMMERERS
7,500 MILES
Butter Wrap
Echo Office
WIND

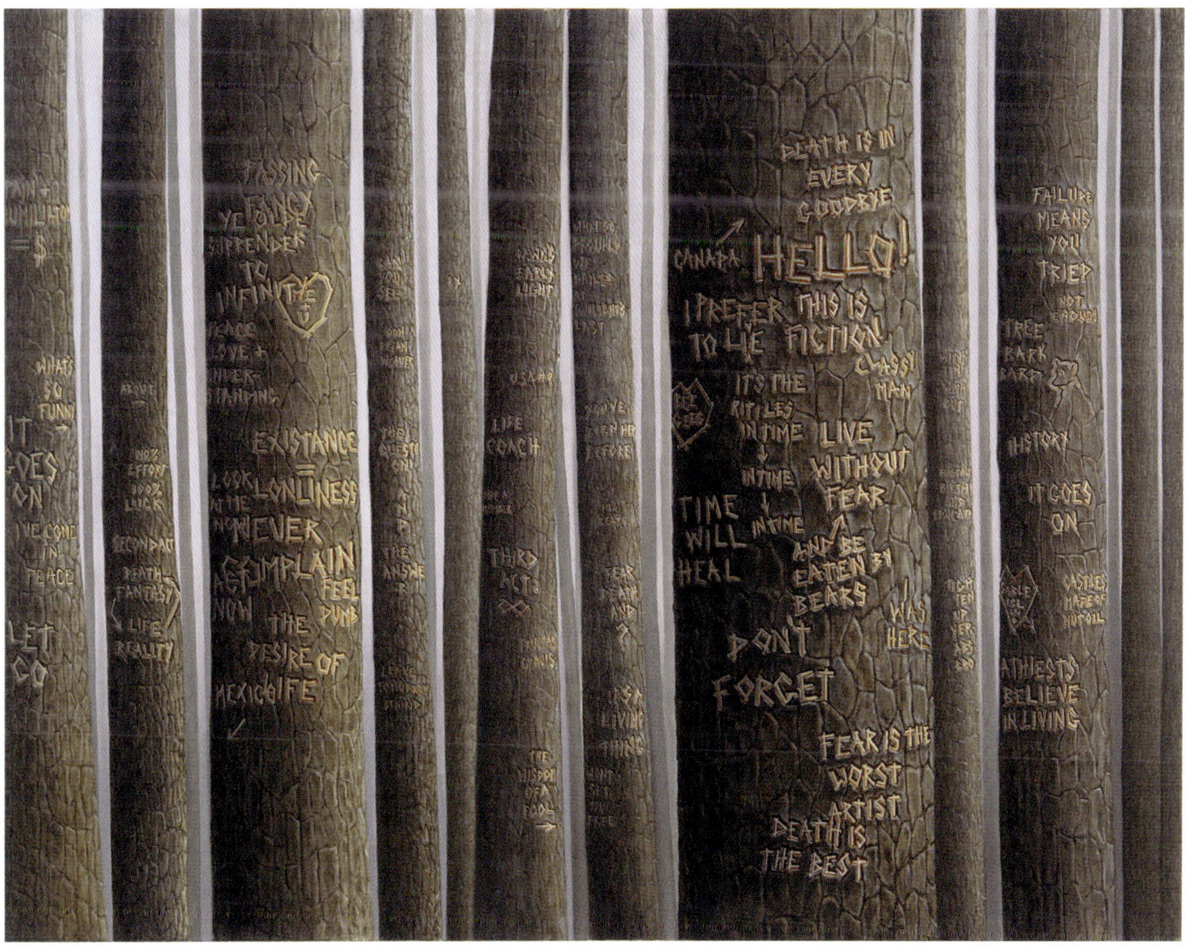
PASSING FANCY
SURRENDER TO INFINITY
EXISTANCE = LONLINESS
NEVER COMPLAIN
FEEL DUMB
THE DESIRE OF LIFE
DEATH IS IN EVERY GOODBYE
CANADA
HELLO!
I PREFER TO LIE
THIS IS FICTION!
CLASSY MAN
LIVE WITHOUT FEAR
AND BE EATEN BY BEARS
TIME WILL HEAL
I WAS HERE
DON'T FORGET
FEAR IS THE WORST ARTIST
DEATH IS THE BEST
FAILURE MEANS YOU TRIED
HISTORY
IT GOES ON
ATHEISTS BELIEVE IN LIVING
LET GO

DEXTER DALWOOD
MARY SHELLEY, FRANKENSTEIN, 2001

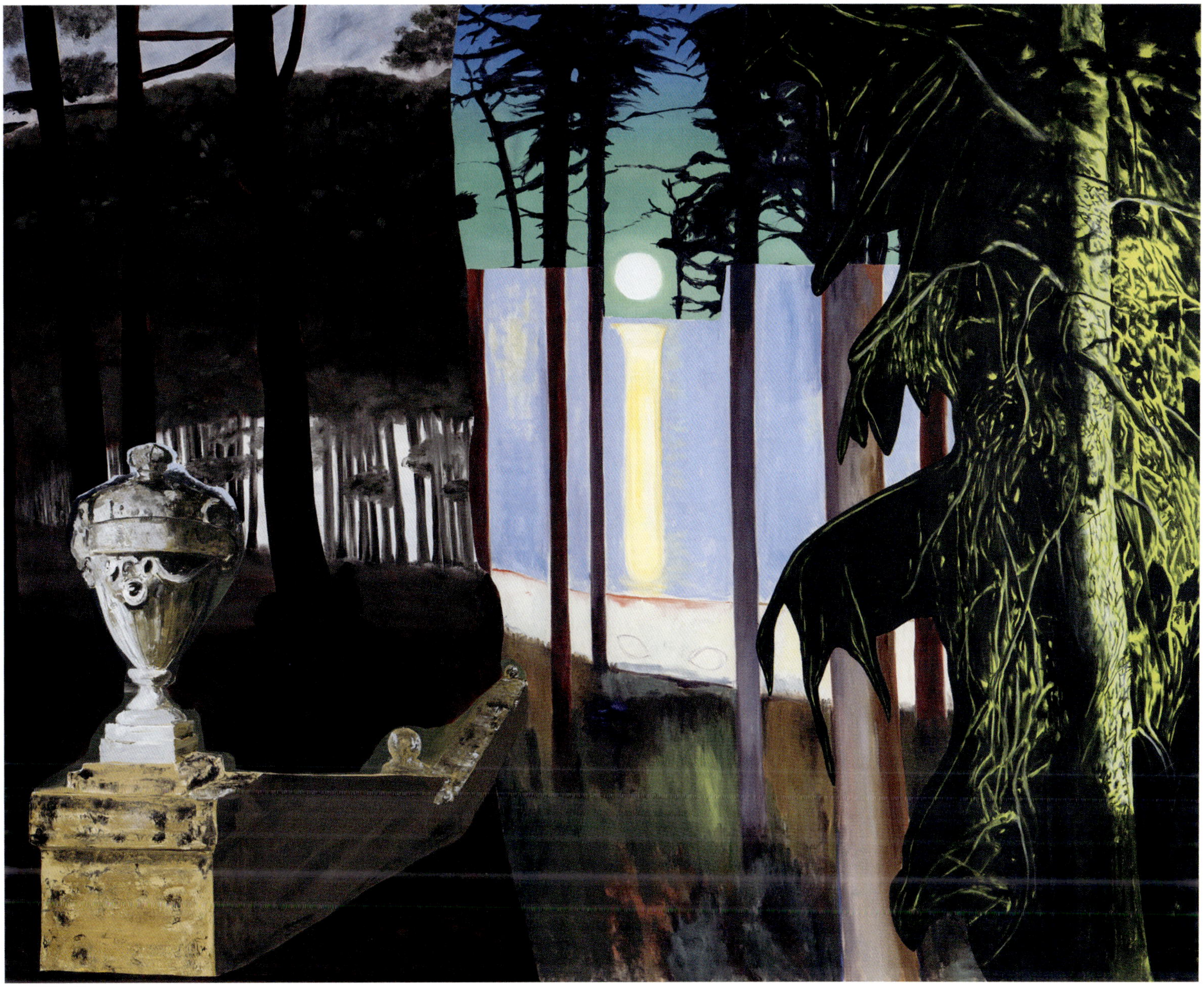

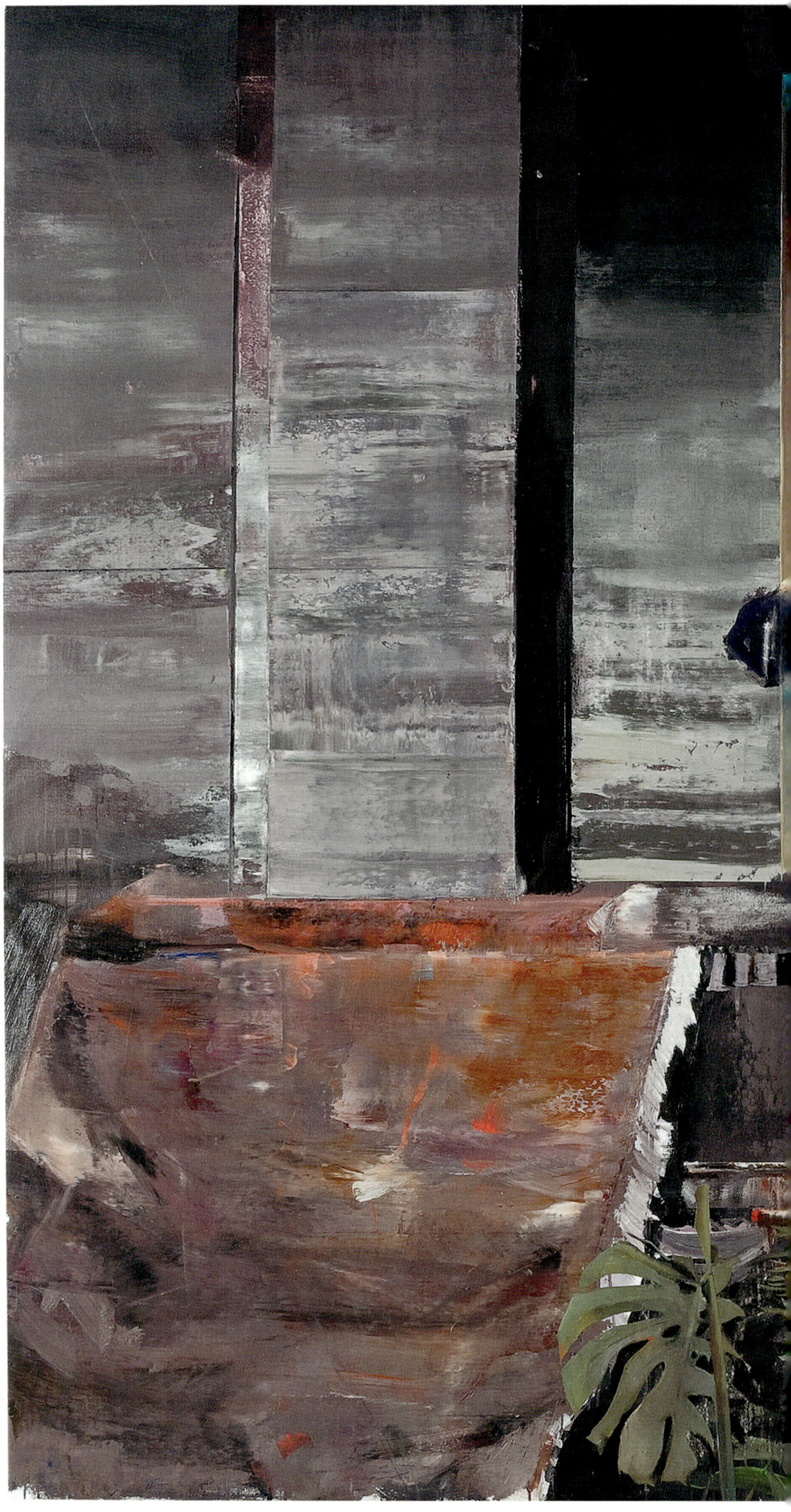

ADRIAN GHENIE
DUCHAMP'S FUNERAL I, 2009

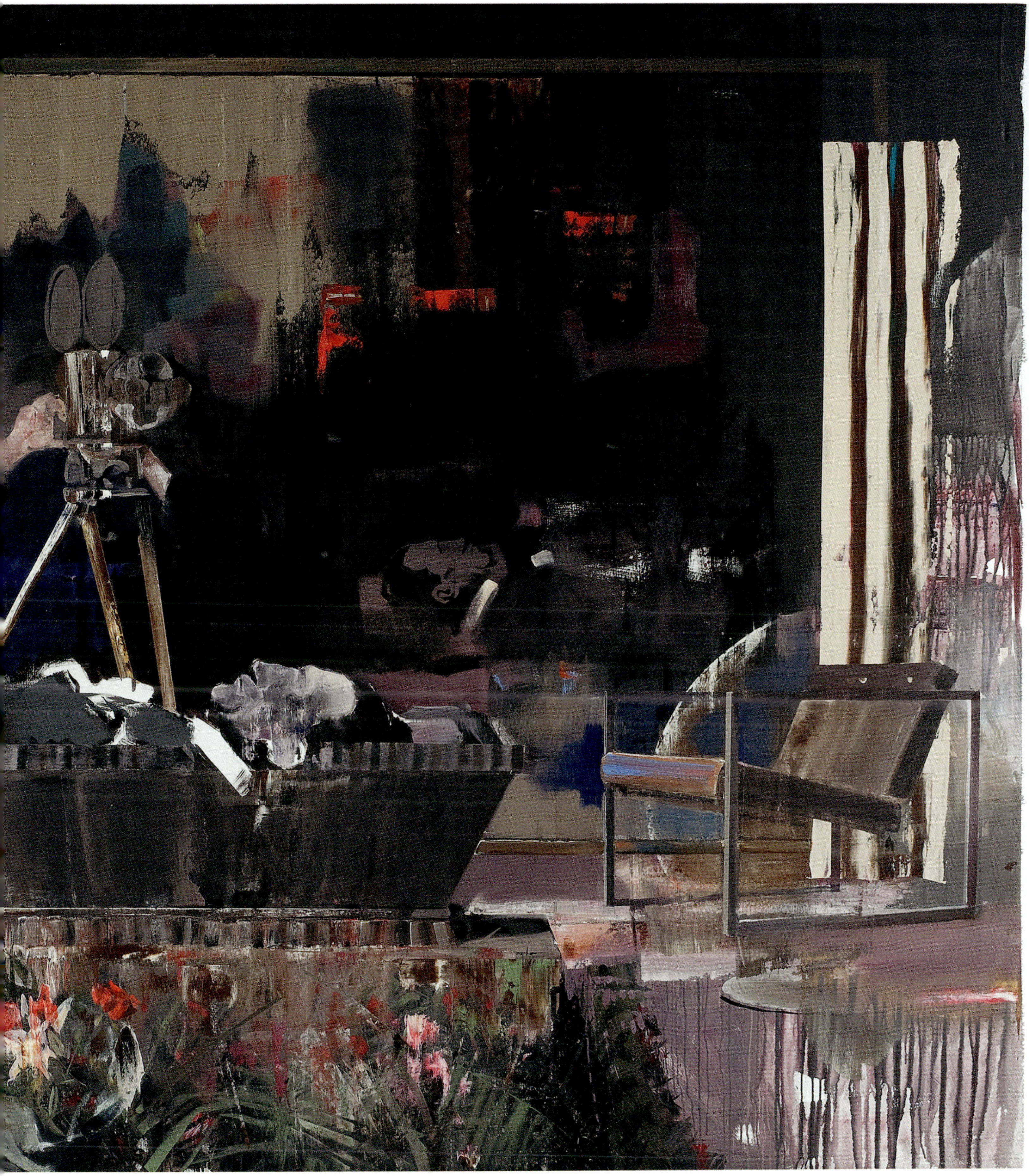

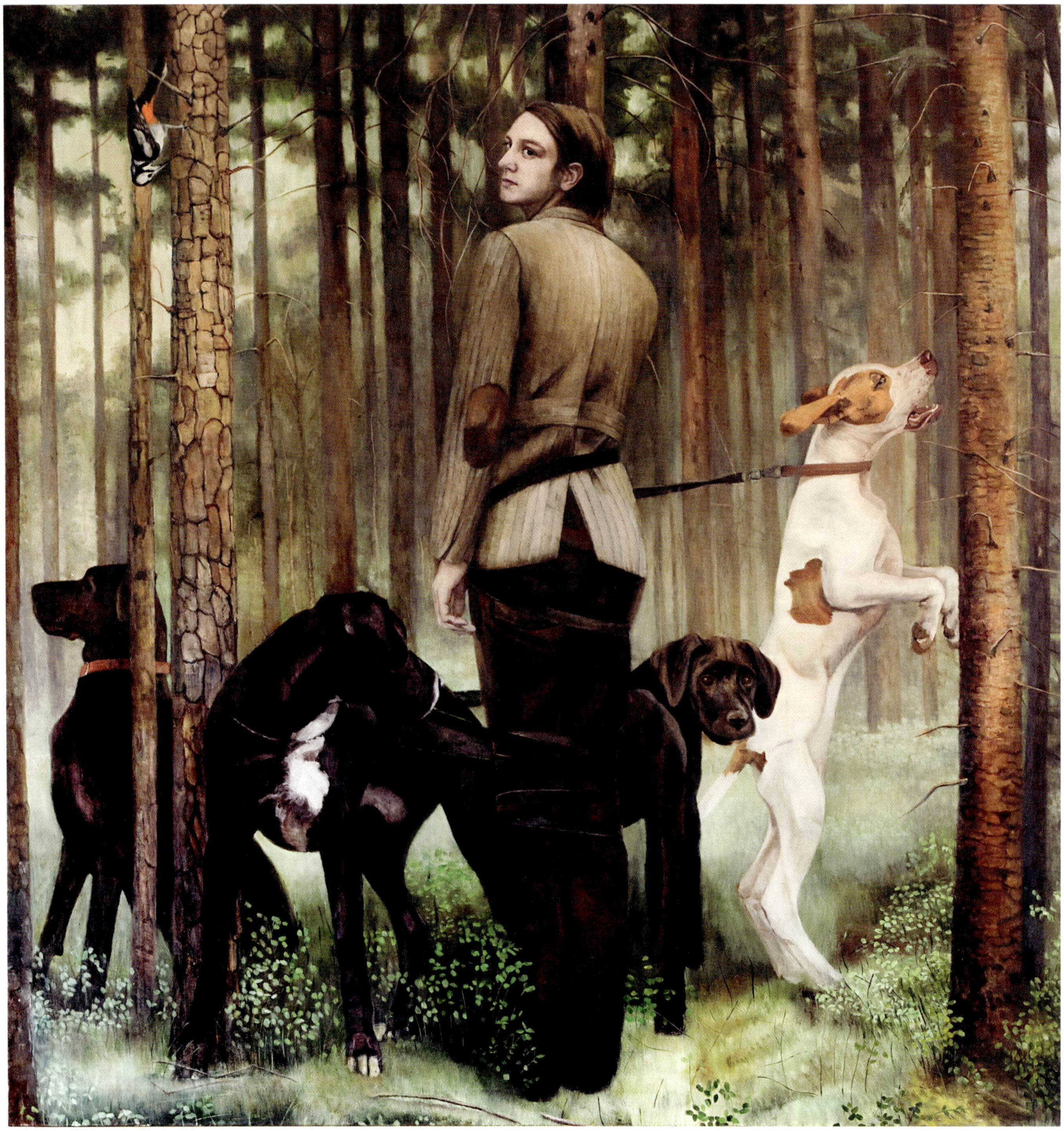

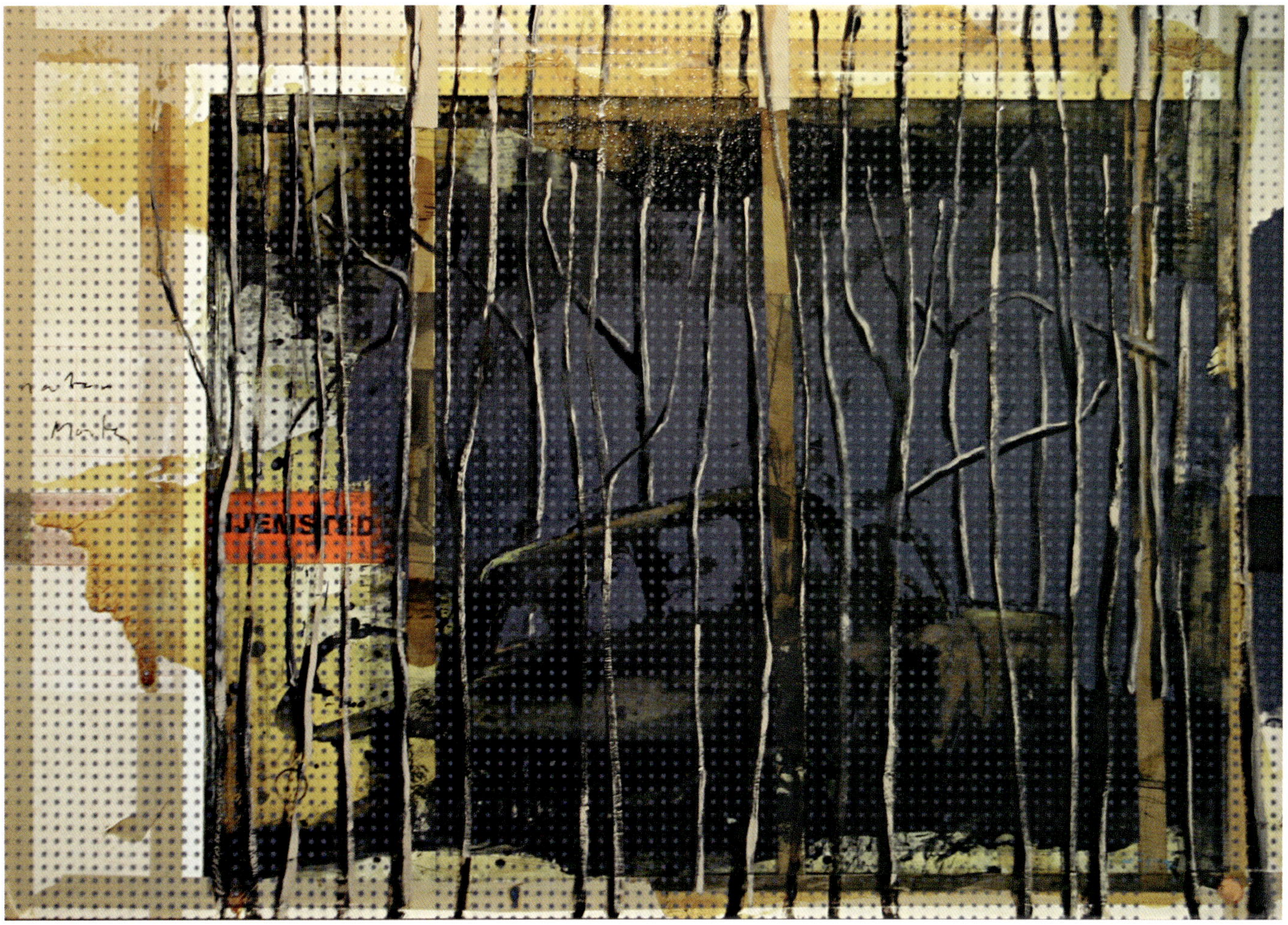

KJELL NUPEN
HJEMSTED NATURE MORTE, 2010

P.120
CHRISTER KARLSTAD
LAND OF GLOOM, 2009

ADRIAN GHENIE
BURNING BUSH, 2014

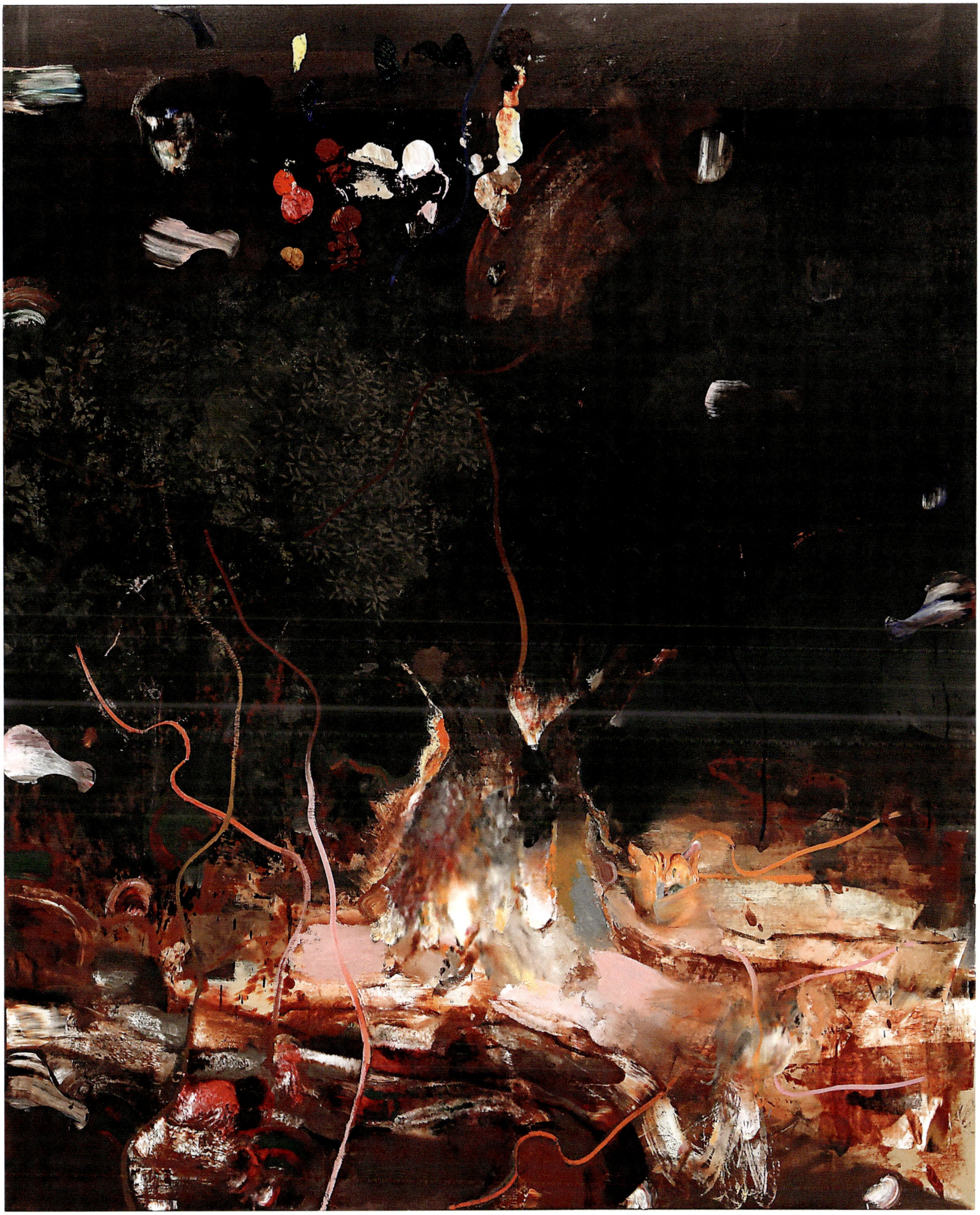

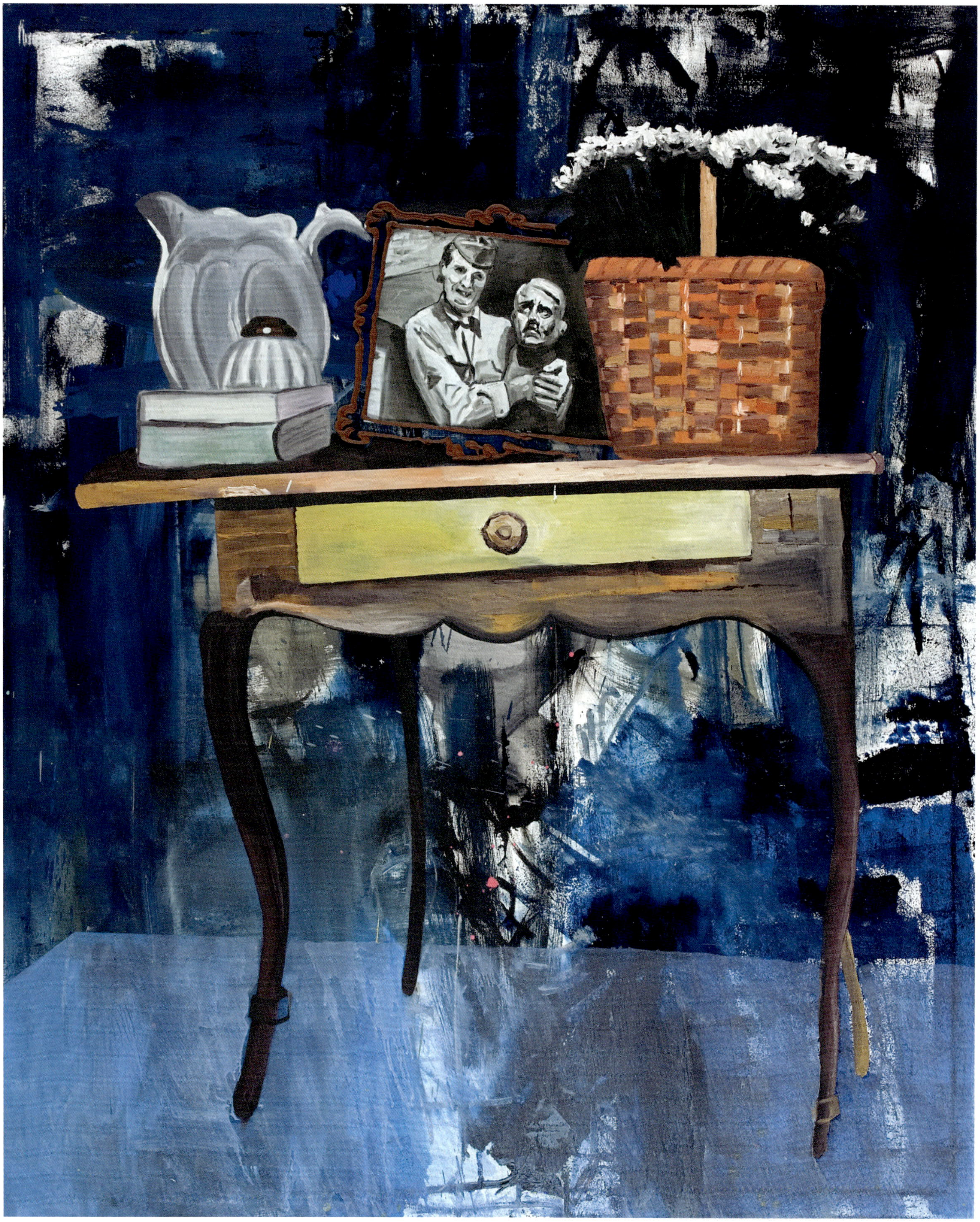

MARTIN KIPPENBERGER
NACHTTISCH, 1985

SVERRE BJERTNÆS
ATELIER, 2013

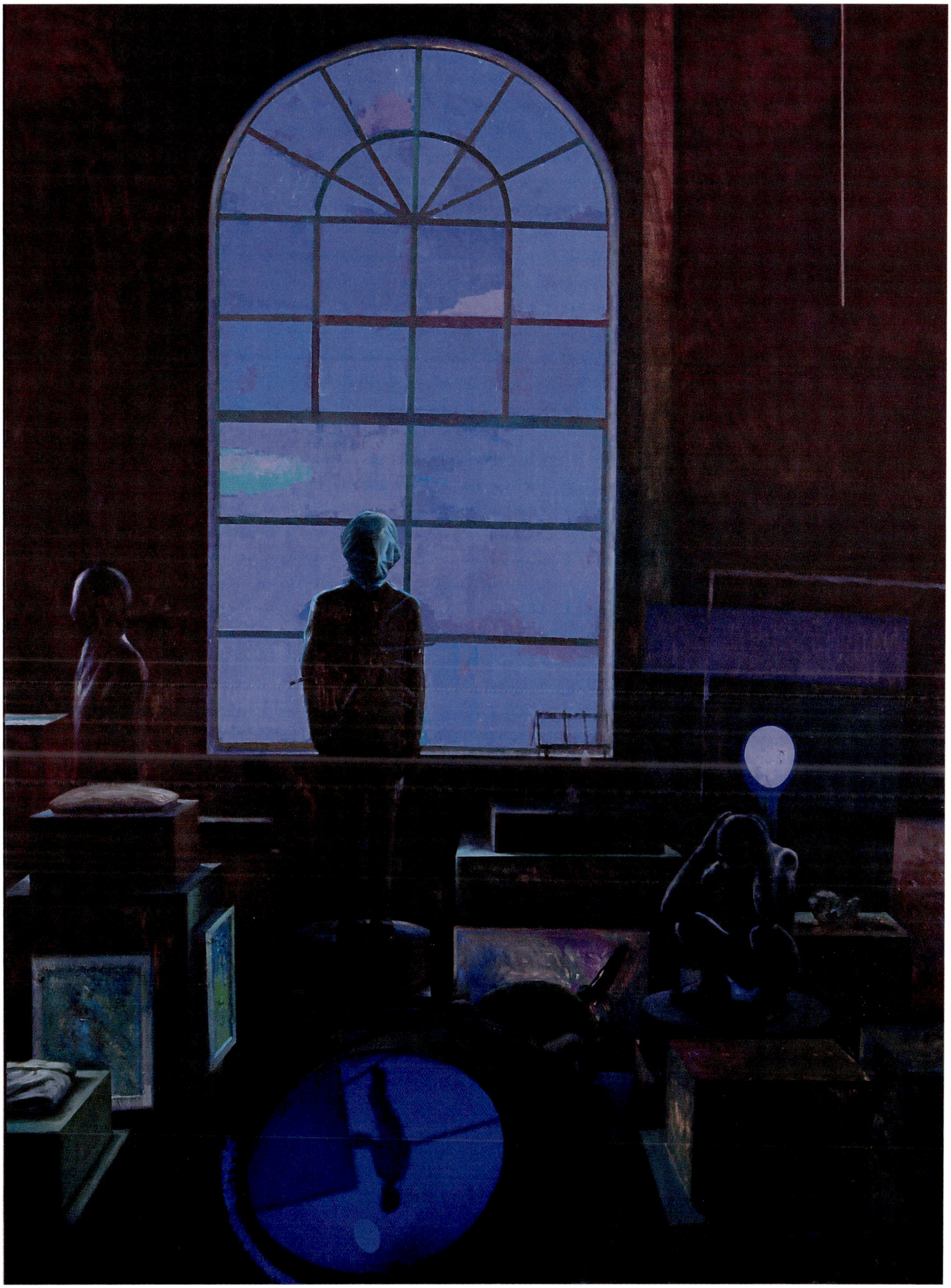

ROSS BLECKNER
BIRDS, 1996

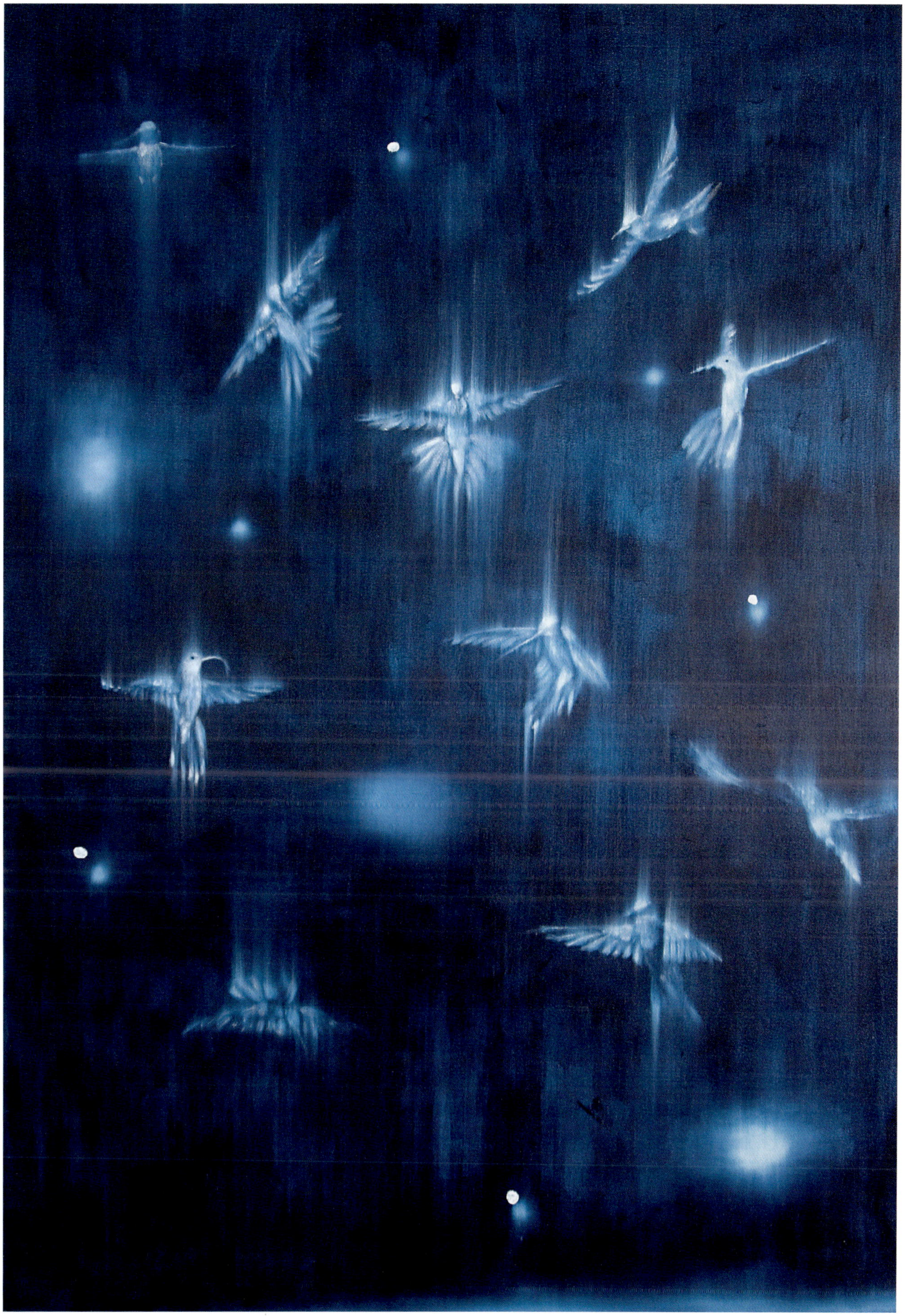

Winter

IV.
WINTER

December typically brings mixed weather and mixed emotions. The calendar year is drawing to a close, and the astronomical calendar heads towards the shortest day of the year in the Northern Hemisphere, the winter solstice on the 21st or 22nd of December. Cold, wintry conditions are forecast for the months ahead. It is also the Christmas holiday season, which is accompanied by a festive spirit, but for some it may also induce a sense of loneliness, isolation and conflict.

The last full moon of the year, known in Europe as the Moon Before Yule, is the full moon before the winter solstice. Some Native American tribes also know it as the Cold Moon or Long Night Moon. Anna-Eva Bergman's *Planète Argent* (*Silver Planet*, 1973) (→ p.135) is composed of a large orb of silver leaf, partially cut off at the top and floating against a striated blue background over a grey horizon line. Silver is associated with both Venus and the Moon.

Winter weather, of course, varies greatly depending on the region. In most northern climates, however, one almost always imagines the winter landscape covered in snow. 'Winter sets out to fill the whole landscape with snow', Karl Ove Knausgård writes in *Om vinteren* (*Winter*, 2017) from his 'Seasons Quartet', 'to cover it, completely so that everyone forgets summer and begins to think that only winter counts.'[4]

Winter scenes, often landscapes featuring mountains, have remained a persistent motif into the 21st century, even as glaciers recede, and snow becomes less frequent and more unpredictable due to global warming induced by humans. Ged Quinn draws on the winter landscapes of Jacob van Ruisdael and Francesco Foschi in *The Insomniacs* (2011) (→ p.136–137), but his snow scenes are warped and include incongruous even jarring elements, both contemporary and historical. Dexter Dalwood's *Wittgenstein's Bathroom* (2001) (→ p.138) is a painting of an imagined interior, partially based on houses that Ludwig Wittgenstein designed and on art historical references to figures such as Bonnard and Munch. The full-height window, a feature of the austere modernist Wittgenstein House in Vienna, frames a view of the snowy landscape with birch trees that is characteristic of Skjolden, Norway, where the Austrian philosopher built himself a remote mountain cabin.

Kjell Nupen adhered asphalt to one half of his canvas to add texture and filled the other half with the simplified image of undulating foothills in his native Norway. Sky and water are rendered in a deep colour he called 'Nupen blue'. His painting, titled *Stille natt—hellige natt* (*Silent Night—Holy Night,* 1994–95) (→ p.139) is overlayed with repeating symbols that acknowledge both the secular and religious sides of Christmas. In 2024, Catherine Opie travelled to Norway to photograph mountains in the winter, seeking to create an intimate connection with the landscape and to capture the deep blue light at sunrise and at dusk (→ p.141). She sees the resulting images as a meditation on 'how the history of blue is used in art' and as a mourning 'that all of us are experiencing as the planet changes so rapidly'.[5]

Influenced by the way in which signage is superimposed on the Los Angeles landscape, most notably the iconic Hollywood sign, *Mountain Standard* (2000) by Ed Ruscha (→ p.143) combines an image of Mount Everest in the Himalayas with a graphic shape that derives from his *Standard Station* (1966)

4. Karl One Knausgard, *Winter*, Vintage, London, 2021, p. 27.

5. 'Catherine Opie: Beginnings and Endings'. *Louisiana Channel*, uploaded by Louisiana Channel, Louisiana Museum of Modern Art, 26 March 2024, https://channel.louisiana.dk/video/catherine-opie-beginnings-and-endings.

to create a visual portmanteau referring to a time zone in western North America.

Bjarne Melgaard conflates winter and mountains with drugs in *Mountain of cocaine* (1995–99) (→ p.144–145). His huge canvas is an abstract field of colour and expressive mark-making in the style of Joan Mitchell, overlayed with a chaotic mix of drawing, collage elements and snippets of conversations or interior monologues—personal references to sex, drugs, music, travels and sportswear. In Johan Knoff's *Pushers, NY* (1981) (→ p.147), loosely painted figures loiter around the doorway of a movie theatre, trying to stay warm while waiting to solicit customers on a cold day. Dragan Zdravković's *Winter Ends* (2014) (→ p.148) depicts a wintery, urban Belgrade landscape painted in a neo-realist manner. The metal drums and other objects in the fenced-off industrial yard are covered by a heavy layer of snow. Although winter does not look as if it is in retreat, a package of green parsley appears incongruously in the extreme foreground.

In 2006, Mette Tronvoll documented the Special Operations Command of the Norwegian Armed Forces at the Rena military camp. Her photograph of elite soldiers (→ p.151), who are trained for anti-terrorism and special operations, shows them masked and dressed in wintertime snow camouflage. Subtle differences in the way the soldiers dress or the equipment they carry impart a sense of individual identity.

Beyond wintry landscapes, interior genre scenes have historically depicted farmers or other labourers working indoors during the winter season to repair their tools and prepare for the spring planting season. Pedro Reyes's sculpture *Navaja Suiza VIII* (*Swiss Army Knife VIII*, 2014) (→ p.152) is a scaled-up version of the multi-use pocketknife, containing an axe, shovel and scythe, among other tools for use around the farm.

If spring is represented by youth in art, then winter is symbolised by old age and death. *Nude with Skeleton* (2002–05) (→ p.153) is a performance on video by Marina Abramović, who lays on the floor with a skeleton resting on top of her body. She breathes slowly; the skeleton rises and falls with each inhalation and exhalation. 'The work is really about facing your own mortality', the artist says, 'it's the way to deal with that fear.'[6] Ross Bleckner's *Candelier & Cherub* (1990) (→ p.155) can be seen as a contemporary vanitas painting, reminding us of our own mortality and the vain pursuit of worldly goods, but also a memorial to those who have died of AIDS-related illnesses. On a more personal level, a precious antique picture frame houses a video and serves as receptacles for personal and collective memories in Ken Matsubara's *Winter Dream—Table* (2011) (→ p.157).

Headlines in the 24 February 2022 edition of *The New York Times* announced the start of the Russian invasion of Ukraine, and the paper also included articles about China's turn away from the world under Xi Jinping and the resignation of prosecutors leading the investigation into Trump's business practices. Rirkrit Tiravanija has mounted these newspaper pages on canvas and stencilled the words 'shine light into dark places' over them in bold yellow block letters (→ p.159). The phrase is associated with the Bible but also with the role of journalism. Tiravanija explains, 'The notion of light in dark places is about getting the truth out'.[7]

6. Marina Abramović, 'Marina Abramović: The Artist Is Present', interview by Glenn Lowry, The Museum of Modern Art, 2010, https://www.moma.org/audio/playlist/243/3132.

7. Rirkrit Tiravanija quoted in Ian Malone, 'A New T-Shirt Capsule Puts Ukrainian Pride Front and Center' *Vogue*, 29 June 2022, https://www.vogue.com/article/ooo-ukrainepride-t-shirt-capsule.

ANNA-EVA BERGMAN
PLANÈTE ARGENT, 1973

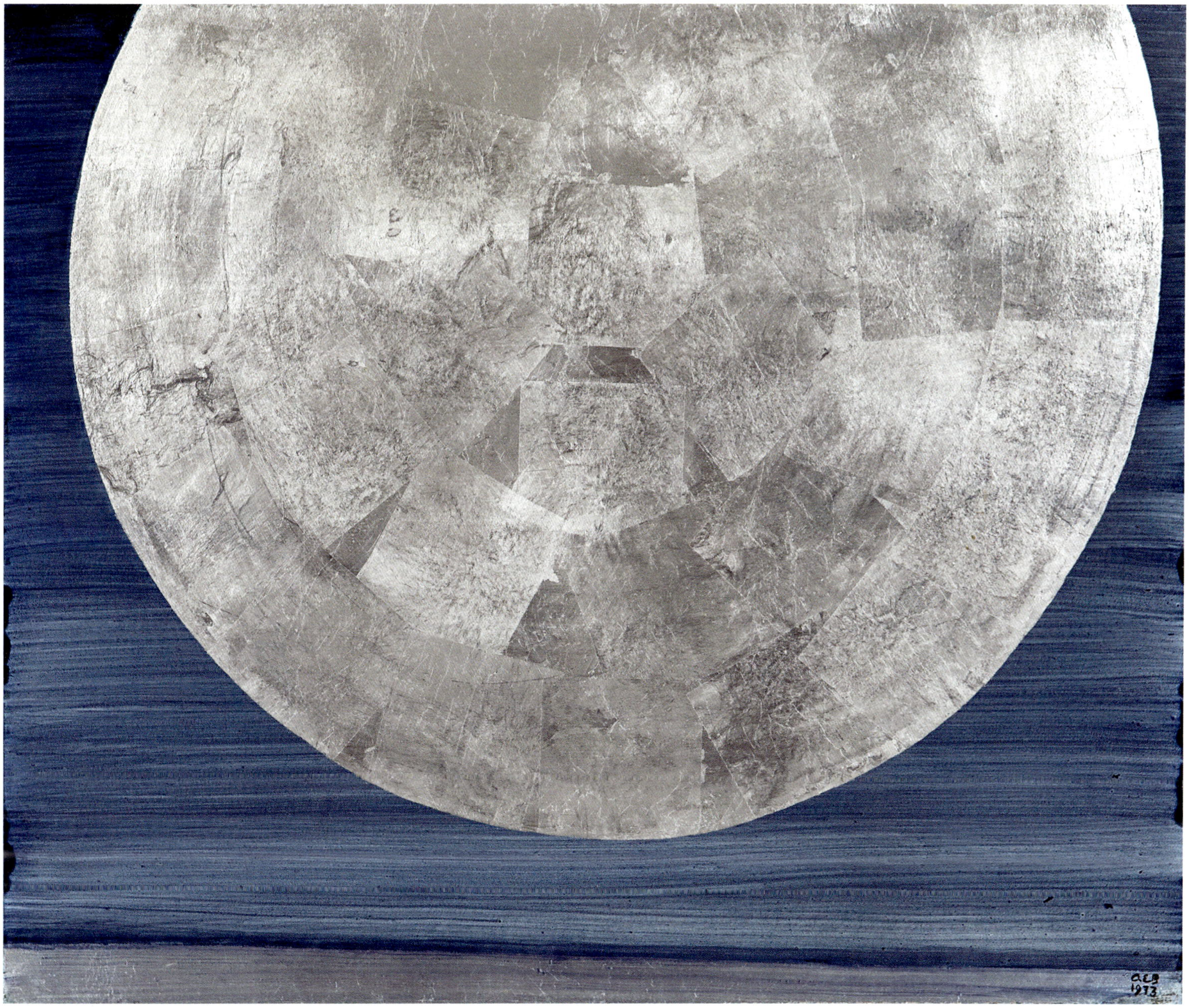

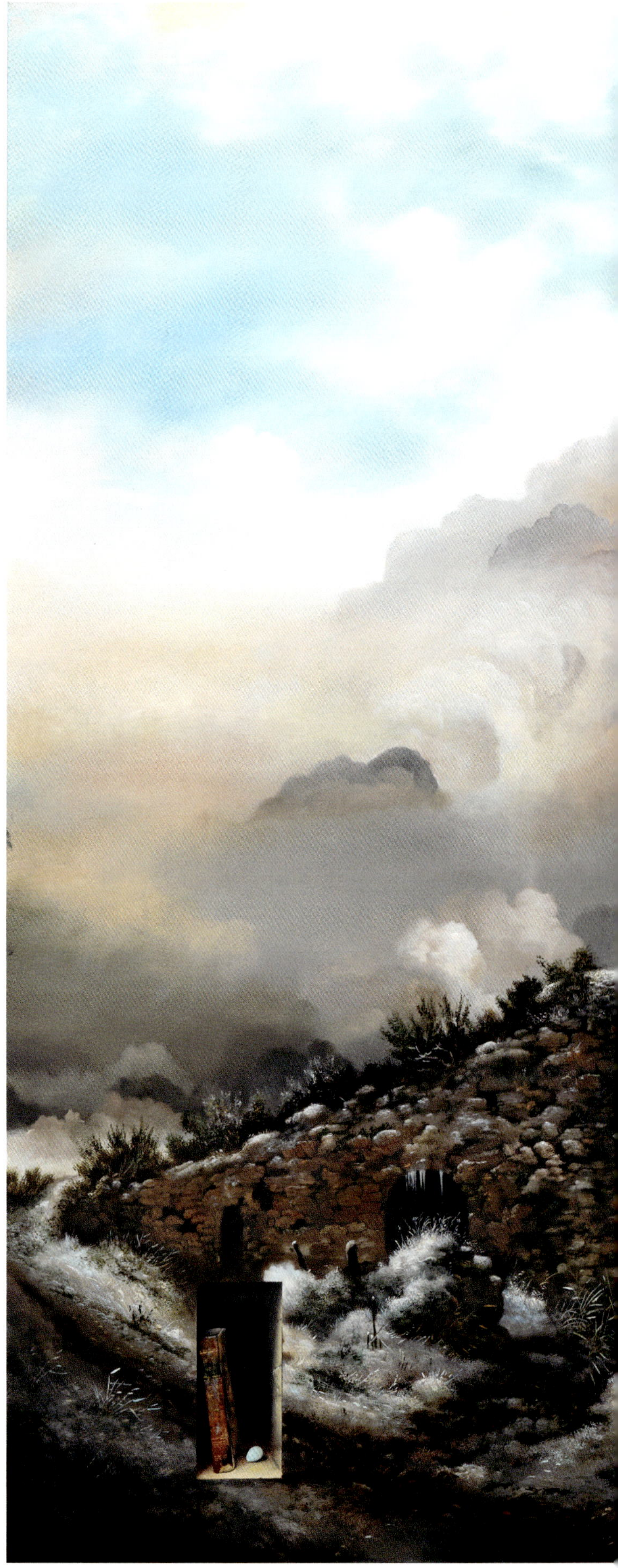

GED QUINN
THE INSOMNIACS, 2011

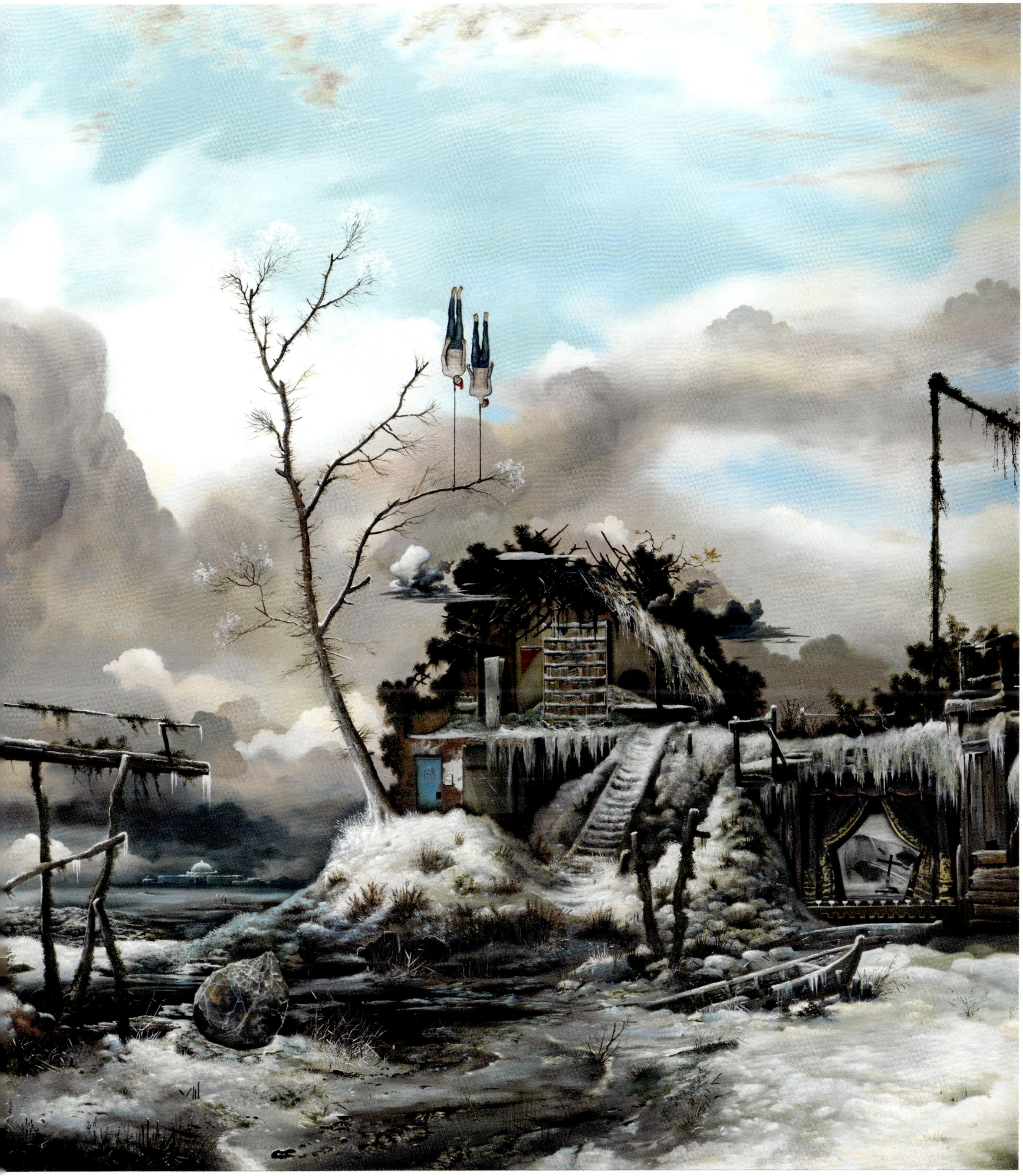

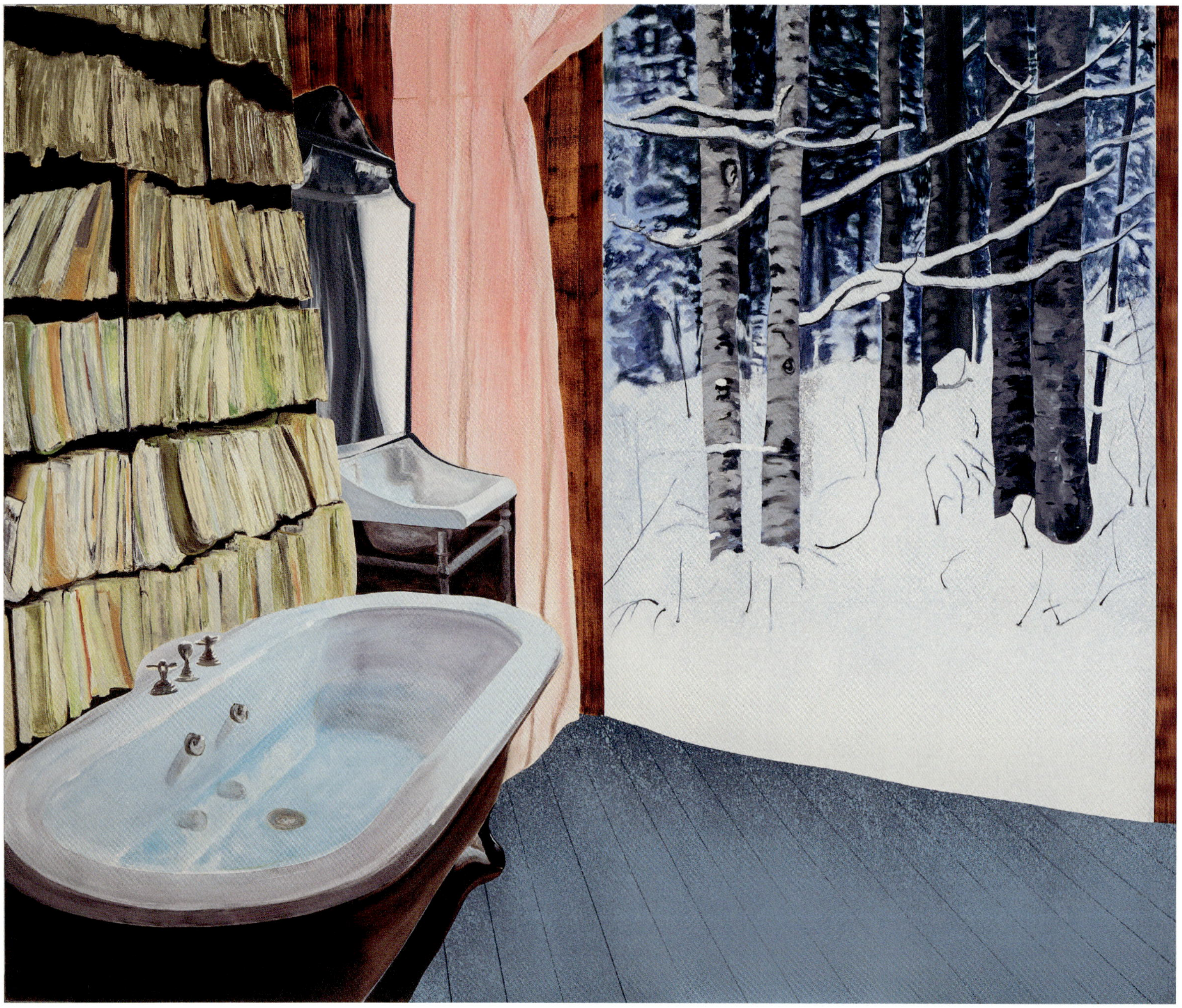

DEXTER DALWOOD
WITTGENSTEIN'S BATHROOM, 2001

P. 139
KJELL NUPEN
STILLE NATT—HELLIGE NATT, 1994—95

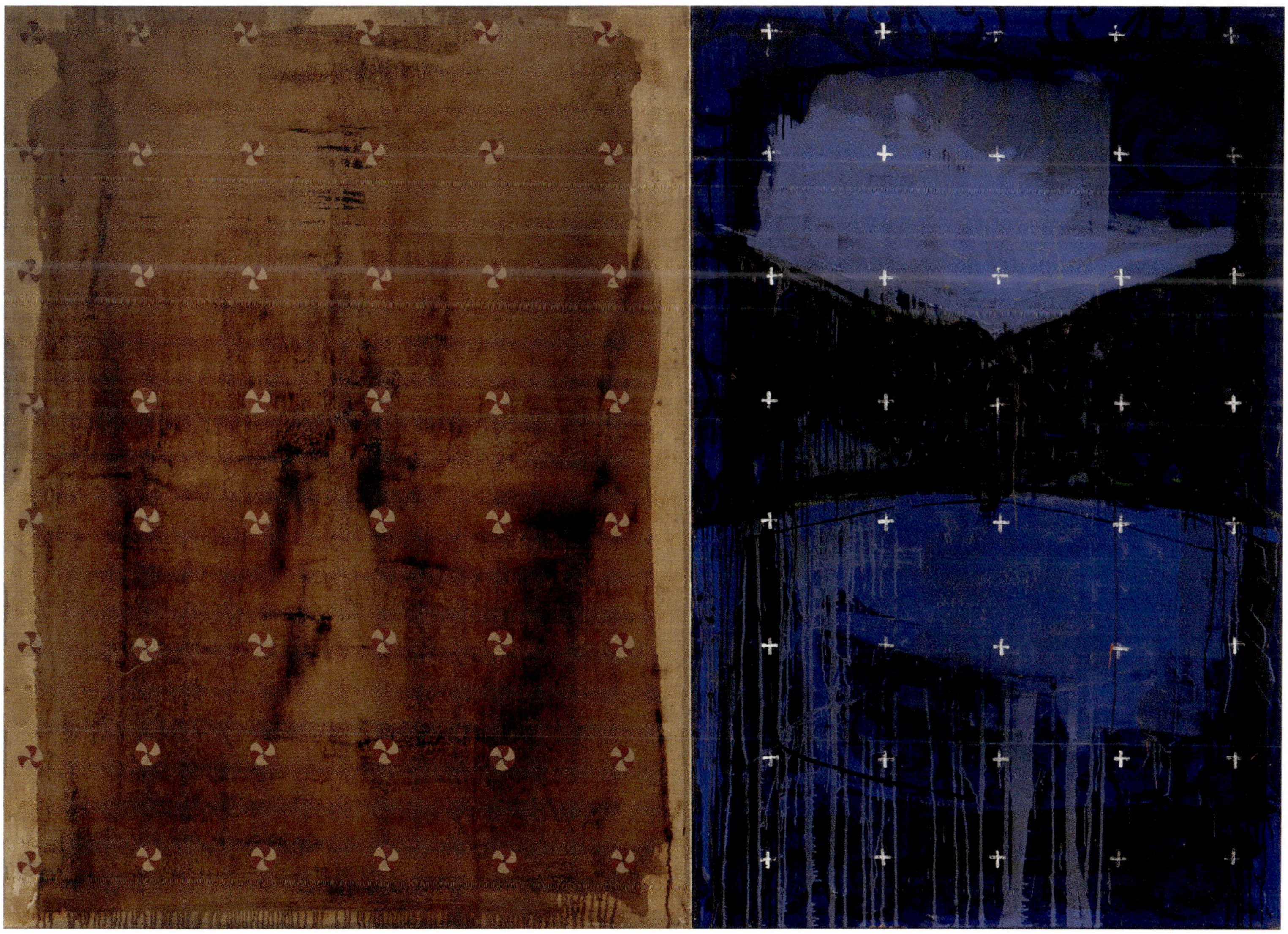

CATHERINE OPIE
UNTITLED #3
(NORWAY MOUNTAINS), 2024

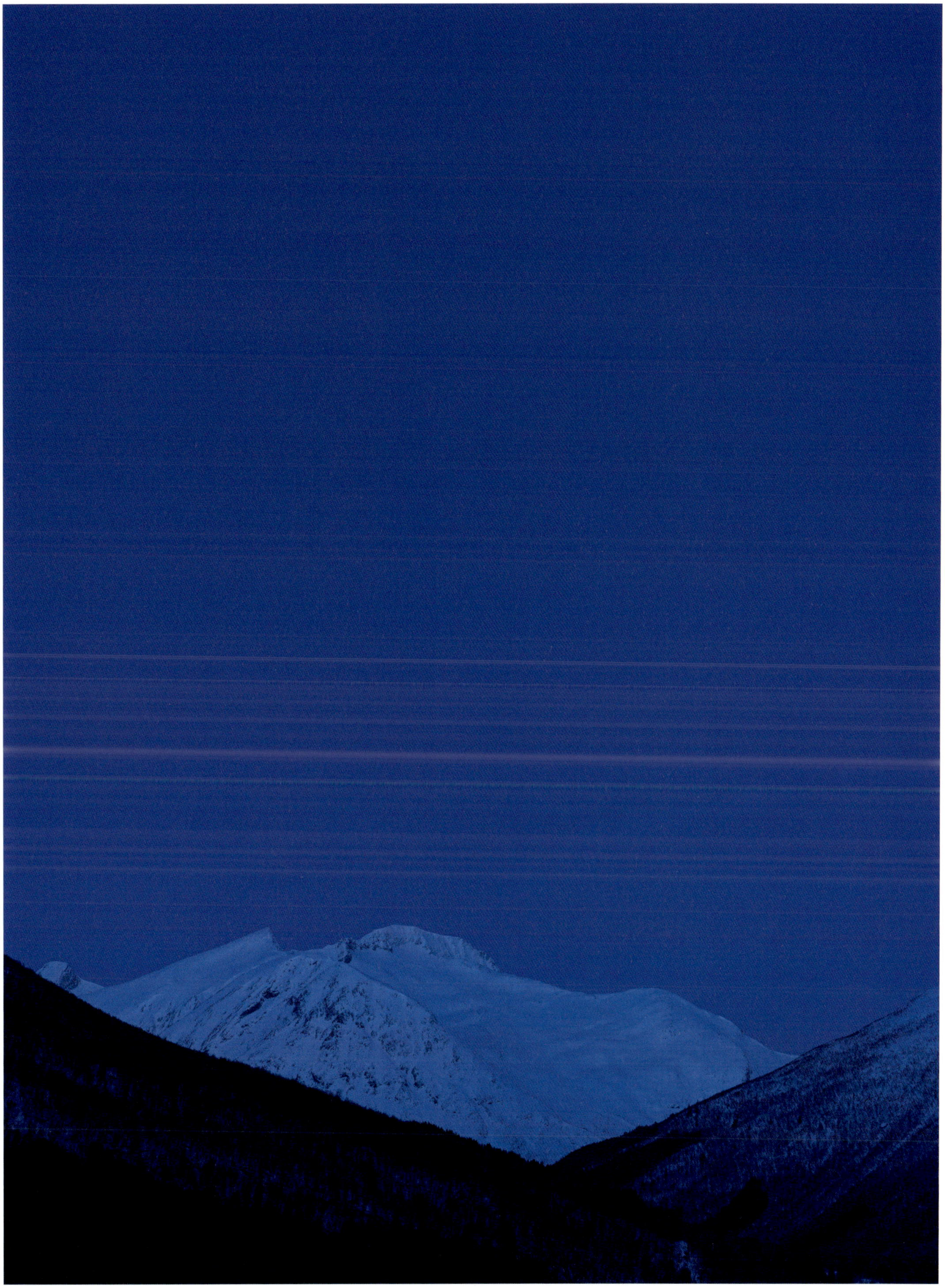

ED RUSCHA
MOUNTAIN STANDARD, 2000

P. 144–145
BJARNE MELGAARD
MOUNTAIN OF COCAINE, 1995–99

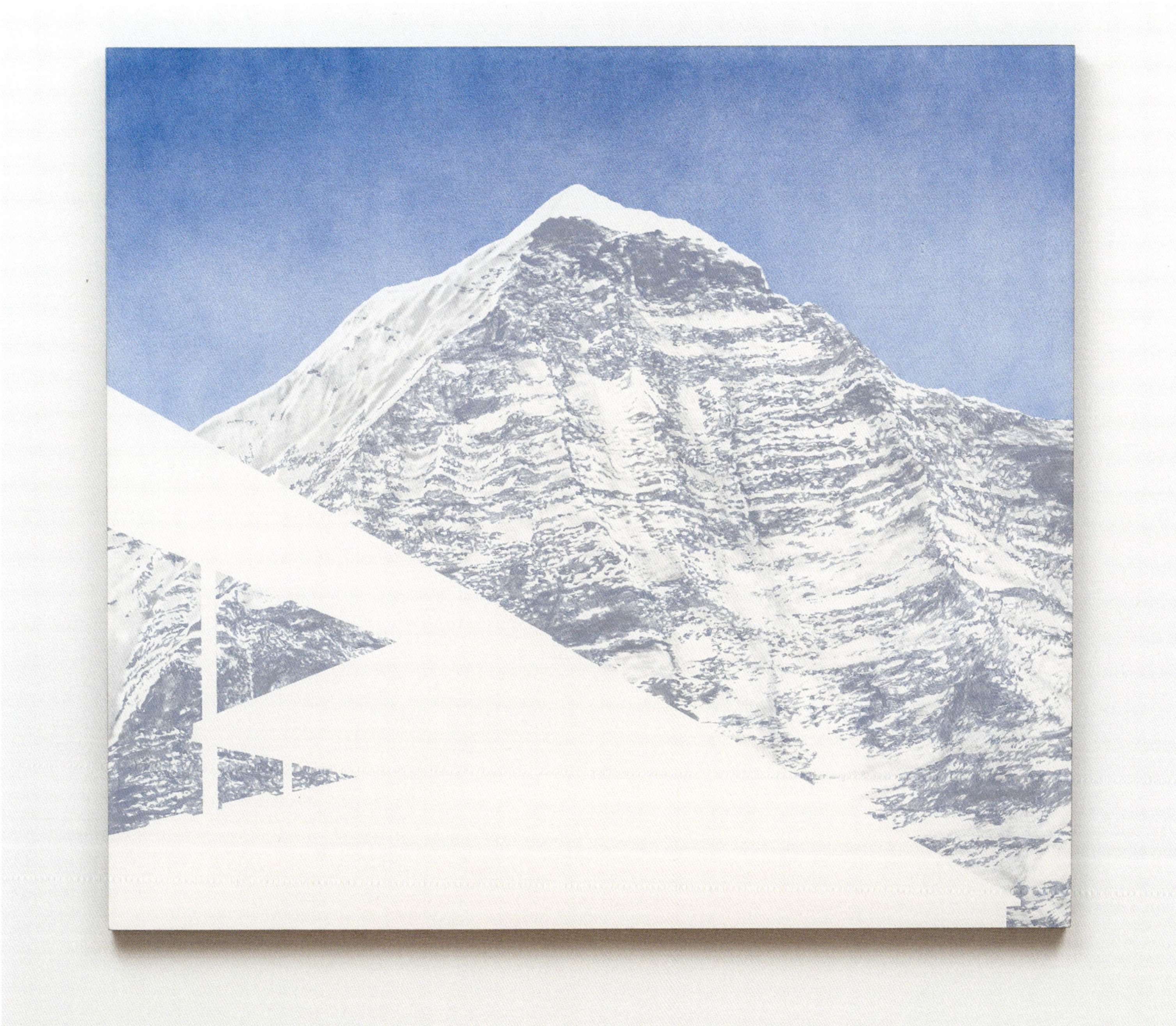

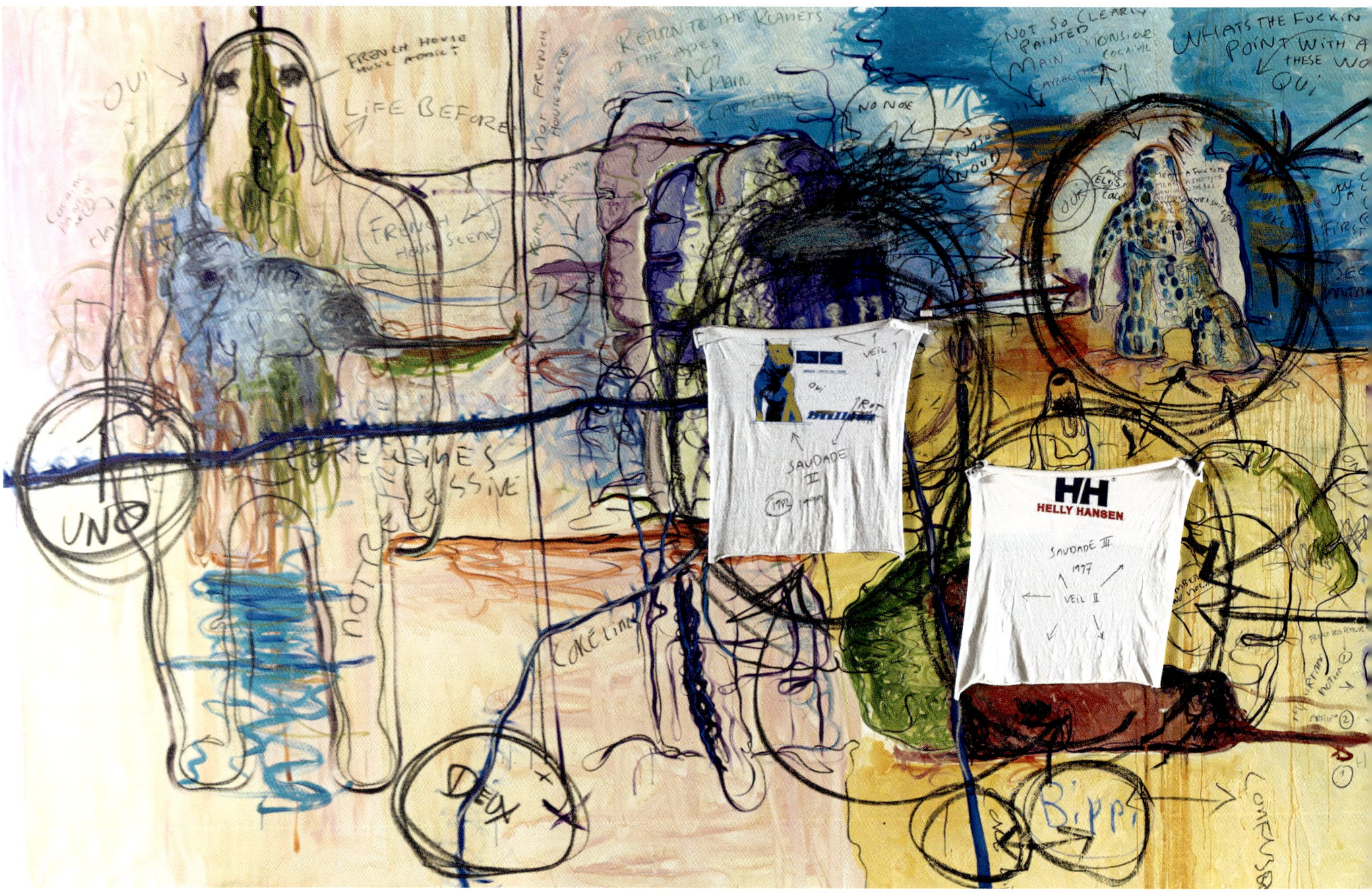
FRENCH HOUSE MUSIC ADDICT
OUI
LIFE BEFORE
NOT FRENCH HOUSE SCENE
RETURN TO THE PLANETS OF THE APES
NOT MAIN CHARACTER
NOT SO CLEARLY PAINTED MAIN MONSIEUR COCAINE
NO NOSE
FRENCH House Scene
UNO
SAUDADE II
VEIL I
HH HELLY HANSEN
SAUDADE III
1977
VEIL II
COKE LINK
DEUX

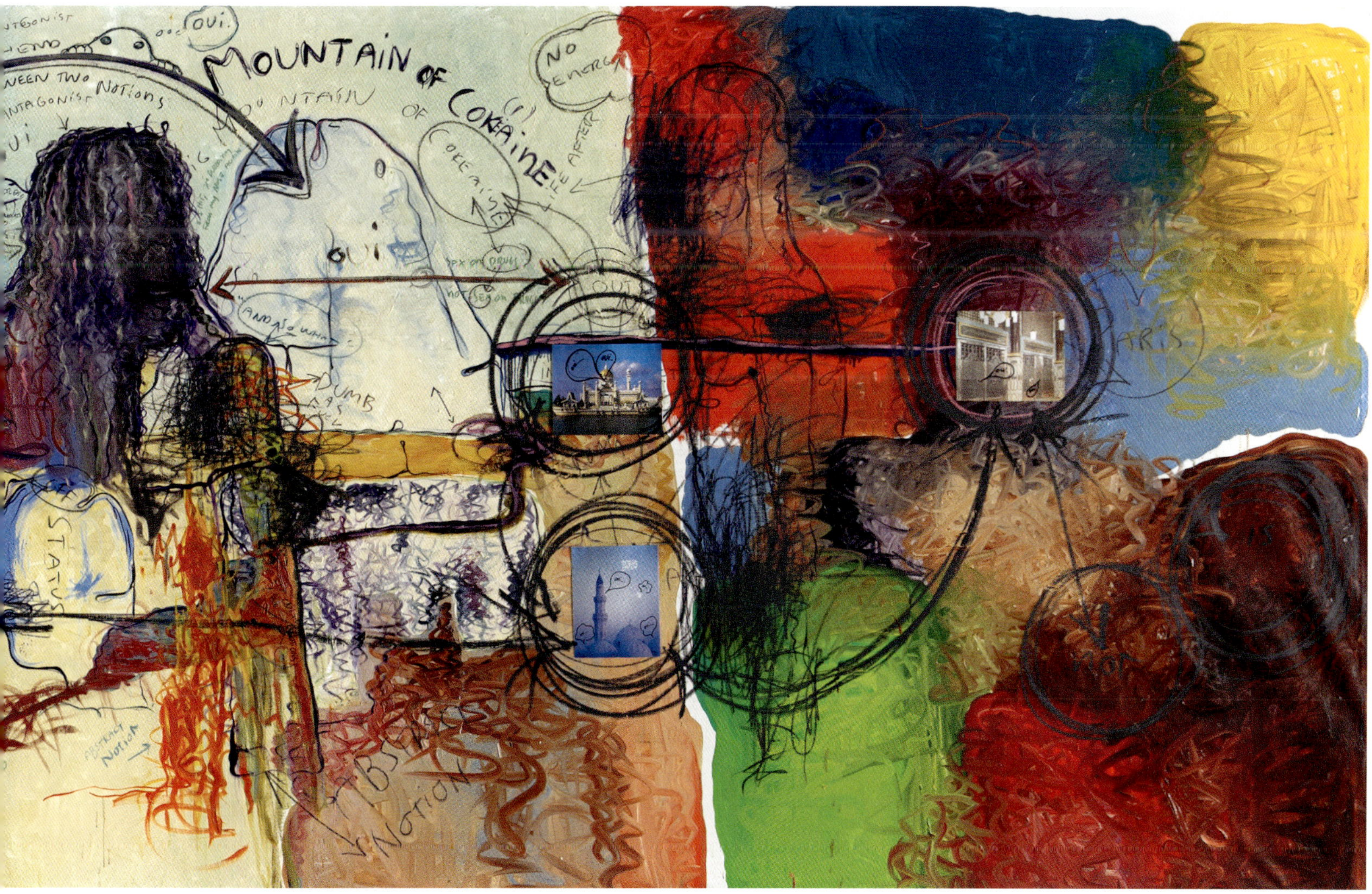
MOUNTAIN OF COKAINE
OUI.

JOHAN KNOFF
PUSHERS, N.Y, 1981

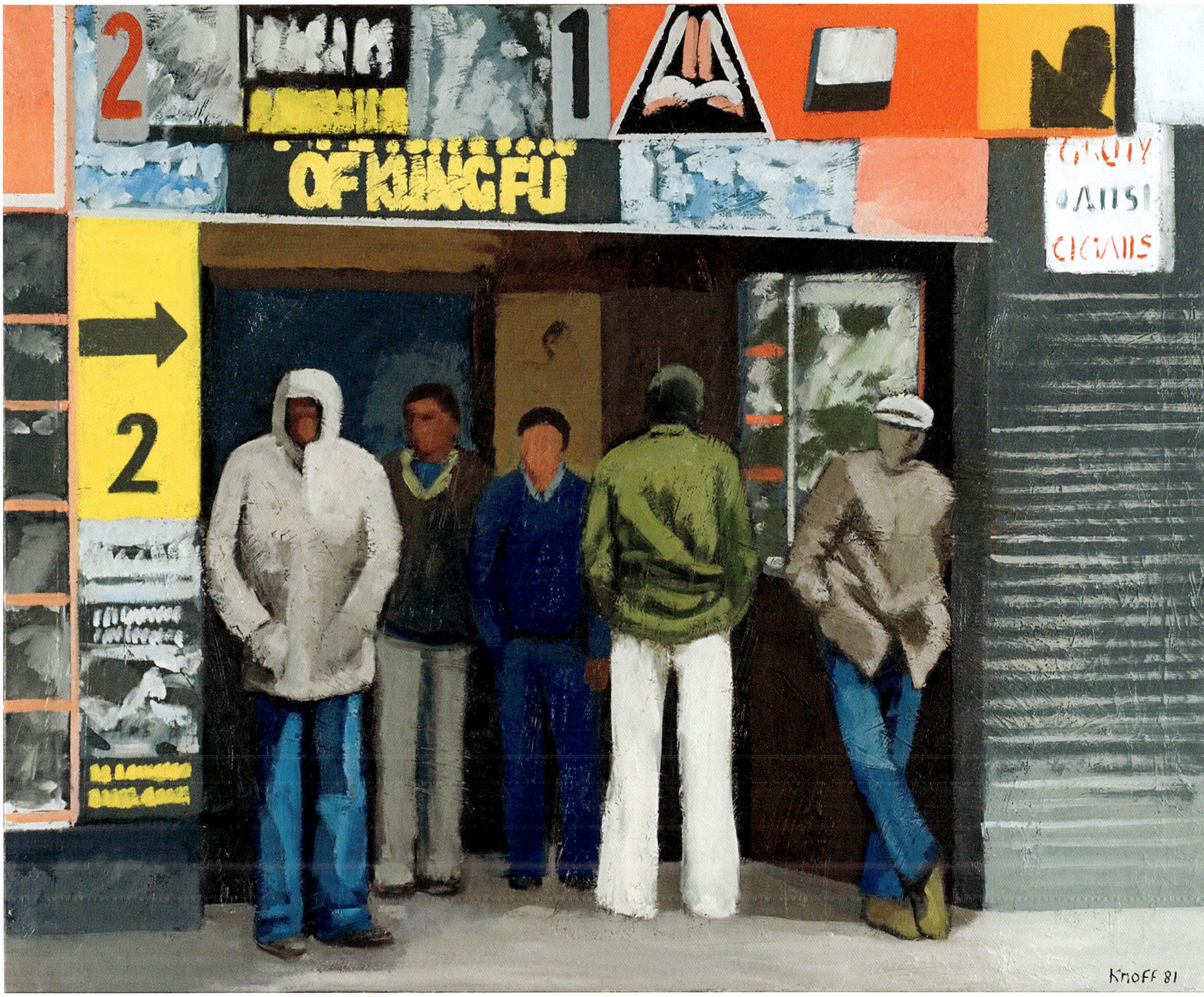
2
1
OF KUNG FU
2
Knoff 81

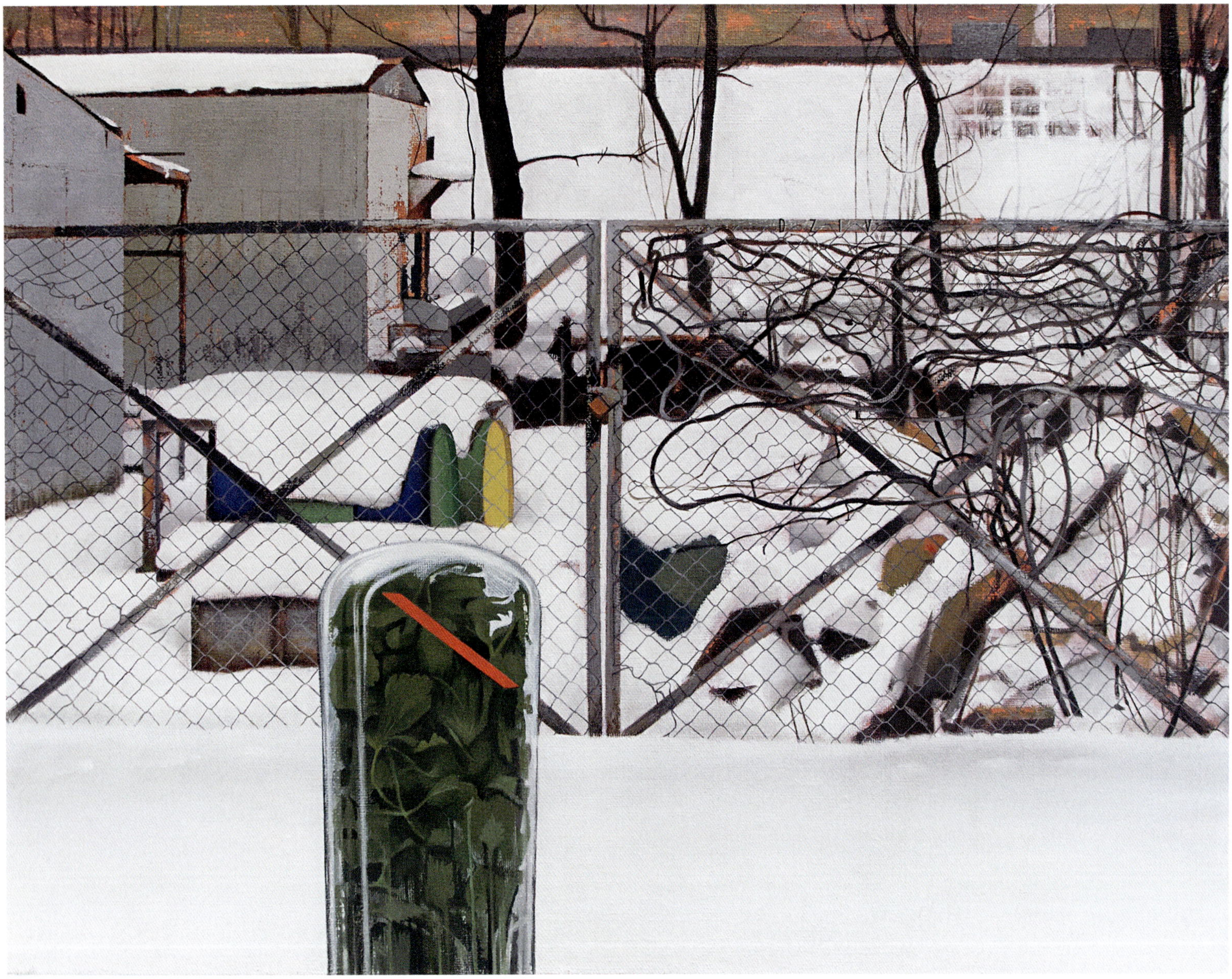

DRAGAN ZDRAVKOVIĆ
WINTER ENDS, 2014

METTE TRONVOLL
RENA 18, 2006

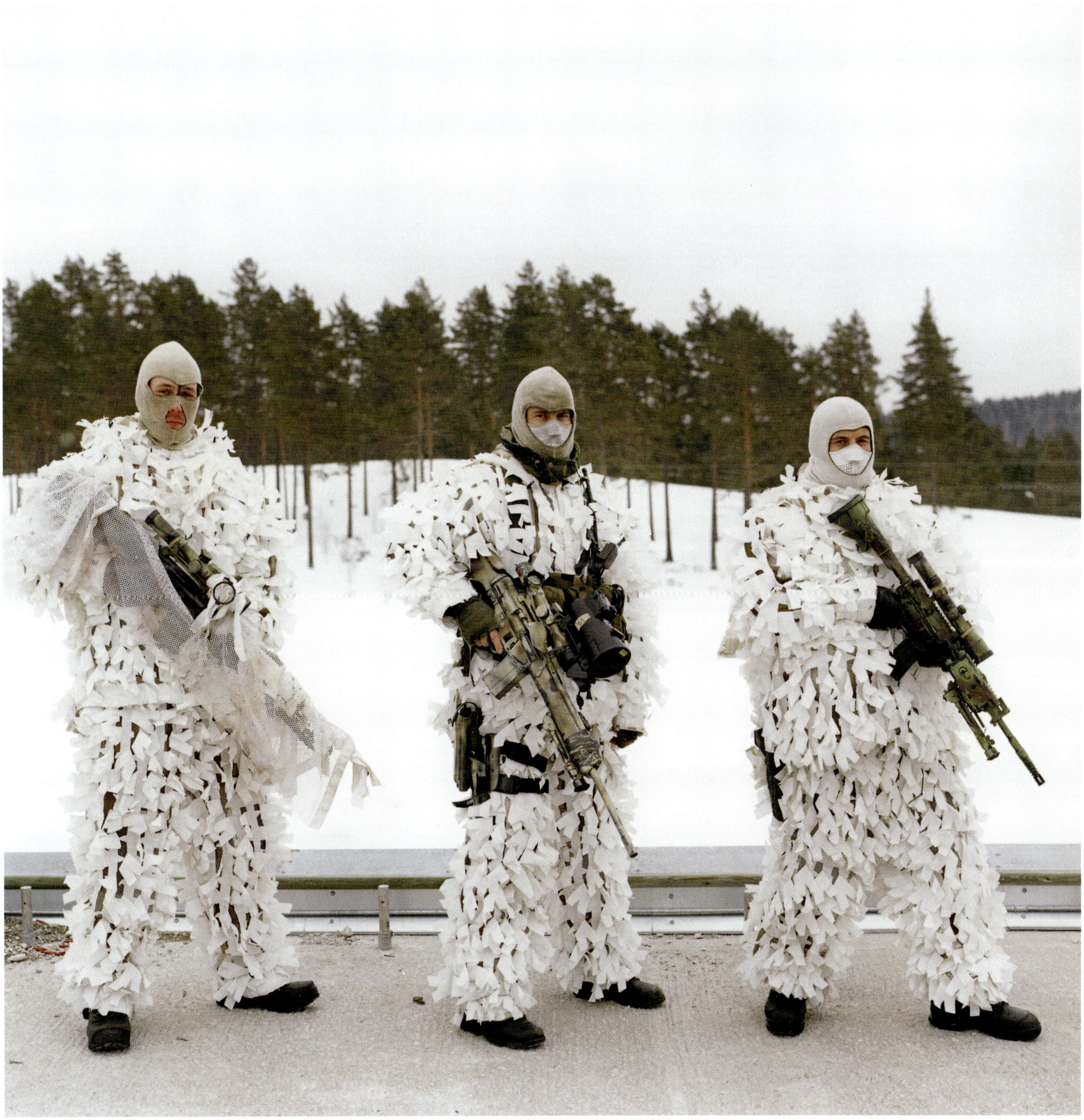

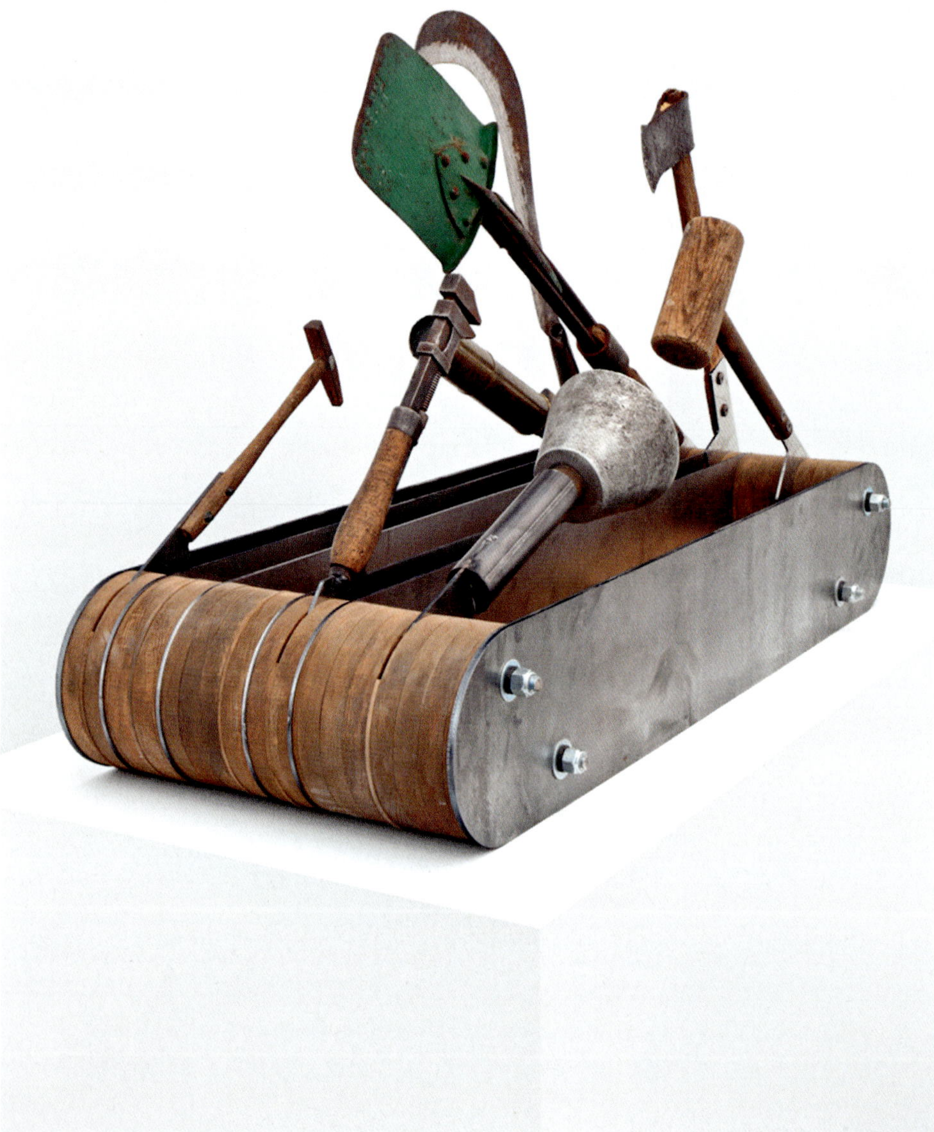

PEDRO REYES
NAVAJA SUIZA VIII, 2014

P. 153
MARINA ABRAMOVIĆ
NUDE WITH SKELETON, 2002–05

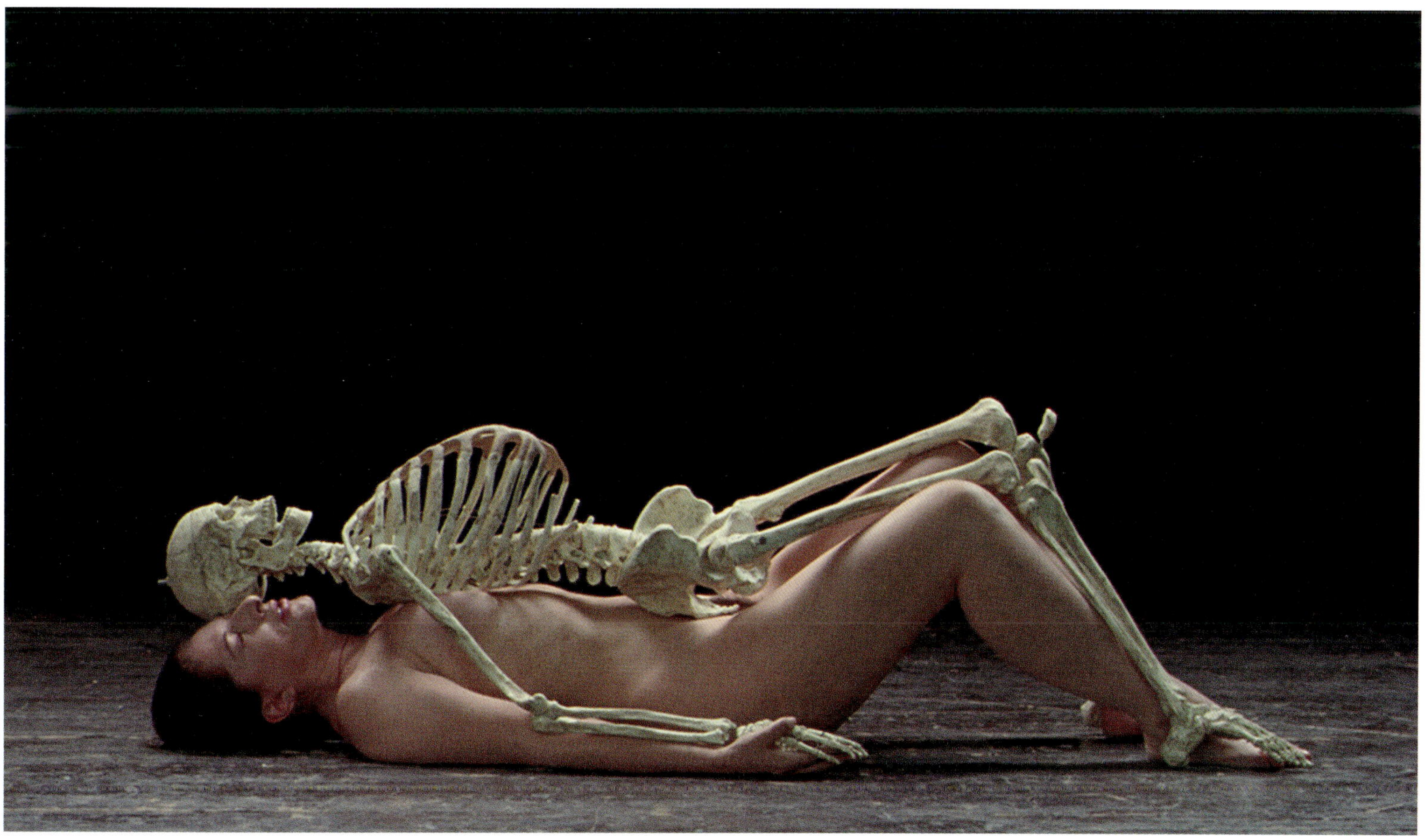

ROSS BLECKNER
CANDELIER AND CHERUB, 1990

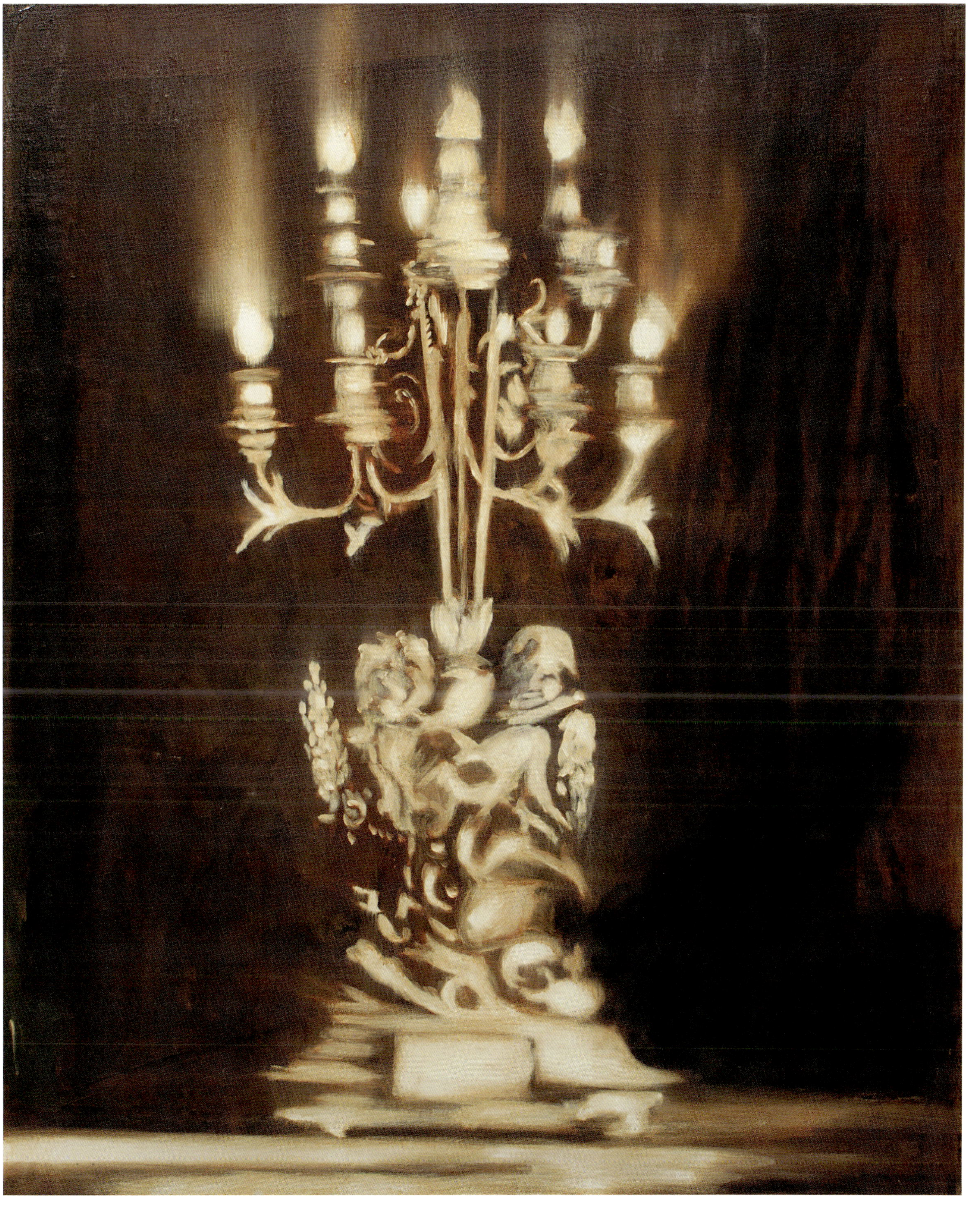

KEN MATSUBARA
WINTER DREAMS—TABLE, 2011

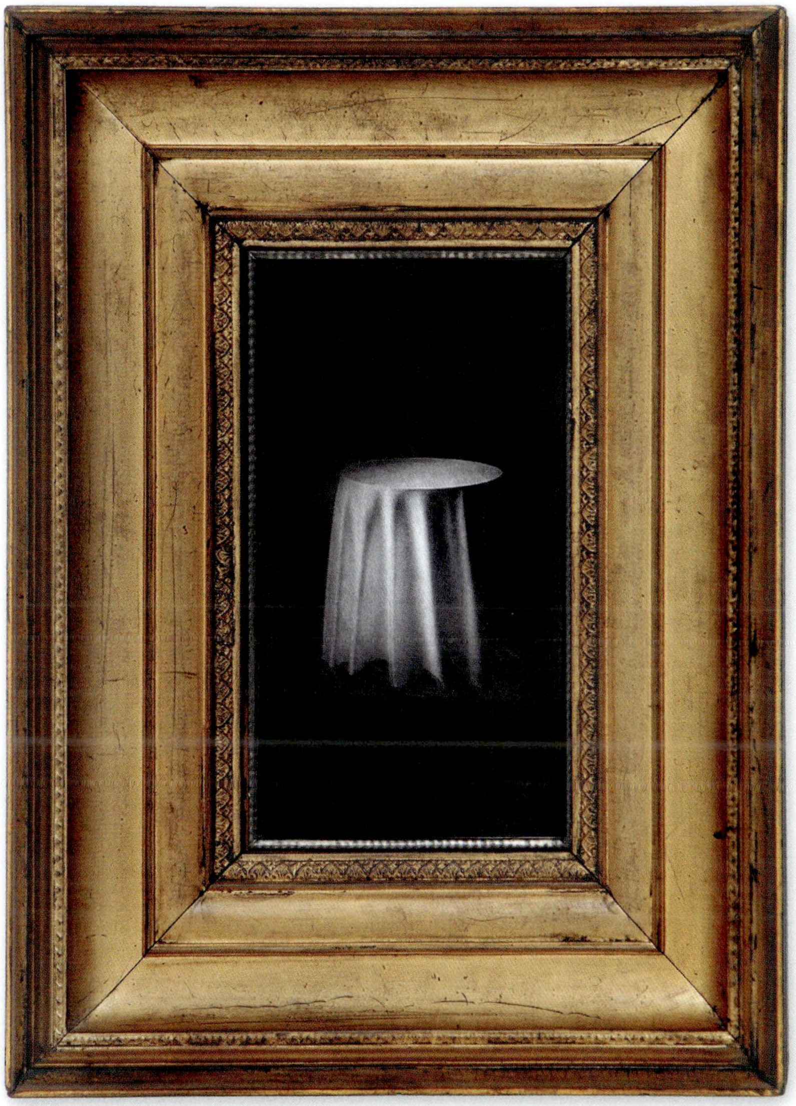

RIRKRIT TIRAVANIJA
UNTITLED, 2023

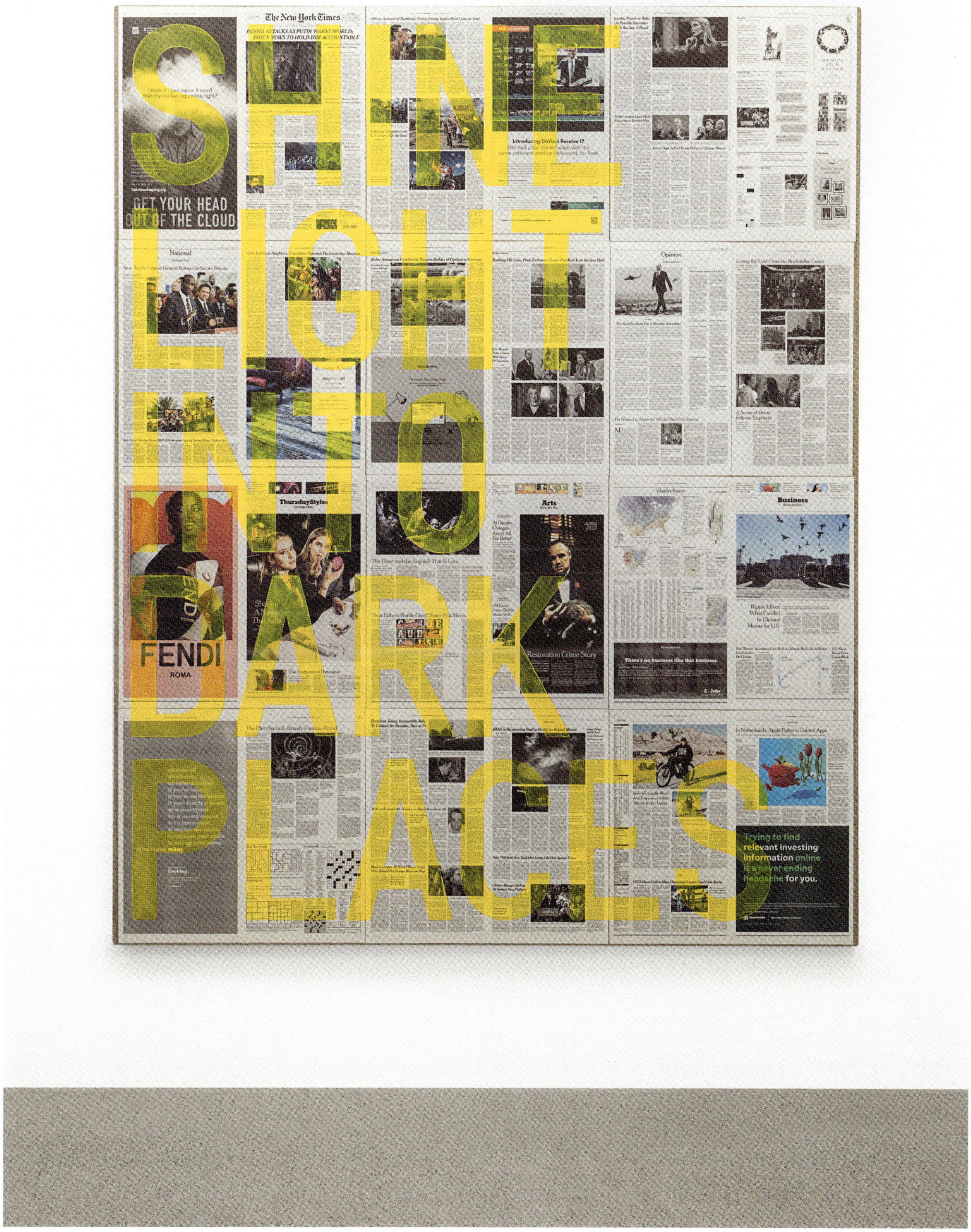
SHINE
LIGHT
INTO
DARK
PLACES

MARYANNE STEVENS

THROUGH NATURE AND THE SEASONS

NORWEGIAN ART c.1820—c.1920

Norwegian art in the 19th and early 20th centuries was shaped by the assertion of Norwegian national identity and a profound engagement with nature, which encompassed both the physical environment and the changing seasons. Increasingly determined to record objectively their direct experience of the external world, artists captured Norway's characteristic features: its fjords, steep mountains, dramatic light, and distinct seasons ranging from a winter marked by ice and snow to the scarcely setting sun of the northern summer nights. Each season was rendered with its specific characteristics, such as the arrival of warmth, the growing season and rejuvenation in spring, and the melancholy of autumn generated by the passing of summer and the anticipation of winter. Furthermore, artists increasingly sought to convey each season's emotional resonance. It was these preoccupations that were to establish a distinct position for Norwegian art within European painting.

The trajectory of Norwegian art was shaped by an open-mindedness, a willingness to learn from other European cultures. At the beginning of the period covered by this essay, Norwegian art was marked by new attitudes to, and appreciation of, the possibility that the range of nature within the cannon of art could be expanded to embrace characteristic elements of Norway: high, bleak mountains, stormy seas, the monotonous flatness of windswept peat bogs and the beauty of rolling meadows. This development was derived from English and German aesthetics and gave licence to the art of Johan Christian Dahl (1782—1857) and Thomas Fearnley (1802—1842). In the second half of the 19th century, access to more centres of professional training and exhibition opportunities on the Continent, from Dresden and Düsseldorf to Karlsruhe, Munich and, most importantly, Paris, ensured that Norwegian art came to be recognised and critically acclaimed both nationally and internationally.

Norway was appreciated as a land of natural variety dominated by its mountains, steep valleys, thundering waterfalls, deep fjords, and the changing seasons:

> Norway, which surpasses every country in Europe in the depths of its fjords, the grandeur of its [mountains], the bleakness of its forests and the savageness of its torrents, is interspersed with valleys and plains teeming with richness and beauty; even while the mountains are black with tempests, and are undergoing the ravages of continued storms, such stillness will prevail on the surface of the neighbouring lake that the surrounding scenery will not cease to be faithfully reflected.[1]

Historically, the mountainous terrain of Norway was considered ugly, unproductive and hence, not worthy to be the subject of art. This attitude was transformed by the elaboration in the 18th century of a new aesthetic term, the sublime, propounded by, notably, the philosophers Edmund Burke[2] and Emmanuel Kant.[3] Rather than generating horror, fear and disgust, mountainous landscapes were seen as inspiring feelings of awe. They could now be celebrated in art. Furthermore, they could be seen as a manifestation of the divine in nature, a romantic proposition which emerged in the early 19th century.

CAPTURING NATURE

Within a burgeoning appreciation of the landscapes and distinct seasons of Norway amongst artists in the opening decades of the 19th century were two of its major exponents: Dahl and Fearnley. Although both artists received their professional training in Copenhagen and Dresden, travelled within Europe and resided outside Norway, both returned regularly. In Norway they made numerous studies outdoors in front of the motif, which informed their finished landscapes created back in the studio. These celebrated the scale and grandeur of the country's nat-

1. Thomas Forster, *Norway and its Scenery*, Henry G Bohn, London, 1853, p. 168.
2. *Philosophical Inquiry into the Origins of our Ideas of the Sublime and the Beautiful, R and J Dodsley, London,* 1757.
3. *Kritik des Uhrteilskraft, Lagarde and Friedrich,* Berlin and Libau, 1790.

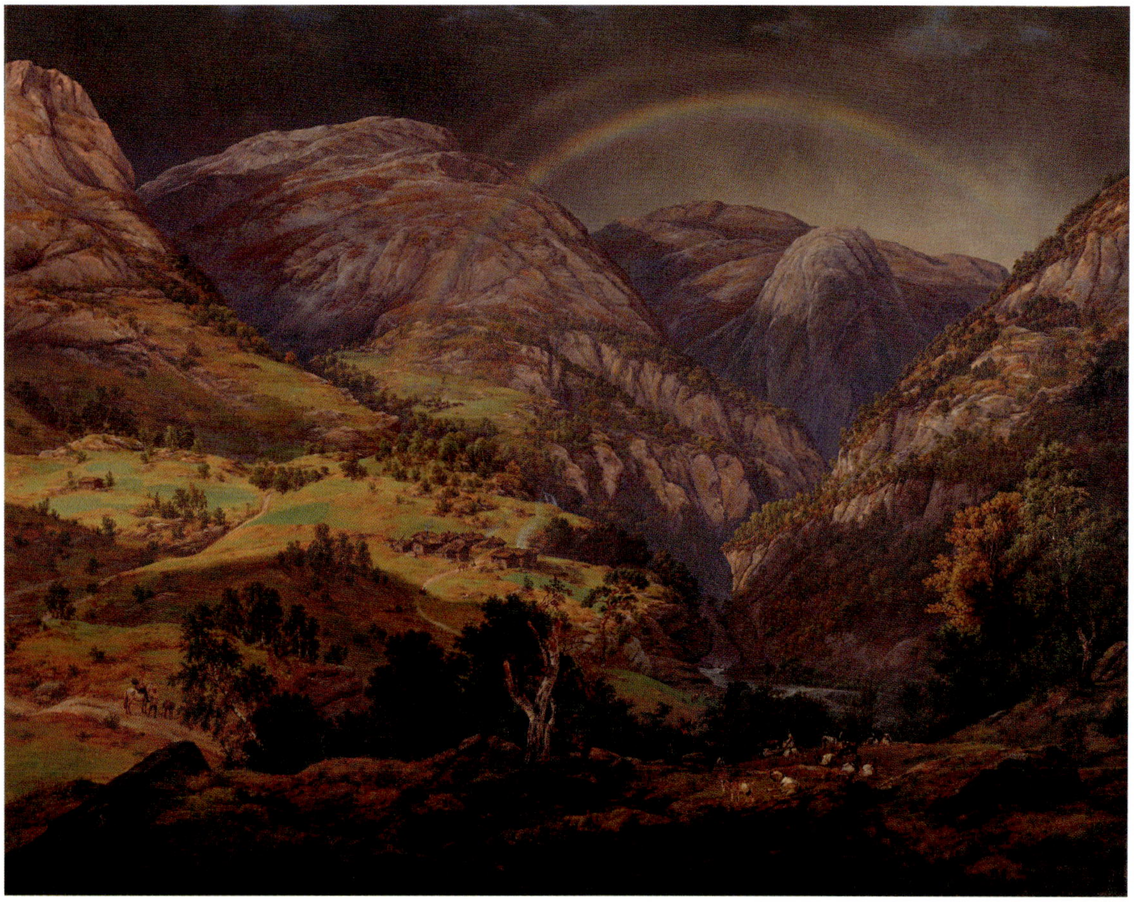

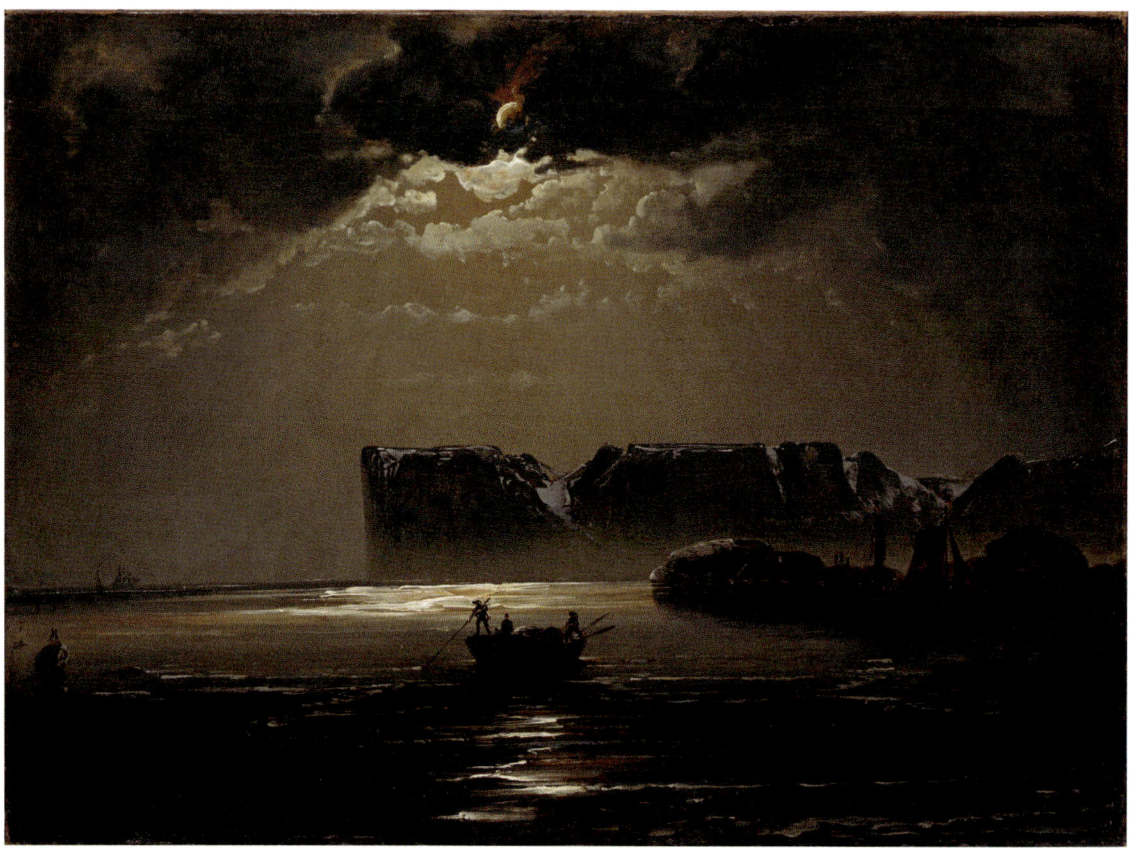

FIG. 1
J.C. DAHL
VIEW FROM STALHEIM, 1842
NASJONALMUSEET, OSLO

FIG. 2
PEDER BALKE, *THE NORTH CAPE BY MOON LIGHT*, 1848
THE METROPOLITAN MUSEUM OF ART, NEW YORK
GIFT OF CHRISTEN SVEAAS, IN CELEBRATION OF THE MUSEUM'S 150TH ANNIVERSARY, 2019

ural features, such as in Dahl's *View from Stalheim* (1842) (FIG. 1) where a summer storm in the mountains has retreated, sun has burst onto the mountain meadows below and nature is blessed by a double rainbow. Fearnley's plein-air study *Gudvangen*[4] (1839) was painted at Gudvangen, at the end of the Nærøyfjord, with quick brushstrokes that conveyed the geological formations of the precipitous valley walls animated by dramatic waterfalls under a hazy blue sky.

Sublime landscapes were also the subject of the slightly younger artist, Peder Balke (1804–1887), whose epic journey to the North Cape in 1832 was to mark his art for the rest of his active artistic career. Using a near monochromatic palette, his views of rocky coasts and mountain ranges (which became increasingly abstracted) were cast in winter, under stormy conditions and illuminated by dramatic shafts of light, as in *The North Cape by Moon Light* (1848) (FIG. 2).[5]

NATURE AND THE SEASONS IN GREATER DEFINITION

The second half of the 19th century was shaped by new developments in European art that demanded a more objective approach to the external world, be it to the natural landscape, light, the seasons or contemporary life. Hans Gude (1825–1903) studied primarily in Germany. Although he held teaching positions in three German art academies, he was committed to Norwegian subjects for his art. His alertness to the seasons and changing weather conditions informed the specificity of location and the observation of light on the water of a fjord or along the coast, as in *Sandviksfjorden* (1879)[6] (FIG. 3), a panoramic view of islands (close to Henie Onstad Kunstsenter) bathed in the silvery light of a summer's evening.

Gude's role as a teacher in Düsseldorf, Karlsruhe and Berlin attracted several Norwegian artists who were to become leading figures in the generation that emerged in the 1880s and became known as the Neo-Romantics. Essentially the product of the disquiet generated by their shared international experience, this younger generation of artists rebelled against the Norwegian artistic establishment.[7] The absence of a national academy of art in Christiania (Oslo) meant that they were obliged to seek their professional training abroad, notably in Paris. As the cultural capital of the world since the 1850s, the city offered tuition in the official École des Beaux-Arts and private academies[8] where instruction was provided by eminent academic artists and was accessible to both male and female students. In addition, the official annual exhibition afforded acclaimed prizes, purchase of work by the French state and the making of reputations that would ensure professional success.[9] Despite the rise of Impressionism during the 1870s, the dominant aesthetic in the ateliers and at the official exhibitions was Naturalism, as executed by French artists such as Jules Bastien-Lepage (1848–1884) and Alfred Roll (1836–1919). Naturalism emphasized a direct, unsentimental approach to the representation of the external world based upon sketching outdoors in front of the motif, a discipline which was also fostered in artists' colonies, established notably in Normandy and Brittany, to which Norwegian artists were drawn. These opportunities enabled, for example, Harriet Backer (1845–1932) to have her work accepted at the Paris Salon,[10] and

4. The Metropolitan Museum of Art, New York, donated by Christian Sveaas, 2020.
5. The Metropolitan Museum of Art, New York, donated by Christian Sveaas, 2019.
6. See also *Funeral Procession on Sognefjord*, c. 1866. Göteborg Konstmuseum.
7. Disquiet with the official artistic establishment also led these artists, headed by Frits Thaulow, Christian Krohg and Erik Werenskiold, to establish a new annual exhibiting body, the Høstutstilling (Autumn Exhibition) in 1882 as an alternative to the official annual exhibition, the Christiania Kunstforening (Christiania Art Society).
8. Notably, the Académie Julian and the Académie Colarossi.
9. The Salon des Artistes Français was augmented by the establishment of other exhibition bodies such as the Salon des Indépendents (1884), the Salon de la Société Nationale des Beaux-Arts (1890).
10. First accepted in 1881 (*Andante*, 1881. Stavanger Kunstmuseum).

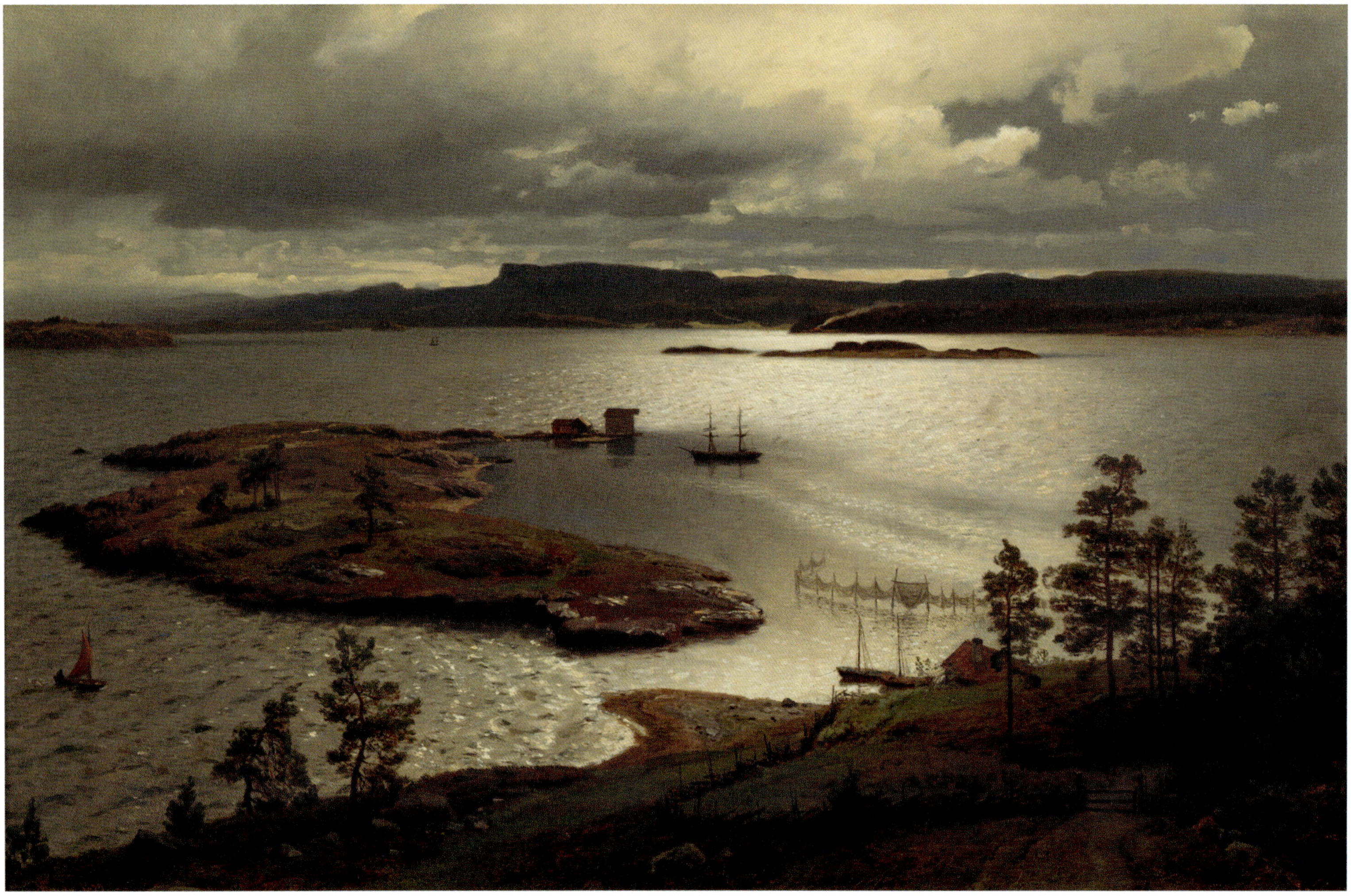

Christian Skredsvig (1854—1924) and Frits Thaulow (1847—1906) to receive official recognition when their work was purchased by the French state in 1881 and 1892 respectively.[11]

The art of the Neo-Romantics was various, but there are certain artistic preoccupations that marked an exceptionally talented generation of both male and female artists. Justifying their almost universal decision to return to Norway to continue the quest for a new and distinct visual language,[12] Erik Werenskiold (1855—1938) declared: 'It is the love of Nature that gives birth to Naturalism, and the love of Nature should lead artists to return to their own country, for they cannot understand, and for this reason, cannot love what is foreign to the same extent as they can what belongs to them.'[13] Yet, given their foreign training, these artists recognised an inherent conflict between the competence and fluency of execution acquired from their French models and the

11. Christian Skredsvig, *Une Ferme à Versoix*, 1881. Musée de Normandie, Caen. Exhibited at the Salon and purchased 1881; Frits Thaulow, *An old Factory under Snow* in Norway, 1892. Musée d'Orsay, Paris. Purchased 1892, exhibited at the Salon, 1893.

12. Certain artists, while returning regularly to Norway, chose to live abroad, e.g, Thaulow lived in France, 1892—1906, and Edvard Diriks (1855—1930) in Paris, 1899—1921, and Christian Krohg taught in Paris at the Académie Colarossi 1901—1909.

13. Quoted in Vibeke Röstorp, *Le Mythe de la Retour*, Stockholms universitets förlag, Stockholm, 2013, p. 258, n. 15.

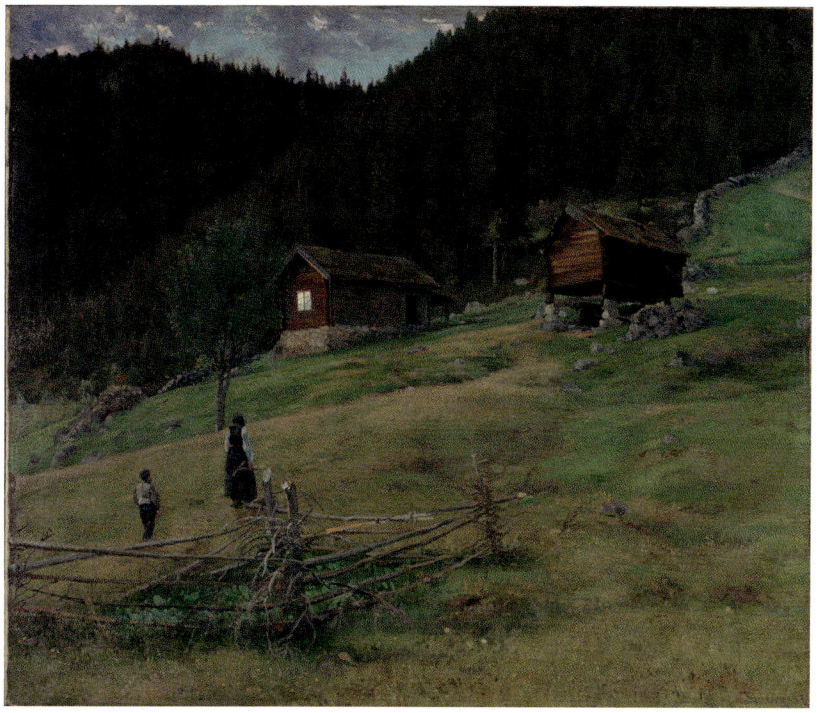

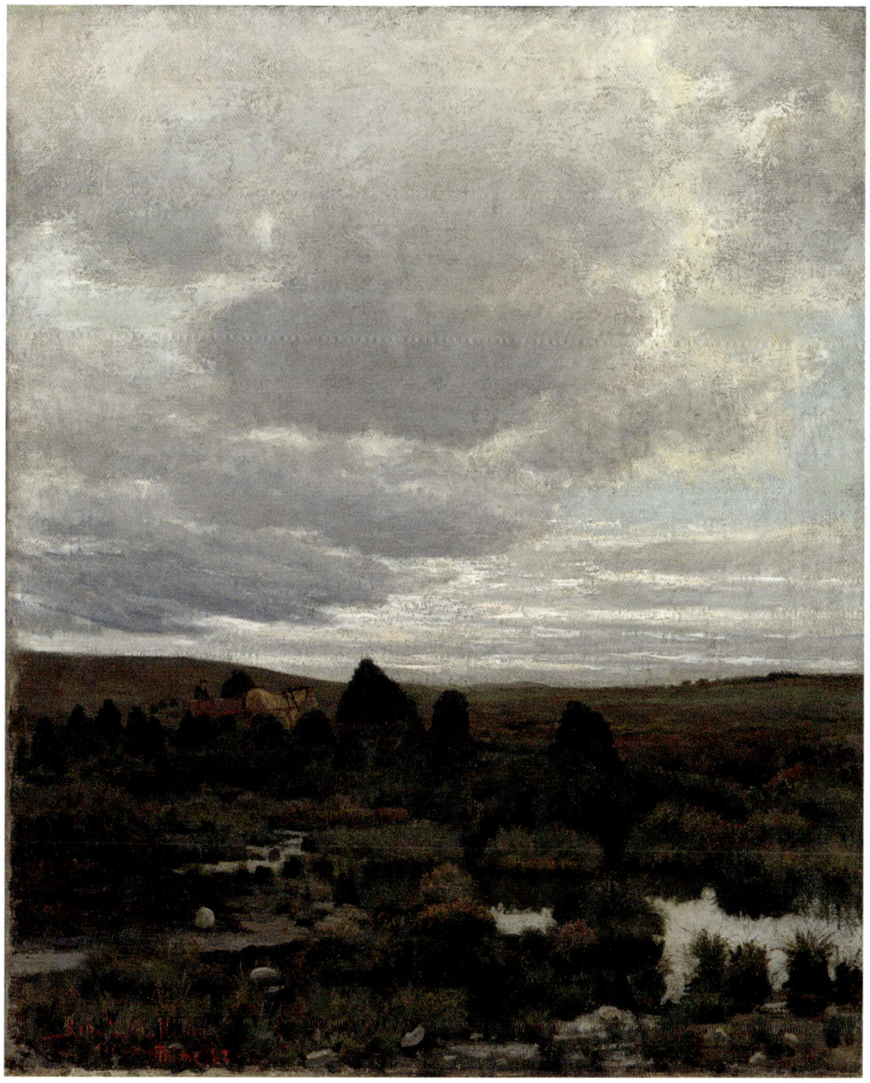

FIG. 3
HANS GUDE,
SANDVIKSFJORDEN, 1879
NATIONALMUSEUM, STOCKHOLM

FIG. 4
CHRISTIAN SKREDSVIG,
THE POET VINJE'S HOME PLASSEN IN TELEMARK, 1887
NASJONALMUSEET, OSLO

FIG. 5
KITTY KIELLAND,
PEAT BOG AT JÆREN, 1882
NASJONALMUSEET, OSLO

making of a distinct national style, which included local iconography, that could immediately identify their art as Norwegian. In reconciling this conflict, they adopted a number of strategies.

QUIET LANDSCAPES AND NORDIC LIGHT

The depiction of the Norwegian landscape and seasons pioneered by Dahl and Fearnley was continued in the dramatic records by Adelsteen Normann (1848–1918) of fjords illuminated by the brilliant intensity of the summer sun and the chilling monumentality of the Lofoten Islands in winter in the work of Otto Sinding (1842–1909). Yet this was broadened to embrace quieter, less dramatic locations, often populated with characteristic traditional buildings, fences and rural activities undertaken by figures wearing local costume, such as Werenskiold and Skredsvig's scenes in Telemark (FIG. 4) and Gerhard Munthe's (1849–1929) depiction of his family home and its environs at Ulvin.[14] Despite the absence of humankind in most of Kitty Kielland's (1843–1914) treatment of the peat bogs of Jæren (FIG. 5), the compositions evoke the distinctive flat, desolate terrain frequently subject to wind and rain of this western coastal region of Norway.[15] Thaulow, despite his international career, became recognised as the painter of winter as he celebrated the local scenery of Norway, often under snow, sometimes making a snow-covered mountainous landscape or a river, fast-flowing or iced over in silent suspense, the unassuming subject of his gaze.[16]

Importantly, these artists' embrace of Naturalism—with its concomitant engagement with the seasons—also involved a re-evaluation of the distinct qualities of light to be found in a country that, contrasted to those in more southern climes, experienced long, penumbral summer nights when the sun hardly set and winters with short days and deep cold nights. Working together in the summer of 1886 at Fleskum, artists such as Kielland, Eilif Peterssen (1852–1928) and Skredsvig explored the agency of the light of the northern summer to add a new dimension to their undemonstrative landscapes, imbuing them with a sense of suspended animation, a calm, a poetry and a distinct mood. Peterssen's *Summer Night* (1886) (FIG. 6) is cast in the fading light of sunset with the sickle moon faintly reflected in the still water of the lake, the trees motionless. Kielland's *Summer Night* (1886)[17] captures the moment after sunset with the sky still tinged with golden and rose hues, which creates an atmosphere of poetic silence. The qualities of the northern light also marked the work of two younger artists, Nikolai Astrup (1880–1928) and Harald Sohlberg (1869–1935). Astrup recorded the dusky glow of the summer night enhanced by the clear atmosphere of a maritime location in his scenes of his home in Jølster, as in *A Clear Night in June* (1905–07).[18] Sohlberg conveyed the luminous effect of winter moonlight on snow in *Winter Night in the Mountains* (1914),[19] first painted as a watercolour in 1911 (now in Christen Sveaas' private collection), which transformed the towering mountains into a symphony of frozen blues that conjure up a landscape of desolation, of a dream-reality.[20]

CONTEMPORARY SCENES

If Naturalism and its focus on the seasons encouraged a closer appreciation of the role of Norwegian light, so, too, it gave license to new subjects and new approaches to genres that, although to a certain extent already explored in Norwegian art in the work, for example, of Adolph Tidemand (1814–1876), gained a new urgency. In keeping with develop-

14. See Erik Werenskiold, *September*, 1883. Nasjonalmuseet, Oslo; Gerhard Munthe, *At the Farm*, 1889. Nasjonalmuseet, Oslo.
15. See *Peat Bog at Jæren*, 1900. Nasjonalmuseet, Oslo.
16. See *Winter at the River Simoa*, 1883. Nasjonalmuseet, Oslo.
17. Nasjonalmuseet, Oslo.
18. KODE Art Museums and Composer Homes, Bergen [Sparebankstiftelsen DNB].
19. Nasjonalmuseet, Oslo.
20. Karl Ove Knausgård conveys the sense of desolation and loneliness generated by a winter landscape by Edvard Munch: 'The fundamental feeling is one of loneliness, of being alone in the world...not actually tangible loneliness, but a wild and existential one. I am here on earth, and I am alone.' 'So Much Longing in So Little Space: The Art of Edvard Munch', Munchmuseet, Oslo, 2017, p. 115.

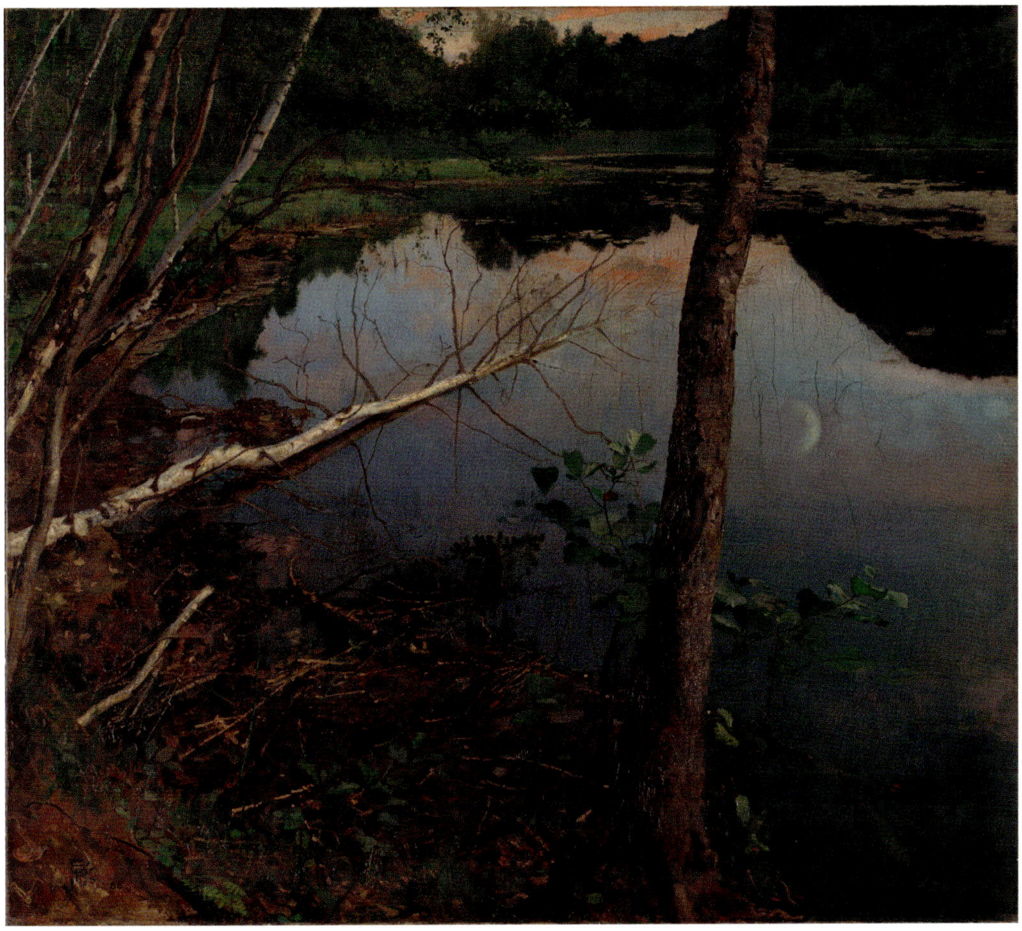

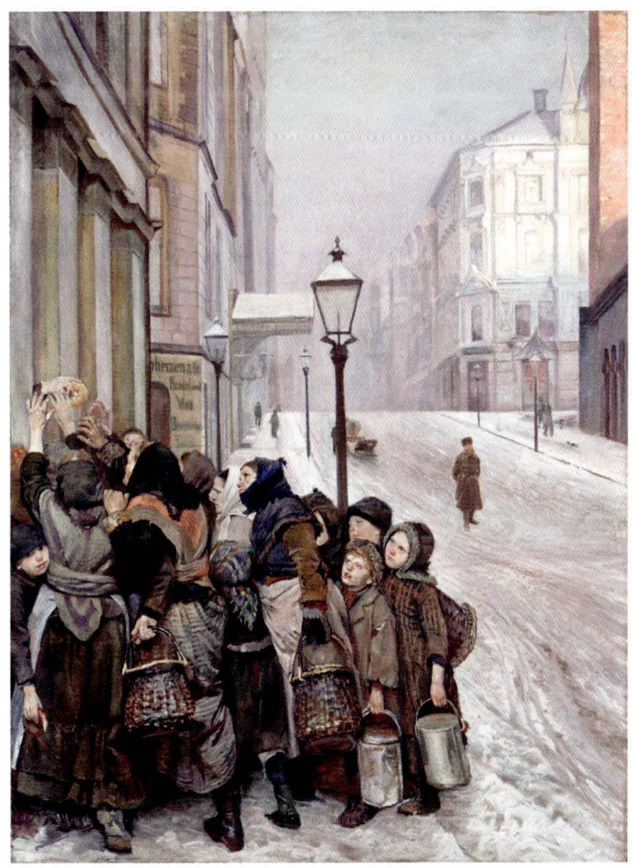

FIG. 6
EILIF PETERSSEN, *SUMMER NIGHT*, 1886
NASJONALMUSEET, OSLO

FIG. 7
CHRISTIAN KROHG, *STRUGGLE FOR EXISTENCE*, 1889
NASJONALMUSEET, OSLO

ments in literature, notably the plays of Henrik Ibsen and Bjørnstjerne Bjørnson, artists acknowledged a broader definition of contemporary genre scenes. While this could encompass subjects set in peasant and bourgeois domestic interiors seemingly devoid of a social critique, as treated by Backer and Gustav Wentzel (1859–1927),[21] others expressed social ills of a rapidly modernising nation, which involved themes such as poverty, both rural and urban, the prevalence and degradation of female prostitution and the harshness and dangers of seafaring life, as proclaimed by Christian Krohg (1852–1925). Indeed, such is Krohg's ability to communicate the harsh cold of winter as it impacts the urban poor in Christiania that the plight of the crowd scrabbling for free food in *Struggle for Existence* (1889)[22] (FIG. 7) becomes synonymous with winter itself.

The generation that succeeded the Neo-Romantics in the early 20th century ushered Modernism into Norwegian art. These artists also trained in Paris, but rather than attending the established academies, they gravitated towards those run by such modernist figures as Henri Matisse (1869–1954). They were also open to the most recent developments in art—from Impressionism to non-naturalism and Fauvism. The impact can be seen in the work of Jean Heiberg (1884–1976), Ludvig Karsten (1876–1926), Henrik Sørensen (1882–1962), Hendrik Lund (1879–1935) and Thorvald Erichsen (1868–1939).

The artist who bridged these two generations was Edvard Munch (1863–1944). Having trained in Christiania and, informally, with Krohg and Thaulow, Munch eschewed a Paris education. The range of his work—from portraits to genre scenes, landscapes and compositions infused with symbolism (FIG. 8)—was always mindful of those distinctive characteristics of the Norwegian visual language, imbued as it was with a sense of locality, the role of individual seasons with their impact on nature, human activity and particular light conditions. The resultant art functioned on two distinct planes: the interplay between the biographical, psychological, and the experiential, in which childhood experiences of illness, loss and death haunted his subjects throughout his career, and a dialogue—one of the definitions of modernist art—between the materiality of a painting or a print where the physical properties—colour, technique and surface—were as important as the image itself.

21. See, for example, Harriet Backer, *Homework*, 1888. Lillehammer Kunstmuseum; Gustav Wentzel, *Breakfast II*, The Artist's Family, 1885. Nasjonalmuseet, Oslo.

22. Nasjonalmuseet, Oslo.

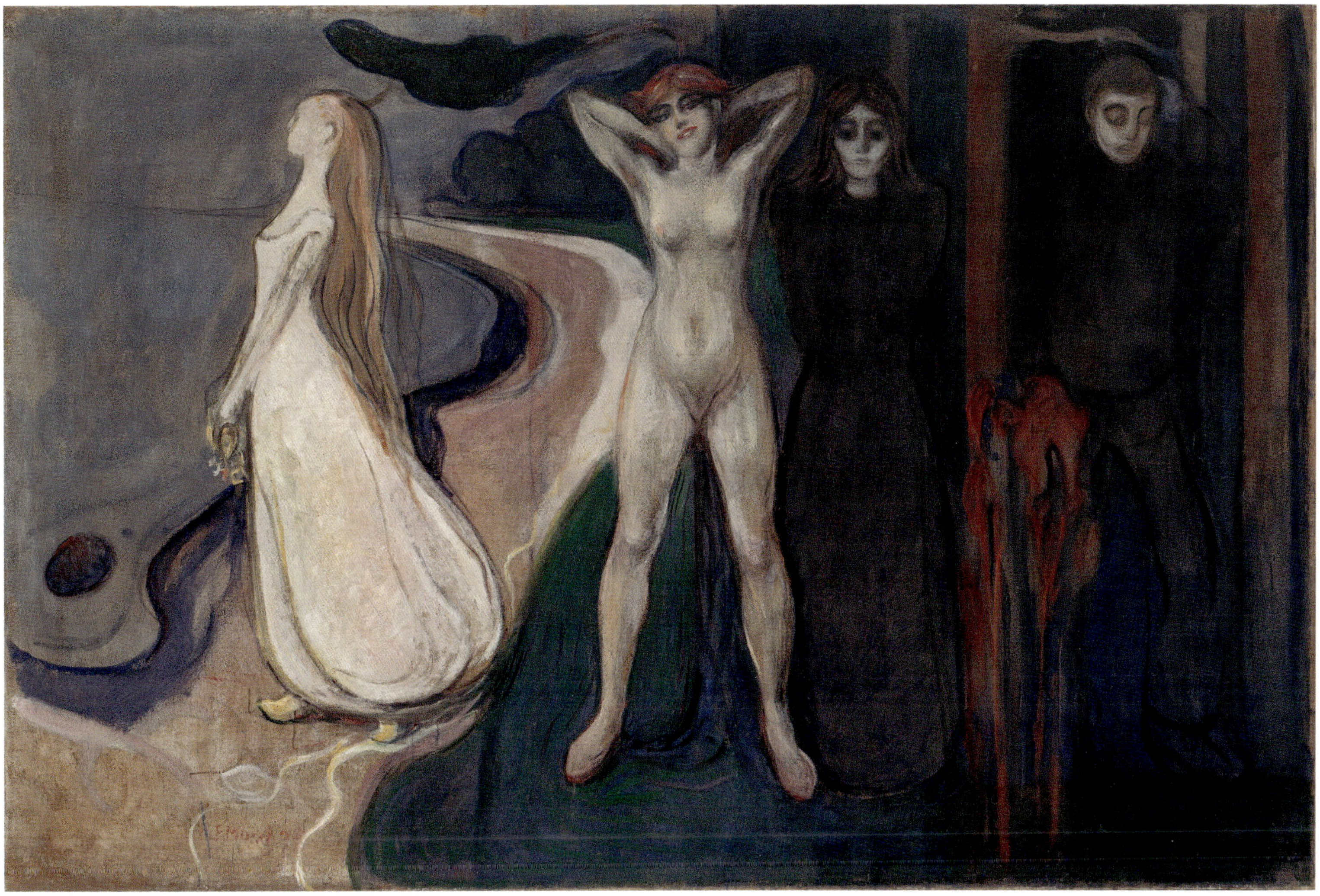

FIG. 8
EDVARD MUNCH, *WOMAN IN THREE STAGES*, 1894
(PART OF THE FRIEZE OF LIFE, 1901)
KODE ART MUSEUMS AND
COMPOSER HOMES BERGEN

LIST OF WORKS

SPRING

Gillian Ayres
Hark Hark the Lark, 1984–90
Oil on canvas, 46 x 31 cm
Christen Sveaas Art Foundation

Julie Curtiss
Le serpent qui danse, 2020
Vinyl and oil paint on canvas
76.2 x 63.5 cm
Private Collection; Courtesy of
Christen Sveaas Art Foundation

Andreas Gursky
Mayday IV, 2000
C-print, 205 x 505 cm
Christen Sveaas Art Foundation

Else Hagen
Oppstilling, 1939
Oil on canvas, 91.5 x 75.5 cm
Christen Sveaas Art Foundation

Mona Orstad Hansen
Downpour, 2013
Acrylic on canvas, 169 x 130 cm
Christen Sveaas Art Foundation

Thorvald Hellesen
Dans, 1921
Oil on canvas, 70 x 89 cm
Christen Sveaas Art Foundation

Thore Heramb
Hage, 1953
Oil on canvas, 50 x 65 cm
Christen Sveaas Art Foundation

Anish Kapoor
Untitled, 2011
Stainless steel and gold, 110 x 110 x 28 cm
Christen Sveaas Art Foundation

R. B. Kitaj
Study for the Waste Land, 1987–90
Oil on canvas, 165 x 140 cm
Christen Sveaas Art Foundation

Edvarda Klaudine Lie
Pike med blomster, 1937
Oil on canvas, 82.5 x 48 cm
Christen Sveaas Art Foundation

Wangari Mathenge
After Eight (There Is A Moment, Fleeting, When One Returns To Self And Feels, As If For The First Time, Alive), 2022
Oil on canvas, 167.6 x 350.5 cm
Private Collection; Courtesy of
Christen Sveaas Art Foundation

Rolf Nesch
Russisk ballett, Stuttgart, 1925
Oil on canvas, 80 x 100 cm
Christen Sveaas Art Foundation

Robin Rhode
Empties (Green), 2007
Set of 12 hand blown bottles
with red plastic crate, 100.5 x 30 cm
Christen Sveaas Art Foundation

Johs. Rian
Pike med grønne epler, 1948
Oil on canvas, 97 x 80 cm
Christen Sveaas Art Foundation

Daniel Schwarz
Walpurgi, 2016
Mixed media on canvas, 140 x 160 cm
Private Collection; Courtesy of
Christen Sveaas Art Foundation

Lars Tiller
Pike med blomst, 1952
Oil on canvas, 70 x 48 cm
Christen Sveaas Art Foundation

Juan Uslé
Al Clarear, 2014
Vinyl, dispersion and dry pigment
on canvas, 274 x 203 cm
Christen Sveaas Art Foundation

Jakob Weidemann
Fugl, 1945
Oil on huntonit board, 120 x 72 cm
Christen Sveaas Art Foundation

Luiz Zerbini
Pica-Pau, 2016
Acrylic on linen, 240 x 240 x 4 cm
Christen Sveaas Art Foundation

SUMMER

Hurvin Anderson
Blue and gold umbrella, 1994
Pencil, oil, metallic paint, glassine
and newspaper collage
on paper, 14.8 x 40 cm
Christen Sveaas Art Foundation

Anna-Eva Bergman
No 4–1960 Un bateau, 1960
Tempera, metal sheet on canvas,
104 x 162 cm
Christen Sveaas Art Foundation

George Condo
Nocturnal Figure Composition, 2004
Oil on canvas, 177.8 x 182.9 cm
Christen Sveaas Art Foundation

Rosson Crow
The Warmth of the Sun, 2014
Acrylic, spraypaint, oil on canvas, 91.4 x 91.4 cm
Christen Sveaas Art Foundation

Carroll Dunham
Wrestlers/ Orange Sky, 2017
Acrylic and pencil on canvas, 94 x 121.9 cm
Christen Sveaas Art Foundation

Judith Eisler
Car Door I (The 10th Victim), 1999
Oil on canvas, 100 x 127 cm
Christen Sveaas Art Foundation

Ida Ekblad
NIGHT FOR DAY, 2022
Oil on linen in artist's frame, 186 x 145 x 5 cm
Private Collection; Courtesy of
Christen Sveaas Art Foundation

Berta Fischer
Xurla, 2016
Acrylic glass, 170 x 190 x 75 cm
Christen Sveaas Art Foundation

Denzil Forrester
Stryder, 1985
Oil on canvas, 274.4 x 412.8 cm
Private Collection; Courtesy of
Christen Sveaas Art Foundation

Theaster Gates
Migration Rickshaw for Sleeping, Building and Playing, 2013
Wood, fabric, Huguenot House wallpaper and wheel, 144.8 x 322.6 x 69 cm
Christen Sveaas Art Foundation

Theaster Gates
Resolution 2: The Only Lasting Resolutions Have Something To Do With James Baldwin, 2013
Wood and decommissioned fire hose, 149.9 x 236.2 x 11.4 cm
Christen Sveaas Art Foundation

Nan Goldin
Jimmy Paulette and Tabboo! In the bathroom, NYC 1991, 1991
Cibachrome print, 50.8 x 71.1 cm
Christen Sveaas Art Foundation

Tewodros Hagos
Journey 32, 2021
Acrylic on canvas, 150 x 130 cm
Christen Sveaas Art Collection

Lubaina Himid
Fish Seller: Safety or Danger, 2023
Acrylic on canvas, 243.8 x 182.9 cm
Christen Sveaas Art Collection

Howard Hodgkin
Night, 2011
Oil on wood, 52.4 x 61.3 x 2.5 cm
Christen Sveaas Art Foundation

Steinar Jakobsen
Street Eclipse, 2004
Oil on aluminium, 150 x 200 cm
Christen Sveaas Art Foundation

Ilya Kabakov
Charles Rosenthal: On the Beach, 1929, 1996
Lamp, wood, oil on canvas, 148 x 186 x 15 cm
Christen Sveaas Art Foundation

Glenn Ligon
Stranger #65, 2012
Oil stick, acrylic, and coal dust on canvas, 213.4 x 152.4 cm
Christen Sveaas Art Foundation

Ibrahim Mahama
UB40 Kofi, 2016
Metal tags and scrap metal tarpaulin on charcoal sacks, 350 x 440 cm
Christen Sveaas Art Foundation

Albert Oehlen
Die Badenden, 1999
Acrylic, oil and lacquer on canvas, 275.6 x 475.8 cm
Christen Sveaas Art Foundation

Robert Rauschenberg
Drizzle, 1999
Vegetable dye transfer on polylaminate, 155 x 125.5 cm
Christen Sveaas Art Foundation

Ed Ruscha
Painkillers, Tranquilizers, Olive, 1969
Oil on canvas, 50.8 x 61 cm
Christen Sveaas Art Foundation

Wilhelm Sasnal
Bar 2, 2007
Oil on canvas, 120 x 160 cm
Christen Sveaas Art Foundation

Vibeke Bärbel Slyngstad
The Nordic Pavilion I, 2009
Oil on canvas, 182 x 260 cm
Christen Sveaas Art Foundation

Aage Storstein
Figurer på badestrand, 1930
Oil on canvas, 77 x 66 cm
Christen Sveaas Art Foundation

Thomas Struth
Mais-Acker, Winterthur, 1992
C-print, 63 x 82 cm
Christen Sveaas Art Foundation

Caragh Thuring
August 2014, 2014
Oil, charcoal, watercolour, oil stick on dyed linen, 213.4 x 274.3 cm
Christen Sveaas Art Foundation

Mette Tronvoll
Boy # 5, 1998
C-print, 73.7 x 89.4 cm
Christen Sveaas Art Foundation

Latifa Echakhch
Night Time (As Seen by Ouch), 2022
Acrylic and concrete on canvas, 200.2 x 150.2 x 2.6 cm
Private Collection; Courtesy of Christen Sveaas Art Foundation

Johs. Rian
Spansk restaurant, 1949
Oil on plate, 54.5 x 45 cm
Christen Sveaas Art Foundation

AUTUMN

Korakrit Arunanondchai
Rains in a tear 1, 2017
Denim, inkjet print and acrylic paint on canvas, 213 x 152 x 4 cm
Christen Sveaas Art Foundation

Sverre Bjertnæs
Atelier, 2013
Oil, permanent marker, resin on canvas, 200 x 140 cm
Christen Sveaas Art Foundation

Ross Bleckner
Birds, 1996
Oil on canvas, 214 x 152.5 cm
Christen Sveaas Art Foundation

Dexter Dalwood
Mary Shelley, Frankenstein, 2001
Oil on canvas, 220 x 275.5 cm
Christen Sveaas Art Foundation

Adrian Ghenie
Burning Bush, 2014
Oil on canvas, 240 x 200 cm
Christen Sveaas Art Foundation

Adrian Ghenie
Duchamp's Funeral I, 2009
Oil on canvas, 200 x 300 cm
Christen Sveaas Art Foundation

Rodney Graham
Sunday Sun, 1937, 2012
Transparency in light box, 88 x 88 x 17.8 cm
Christen Sveaas Art Foundation

Thore Heramb
Regnværs. Gaustad gård, 1951
Oil on board, 73 x 60 cm
Christen Sveaas Art Foundation

Howard Hodgkin
Venice Rain, 1984–87
Oil on wood, 58.4 x 58.4 cm
Christen Sveaas Art Foundation

Christer Karlstad
Land of Gloom, 2009
Oil on canvas, 160 x 155 cm
Christen Sveaas Art Foundation

Martin Kippenberger
Nachttisch, 1985
Mixed media on canvas, 180 x 150 cm
Christen Sveaas Art Foundation

Sean Landers
Dark Trees (Hello!), 2014
Oil on linen, 127 x 165.1 cm
Christen Sveaas Art Foundation

Stein Mehren
Borealis, 1993
Oil on canvas, 65 x 54 cm
Christen Sveaas Art Collection

Kjell Nupen
Hjemsted Nature Morte, 2010
Oil, paper, wood, 141.5 x 191.5 cm
Christen Sveaas Art Foundation

Laura Owens
Untitled, 2015
Silkscreen inks, flashe, charcoal, acrylic and gesso on linen, 351 x 264.2 x 8.5 cm
Christen Sveaas Art Foundation

Robin Rhode
Untitled, Harvest, 2005
Video
Christen Sveaas Art Foundation

WINTER

Marina Abramović
Nude with Skeleton, 2002–05
Colour video without sound,
15 minutes 46 seconds
Christen Sveaas Art Foundation

Anna-Eva Bergman
Planète argent, 1973
Oil and silver leaf on board, 60 x 73 cm
Christen Sveaas Art Foundation

Ross Bleckner
Candelier and Cherub, 1990
Oil on canvas, 132 x 107 cm
Christen Sveaas Art Foundation

Dexter Dalwood
Wittgenstein's Bathroom, 2001
Oil on canvas, 234.9 x 279.4 cm
Christen Sveaas Art Foundation

Johan Knoff
Pushers, N.Y, 1981
Oil on canvas, 95 x 120 cm
Christen Sveaas Art Foundation

Ken Matsubara
Winter Dreams-Letters, 2011
Mixed media (antique box), 17 x 10 x 3.7 cm
Christen Sveaas Art Foundation

Bjarne Melgaard
Mountain of cocaine, 1995–99
Oil on canvas, 200 x 656 cm
Christen Sveaas Art Foundation

Kjell Nupen
Stille natt–hellige natt, 1994–95
Oil, harpix, pavement on canvas, 195 x 280 cm
Christen Sveaas Art Foundation

Catherine Opie
Untitled #3 (Norway Mountains), 2024
Pigment print, 195.6 x 147.3 cm
Christen Sveaas Art Collection

Ged Quinn
The Insomniacs, 2011
Oil on canvas, 200 x 295 cm
Christen Sveaas Art Foundation

Pedro Reyes
Navaja Suiza VIII, 2014
Metal and wood, 100 x 40 x 17 cm
Christen Sveaas Art Foundation

Ed Ruscha
Mountain Standard, 2000
Acrylic on canvas, 163 x 183 cm
Christen Sveaas Art Foundation

Rirkrit Tiravanija
Untitled, 2023
Oil on newspaper on linen, 226 x 185 x 3 cm
Christen Sveaas Art Collection

Mette Tronvoll
Rena 18, 2006
C-print, 150 x 150 cm
Christen Sveaas Art Foundation

Dragan Zdravković
Winter Ends, 2014
Oil on jute fabric, 100 x 130 cm
Christen Sveaas Art Foundation

CONTRIBUTORS

WILLIAM FLATMO

William Flatmo is the Director of Christen Sveaas Art Foundation in Oslo. Since 2010 he has been director of Christen Sveaas Art Collection and curator of the sculpture park at Kistefos where he has overseen its development, working closely with several of the world's leading artists and galleries. He is currently a board member of Stiftelsen Bergenssølvet and has held various other board positions within the arts. Before taking on his current roles, he held various positions within the gallery and museum sector. He holds degrees from the University of Oslo and Sotheby's Institute of Art and is currently pursuing an MA in curating at the University of Oslo.

MARYANNE STEVENS

MaryAnne Stevens (BA Cantab., MA Lond., Hon. FRIBA) is an independent art historian, scholar, curator, and consultant. She specialises in 18th–, 19th– and early 20th–century art, with particular reference to British, French and Nordic art in the second half of the 19th and early 20th centuries. After holding university posts, she became Director of Academic Affairs at the Royal Academy of Arts, London, where she had responsibility for Learning, the Collections, Library and Archive, Architecture and Exhibitions. She currently runs courses on Early Modernism and on Nordic Art 1814 – c. 1920 at the Courtauld Institute, London and has curated exhibitions, and written about, such Nordic subjects as Vilhelm Hammershøi and Nikolai Astrup. Her most recent curated exhibition, *After Impressionism: Inventing Modern Art* was presented at the National Gallery, London in 2023.

LYDIA YEE

Lydia Yee is a London-based curator and art historian. She is currently senior curatorial advisor to YDP (Yan Du Projects) and a member of the external faculty for New Curators. Yee previously held curatorial positions in London and New York, including Chief Curator, Whitechapel Gallery; Curator, Barbican Art Gallery and Senior Curator, The Bronx Museum of the Arts. A recipient of the Asian Cultural Council Individual Fellowship (2024–25) and a member of the Turner Prize jury (2024), Yee was also co-curator of Frieze Talks (2018–19) and British Art Show 8 (2015–17).

IMPRINT

THIS CATALOGUE HAS BEEN PUBLISHED ON THE OCCASION OF THE EXHIBITION

THROUGH THE SEASONS. CHRISTEN SVEAAS ART FOUNDATION

HENIE ONSTAD KUNSTSENTER
24 APRIL—7 SEPTEMBER 2025

EDITOR:
MARTINE HOFF JENSEN

PHOTO EDITOR:
ANJA GRØNER KROGSTAD

COPY EDITOR:
KATIA STIEGLITZ

TEXTS:
WILLIAM FLATMO,
LYDIA YEE, AND
MARYANNE STEVENS

DESIGN:
ANETTE L'ORANGE
(BLUNDERBUSS)

COVER: HOWARD HODGKIN
NIGHT, 2011 (DETAIL)
© HOWARD HODGKIN
/BONO, OSLO 2025

TYPE: SELF MODERN, SUISSE INT'L
PAPER: ARCTIC VOLUME
REPRO: J.K MORRIS
PRINTED BY: LIVONIA PRINT SIA,

FIRST EDITION: 800 / 2025
PRICE: € 35 / $ 40
ISBN: 978-88-6749-682-2

PUBLISHED BY:
HENIE ONSTAD KUNSTSENTER
SONJA HENIES VEI 31
1311 HØVIKODDEN, NORWAY
HOK.NO

MOUSSE PUBLISHING
CONTRAPPUNTO S.R.L.
VIA PIER CANDIDO
DECEMBRIO 28,
20137, MILAN ITALY

DISTRIBUTED BY:
MOUSSE PUBLISHING

AVAILABLE THROUGH:
MOUSSE PUBLISHING, MILAN
MOUSSEMAGAZINE.IT

CREDITS:
P. 25: Courtesy of the artist and Frith Street Gallery, London. Photo: Steve White
P. 43: Courtesy White Cube. Photo: Prudence Cuming /Associates Ltd
P. 56, 68, 117, 139: Photo: Øystein Thorvaldsen
P. 59, 135: Photo: Nina Ansten / Vestfossen Kunstlaboratorium
P. 61, 69, 74, 91, 96, 143, 169: Photo: Dag Fosse /KODE
P. 66–67: © Sotheby's 2025
P. 75: © Glenn Ligon; Courtesy of the artist, Hauser & Wirth, and Thomas Dane Gallery. Photo: Ronald Amstutz.
P. 77: Courtesy White Cube. Photo: Edouard Fraipont
P. 81: Photo: Andy Keate
P. 87: Courtesy of the artist and Peder Lund
P. 88: Photo: Stephen White
P. 94: Photo: Sebastiano Pellion Di Persano
P. 97: Photo: Uli Holz
P. 106: Courtesy of the artist; Bangkok City Gallery; Carlos/Ishikawa, London; C L E A R I N G, New York; and Kukje Gallery, Seoul. Photo: Stephen James
P. 113: Photo: Ken Adlard
P. 123: Courtesy Tim Van Laere Gallery, Antwerp–Rome
P. 141: Courtesy Regen Projects, Los Angeles and Lehmann Maupin, New York, Seoul, and London
P. 153: Courtesy of the Marina Abramović Archives
P. 159: Photo: Jiayun Deng /Galerie Chantal Crousel
P. 162, 165, 167: Photo: Børre Høstland / Nasjonalmuseet, Oslo
P. 164: Photo: Cecilia Heisser / Nationalmuseum

Henie Onstad

Christen Sveaas' Kunststiftelse

MOUSSE PUBLISHING